Young British Muslim Voices

Young British Muslim Voices

Anshuman A. Mondal

Greenwood World Publishing
Oxford / Westport, Connecticut
2008

First published in 2008 by Greenwood World Publishing

1 2 3 4 5 6 7 8 9 10

Greenwood World Publishing
Wilkinson House
Jordan Hill
Oxford OX2 8EJ
An imprint of Greenwood Publishing Group, Inc
www.greenwood.com

British Library Cataloguing-in-Publication Data: a catalogue record for this
book is available from the British Library

Library of Congress Cataloguing-in-Publication Data

Mondal, Anshuman A. (Anshuman Ahmed), 1972–.
Young British Muslim voices / Anshuman A. Mondal.
   p. cm.
Includes bibliographical references and index.
ISBN-13: 978-1-84645-019-8 (alk. paper)
  1. Muslims – Great Britain. 2. Muslims – Great Britain – Social conditions.
3. Muslims – Great Britain – Economic conditions. 4. Great Britain – Ethnic
relations. I. Title.
DA125.M87M66 2008
305.6'970941 – dc22

                                                            2008019664

Designed by Fraser Muggeridge studio
Typeset by TexTech International
Printed and bound by South China Printing Company

In memory of my father Dr Ansar Ali Mondal 1943–2008

Contents

Acknowledgements

A book of this kind accrues many debts; it is made possible only by the goodwill and favours of numerous people. My sincere thanks are due, first and foremost, to those young Muslims who appear in this book for taking the time and making the effort to talk to me at such length. In the end, I acquired nearly 50 hours of recorded interviews and I only hope I have done justice to their generosity of time and spirit. I would also like to thank Dr Raisa Malik and Saiqa Hameed of the Pendle Women's Forum, Rauf Bashir of Building Bridges in Nelson and Raza Yasin of the Pendle Pakistani Welfare Association for helping to find me some interviewees in Lancashire; likewise, to Rushanara Ali of the Young Foundation, Asim Siddiqui of the City Circle, Madeleine Bunting of *The Guardian*, Lord Amir Bhatia, chair of the Ethnic Minority Foundation, and Dr Christina Julios, director of Policy and Research at the British Edutrust Foundation. I would also like to thank Lord Bhikhu Parekh for his support and encouragement over a very convivial dinner in Newcastle right at the outset of this project. The School of Arts at Brunel University made it possible for me to make a number of journeys to various parts of the United Kingdom by funding my travel and accommodation expenses – much of this book would not have been possible without that assistance. Similarly, I would like to express my gratitude to Simon Mason, my commissioning editor, who not only approached me with the idea but had faith in my handling of the project from the beginning and also provided funds so that the best interviews could be fully transcribed, thereby saving a great deal of time. Kerry Cable at Business Friend provided prompt and accurate transcription services, for which many thanks. I am very grateful to my friends Peter Morey and Amina Yaqin for inviting me to present some of this work at their 'Framing Muslims' seminar series; the encouraging feedback I received there was precisely the kind of boost I needed. I would like to thank my parents, who as always have supported me in countless ways. Finally, as always, my heartfelt gratitude goes to my wife Joanna, whose love and companionship has sustained me from the beginning to the end.

Something is happening here but you don't know what it is,
Do you, Mr Jones?

—Bob Dylan, *Ballad of a Thin Man*

So will the real, the Real Great Britain step forward?

—Asian Dub Foundation, *Real Great Britain*

The crisis consists precisely in the fact that the old is dying and the new cannot be born; in this interregnum a great variety of morbid symptoms appear.

—Antonio Gramsci, from *The Prison Notebooks*

Preface

This book began with a conversation. In fact, it began with two conversations. The first was with my publisher who wanted to sound me out on a book about the thoughts and opinions of young British Muslims. I thought it was a great idea, but I was reluctant to take it on myself. I had just finished one book and was not so keen on beginning another immediately. Also, I surmised that this would be a work more suited to a journalist than a literary scholar. I am more accustomed to working in a library than racing around the country; professionally speaking, I was used to conversing with books rather than people. I declined and gave him a couple of names he might want to contact instead.

Later that week, one of my students came to see me about an academic matter. She was wearing a *hijab*. As she was making ready to leave my office, I asked her if she would mind talking to me briefly about being a young Muslim on campus and soon enough she began to tell me how she felt about certain contemporary issues (this was in early 2006). Who knows what prompted me to do this – perhaps the earlier conversation had lingered in my subconscious?

Half an hour later she was gone (and she does not make an appearance in this book), but I began to dwell on what she had told me. I realised that I knew little about the kind of life she led. I also realised that a gulf separated my ways of thinking from hers – even though, as her tutor, one of my jobs was to help her acquire knowledge! – and that in many ways, both trivial and profound, our lives were very different.

Though I am of part-Muslim parentage, I was not raised among Muslims. My parents rarely socialised with any and I spent my formative years in an English boarding school far removed from the social environments of most young British Muslims. My education was wholly secular and I have never been of a religious persuasion. For many years, I had few Muslim friends and those I did come to know were of a similarly secular outlook.

My interest in Islam has, until now, been of a bookish kind. I began researching the history of nationalism in early twentieth-century India and Egypt as a doctoral student in London, and this helped me understand something of the lives and ideas of Indian and Arab Muslims during that period. I came to understand the origins of what we used to call Islamic 'fundamentalism' in Egypt in the 1930s, but until that conversation with my student in 2006, I knew little about the Muslims who lived and grew up – as I had – in Britain in the late twentieth and early twenty-first centuries. I certainly knew none who prayed five times a day or wore the *hijab*. I realised that I wanted to know more. The following day, I called the publisher and told him I had changed my mind.

This book takes its place alongside others that have sought to meet the demand for more knowledge about Islam and Muslims since the atrocities of 11 September 2001. This interest has been double-edged. Sometimes the knowledge offered and absorbed has merely confirmed prejudices and reinforced stereotypes about the Muslim 'Other'. But there has also been a genuine desire amongst many people to open themselves to different ways of thinking and being, to take on board Muslim perspectives, ideas and experiences.

Since the London bombings of 7 July 2005, there has been a slew of books about British Muslims, and this is one of them. It is, however, somewhat different from all of them. It is not a memoir like Rageh Omaar's *Only Half of Me*, Sarfraz Manzoor's delightful *Greetings from Bury Park* or Imran Ahmad's *Unimagined: A Muslim Boy Meets the West*. Nor is it an academic work such as Humayun Ansari's *The Infidel Within* or Tahir Abbas's *Muslim Britain: Communities under Pressure*. It is not even very similar to Philip Lewis's *Young, British and Muslim*, which was published whilst I was in the latter stages of writing this book. These scholarly works strive for an objectivity that is sorely needed but that, for better or worse, is not the purpose of this book.

Essentially, this book is a record of many conversations with young British Muslims from a variety of ethnic, cultural and regional backgrounds. I spoke to more women than men (the split was probably 60:40) and to working class as well as professional Muslims. Two or three were barely into their adulthood, but a few, on the other hand, were on the threshold of their thirties.

Unlike an academic sociology, this book makes no claim to representativeness. It is a subjective account of my encounters across Britain with a group of people about whom so much is said but from whom so little is heard. It is an attempt to bring what they have to say into the public domain, not in response to a news agenda which predetermines the range of views suitable for presentation, but as a result of listening carefully to their life stories, their ideas and opinions, their desires and their motivations, fears and anxieties.

This book is also *not* an attempt to explain the rise of political 'extremism' amongst a certain group of young British Muslims. It is not concerned with those people at all because they already attract enough attention from a news media hungry for sensation. The success of Ed Husain's *The Islamist*, despite its many flaws, demonstrates the understandable appeal and presence of 'Islamic extremism' as a trope in current public discourse, but that is not my concern here.

The young men and women I spoke to were all practising and self-confessed Muslims. They all considered themselves to be part of the silent majority of British Muslims – if ever this phrase was appropriate, it is in this instance – who show up in statistics and opinion polls but whose views are never given much space for elaboration. These views are more complex than many people might imagine, and sometimes misunderstandings arise because they are not given due attention – as the fear over the apparent support for *Shariah* law amongst over a third of young Muslims demonstrates. Such views need to be put in context. They need to be clarified by Muslims themselves; without control over their discourse, terms which are not problematic within their own interpretative communities or are taken to mean certain things by them (such as *jihad*) can be mistranslated and misconstrued. This helps no one but the extremists on both sides.

One final comment: just as I have already disavowed any claim to representativeness so too do I acknowledge the problem of representation in any effort, such as this one, to showcase the views of others. The voices that appear in this text are not, of course, presented without mediation. My presence as author, editor and interlocutor is inevitably to be reckoned with. This is an ethical task, one which charges the author with a great responsibility to vouchsafe the integrity of his subjects and the trust of his readers. I have sought to present and contextualise the views of the young men and women to whom I spoke to better able the reader to understand them; this, of course, requires a judgment in each and every instance and I leave it up to readers to determine whether I have been successful. But I have also sought to analyse their words, where necessary, against the backdrop of larger contemporary concerns, to tease out significances and inferences. At times I have put forward my own arguments; some of these span the whole book, others have a more local jurisdiction within the context of a particular passage. Again, I leave the readers to make of these what they will.

Chapter 1
Why Islam?

Not so long ago it was believed by many that successive generations of British Muslims would, like the rest of British society, become less and less religious. It seemed a plausible hypothesis at the time. After all, church attendance has been in steep decline for some time, and it was believed that Islam would go the same way as Christianity and become, if anything, a privatised, personal religion. Whatever comforts Islam might have offered the first-generation migrants would soon become unnecessary for their children and grandchildren, born on British soil and raised in its social, cultural and political climate. Islam would become an exotic vestige, an echo from another world and another time.

Perhaps it was complacent – arrogant even – to imagine that the culture and religion of their parents would hold no attraction for them once these young men and women had sampled and had become accustomed to British social and cultural mores. Whatever it was, I myself, and many others like me – the second-generation British Asians who grew up in the 1970s and 1980s, whether Muslim, Hindu or Sikh – fully subscribed to it. Despite the presence of angry young men burning copies of *The Satanic Verses* in 1989, the lingering impression for many of my generation was that the protest was led by disgruntled and rather forbidding old men with clipped white beards and betel-stained teeth, glassy-eyed with righteous indignation. These men represented the archetypal Other – exotically attired, speaking broken English in thick 'foreign' accents and fanatically propagating the rhetoric of the mullahs in Tehran. They came to represent (unfairly, as it happens) an older generation whose attachment to Islam sat uneasily within a multicultural and multiracial society.

I imagined the young men in the crowd to be merely letting off steam, expressing their dissatisfaction and frustration at being at the bottom of the pile and railing against racism, unemployment and class inequality, but not really bothered about a book they had not read nor ever would. Later I found this image reflected in the character of Millat Iqbal in Zadie Smith's *White Teeth*, who goes to that very Bradford protest for precisely those reasons. I did not for one minute think that they were a portent of the future. Instead, I thought that they were an aberration; the future belonged to people such as Milly, the Asian character in the television series *This Life*, a successful career woman whose Muslim identity is reduced to a barely discernible residue (there is the briefest mention of her full name, Jamila).

Ironically, it is people such as Milly (and myself) who have become the aberrations. All the evidence suggests that religiosity is growing amongst young British Muslims. A recent report published by the think-tank Policy Exchange notes that far from declining, Islam remains 'the most important thing in my life' for 86 percent of Muslims, and this is roughly similar for all age groups.[1] Beyond this broad similarity across generations, it is also clear that the younger generation of British Muslims are, according to a range of criteria, in fact much more religious than their parents. For example, 19 percent of 55 year olds and above would prefer to send their children to an Islamic state school compared with 25 percent of 45–54 year olds and 37 percent of 16–24 year olds. There is also a marked difference in the preference for *Shariah* law between the different age groups. According to the report, 37 percent of 16–24 year olds, 32 percent of 25–34 year olds, 26 percent of 35–44 year olds, 16 percent of 45–54 year olds and 17 percent of 55 year olds and above prefer Muslims in Britain to live under *Shariah* law rather than British law. The contrast between the youngest generation and 45 year olds and above is particularly striking.[2]

So how did we get it so wrong? Why have these young British men and women turned to Islam and what is its appeal? The authors of the Policy Exchange report have joined a host of commentators and politicians who point the finger at multiculturalism, as well as 'a more fundamental shift in cultural attitudes'.[3] Whilst opinion polls and questionnaires can provide useful data, they can be limited in helping to explain complex social, psychological and cultural processes, and our reliance on them can be misleading. The framing of questions can often distort the picture that emerges and tell us more about the preoccupations of the researchers than their subjects. Sometimes it is the smallest details which enable us to draw the bigger picture with greater clarity, and this, in turn, involves listening carefully, with an open mind, to what people have to say. So what do young British Muslim men and women say about their reasons for turning to Islam?

* * *

Nearly all the young men and women I spoke to confirmed the view that they were more religious than their parents, but it soon became clear that although Islam was indeed an important part of their parents' lives, they were not really practising or 'devout' Muslims in the same way that their children are.

The older generation rarely imposed religion upon their children. Munizha, a 21-year-old student in Slough, recalled that she didn't take much notice of Islam during her childhood and adolescence mainly because her family were not very religiously observant. 'Growing up in a Pakistani family', she said, 'I think a lot of Islamic values are rooted in your cultural values as well so I wouldn't say I was a strong, practising Muslim when I was younger. I mean, we obviously fasted and we knew about the five pillars and stuff but I didn't really pray, though obviously that was part of the background – you know everybody has to pray five times a day but you didn't do it. I don't know why we didn't do it, I guess it was because we didn't have that example because our parents didn't give any importance to it and grandparents didn't either and you didn't hear of other people doing it.'

Another student from Slough, Aisha, whose parents were perhaps slightly more practising than Munizha's, remembered that 'you were always taught the basics about, you know, praying, believing in God, but nothing was ever enforced upon us; they didn't sit us down saying this is what you have to do, that is what you have to do'.

This is a refrain that I heard often: that their parents did not impose religion upon their children, they 'didn't force it down our throats'. As it happens, Islam did make an impression on the young Aisha but in the rather more relaxed and accessible form of stories about the Prophet and other key figures in Islamic history, which she would then dwell on and share with her friends. 'We would have family time together at the dinner table and then my dad would tell certain religious stories and my mum would as well,' she said. Sharing these stories with her friends led her to ask questions about them and, eventually, her interest in Islam grew as she sought out more and more answers.

Others had a more unusual, even idiosyncratic, relationship to Islam during their childhood. Shaheen, who now works as an accountant in a major City firm, admitted that Islam was practised at home in a 'superficial' way. 'My mum would say words like *bismillah* ["in the name of Allah"] and that kind of thing. She would pray occasionally. My dad – well, it was ironic because he had performed *Umrah* [the minor pilgrimage to Mecca, as distinct from the full *hajj*] and continued to perform *Umrah* even though he would, like, drink and stuff.'

Shaheen was aware that her class was perhaps a decisive factor in this; born in Karachi to well-off parents, they led a 'very glamorous life, you know, my mum was always very well dressed, lovely jewellery, and my dad [who was an airline pilot] was very glamorous. They would have these lovely parties with alcohol flowing. At the same time, mum … was trying to be very, very strict, saying "you can't go here, you can't go there." In other respects, she wouldn't care what I wore, and we were allowed to eat McDonalds, we could eat any food as long as we didn't eat pork. So there were some boundaries but it was very difficult to say where those boundaries were drawn.'

Some of their parents did perform the basic rituals of Islam but in other respects were not very religious. Razia, a British-Bangladeshi, for example, said that her parents pray five times a day, but 'nobody in my family is particularly religious'. They do not like the fact that she has started to wear a *hijab* and 'they think I have a reason for it other than my religion'. She thinks that this is because religion for her parents and the rest of her family is all about the impression they give to other people, 'a lot of my relatives, including my own immediate family, they tend to do things because they want other people to perceive them in a certain way'. This seems to have filtered down to her generation too. Her cousins, for instance, 'pray five times a day, they do this, they do that, so that people think they're religious but then they do all these other bad things that people don't know about'. She was particularly dismissive of her sister who started covering her head about a year ago but has continued to 'misbehave' with 'boys and drinking and smoking and stuff like that'.

This suggests that for many Muslims of the older generation, the observance of Islam was less about piety and more to do with participation in communal life. Whether sincerely undertaken or not, the performance of rituals, the attendance at mosques and the undertaking of fasting during Ramadan were aspects of a social life which established a semblance of community for the older generation of South Asian migrants, and the dense network of relationships that such activities helped to sustain would provide them the stability and support they needed in an unfamiliar environment. Munizha noted, for example, that even though her family and her neighbours did not pray normally, they nevertheless did so during Ramadan. It seems that this *collective* observance is what motivated the older generations in their adherence to Islam rather than any particular sense of personal religiosity.

In hindsight, the belief that succeeding generations of migrant families would be less religious than the first generations was based on a false premise, namely that the first generations were, in fact, religious in the first place. Rather, Islam was merely one dimension of a cultural and communal life that they took for granted and which provided the background to their passage through life and its major events and turning points. Instead of forcing their beliefs and practices down their children's throats, they may have simply been content to let them absorb Islam in the same attenuated form they had done.

This might, in fact, have enabled their children and grandchildren to grow into Islam, because they would not have to come up against the weight of parental expectation. As the young Muslim artist Yara el-Sherbini told me, 'people I see who've had religion thrust upon them find it very difficult to ever find themselves choosing to believe in something because it's been pushed upon them and they reject it, and I don't think *that* in any way allows them to breathe in a religion'. Her father, ironically, has a passion for religion and is currently translating a book on 'misinterpretations and misunderstandings of the Bible, the Torah, and the Qu'ran'. However, although she grew up in a household 'where religion was prominent in a way, it was never, ever pushed upon us or actually it wasn't even a big thing in our house but it was a quiet underlying thing by which we found our morals and knew ourselves'.

It is therefore true that 'the rising interest in religion amongst second and third generation British Muslims is not an outcome of parental or community influence'.[4] Indeed, the opposite seems to be the case. Although it would be fanciful to suggest that all older Muslims were relatively less religious, it is reasonable to assume that the majority of those first-generation Muslim immigrants, coming over from rural Pakistan and Bangladesh to do low-paid, labour-intensive work and having to adjust to an alien environment, hostile people and unforgiving weather, would have had neither the time nor the inclination to concentrate on less worldly matters. But perhaps by not being particularly religious themselves, by allowing their children the room to 'breathe' in their religion, the older generation of Muslims in Britain were, in a way, indirectly responsible for the greater religiosity of their offspring. Like other younger generations throughout history, their children may have responded by simply taking the opposite route

to them. However, this is but one dimension of a reality that is in fact
a lot more complex.

* * *

In November 2006, I visited The Islamic Foundation, which is based
on the outskirts of the village of Markfield, a few miles north of Leicester.
The foundation's quiet campus is surrounded by fields, a pastoral idyll
seemingly far removed from the dense urban environments within which
most British Muslims spend their lives. In fact, the foundation is an
important centre of research into Islam and Muslims. It has one of the
finest libraries on Islam in Europe with historical collections of texts of
the Qu'ran and the Hadith (the archive of sayings and exemplary deeds
attributed to the Prophet Muhammad which, along with the Qu'ran,
constitute the major components of the orthodox tradition known as
the *sunna*[5]) but also important texts on the *Shariah* and contemporary
Muslim life. In a corner of the campus is the foundation's publishing
house, which publishes a wide range of materials related to Islam, from
scholarly monographs to children's books. It also runs the Markfield
Institute of Higher Education, a kind of 'Islamic university' that is
affiliated to Loughborough University, specialising in postgraduate
courses and offering students the chance to undertake doctoral research
on Islam.

Sughra Ahmed works for the Islamic Foundation's Policy Research
Unit, which is working on three major research projects at the moment:
Muslim youth, citizenship and integration, and extremism and
radicalisation. Her focus is on Muslim youth, looking at the issues that
young Muslims face today, how they tackle them and whether the fact
that they are Muslim means they experience life any differently from any
other young person. The project was at an early stage, but I asked her for
her impressions of the kind of lives young British Muslims are leading.
'I don't know if there's been too many surprises', she said before adding,
'In terms of the issues, perhaps they are not so different from those facing
all other young people in Britain, but in terms of how they deal with it,
they have a whole host of new issues to try and deal with as well.'

Such as?

'Well, being in the limelight, for example, in the media you know? For
a young person who's already struggling to find themselves I think that's
an added pressure – how people perceive them. That's quite an issue when
you're growing up and perhaps you're a teenager or in your twenties and

you're trying to understand who you are as a person, and then when other people are sort of labelling you at the same time the pressure is increased much more. That's the kind of thing we're coming across.'

I began to wonder what effects these new pressures might be having on young British Muslims and how they might be playing themselves out.

The previous week I had been in Pendle, an area comprising a number of troubled and deprived industrial towns that have often been spoken of as possible hotbeds of recruitment for Muslim radicals; towns such as Burnley, Brierfield, Nelson and Colne. Close by is Blackburn, and Oldham is not so very far away; just over the Pennines, some 20 or so miles away, is Keighley, which has seen a surge in support for the racist British National Party (BNP), and just beyond that is the sprawling conurbation of Bradford and Leeds. All these towns have large immigrant populations originally from South Asia, and most of them are Muslims. In the summer of 2001, just before 9/11, race riots flared across towns in this region, principally in Oldham, Burnley and Bradford, and concerns about racial and ethnic segregation began to be raised following the publication of the Cantle Report into these disturbances. The 9/11 incident added fuel to a still simmering fire, and this part of the world has rarely been out of the spotlight since, not least because three of the 7 July bombers hailed from Beeston, a suburb of nearby Leeds. A few days prior to my visit to Pendle, Jack Straw made some comments about Muslim women, which intersected the two arcs of contemporary concern about terrorism and segregation, both of which converge on Muslim communities, especially those inhabiting these northern towns. The pressures to which Sughra referred would surely be at their most intense in places such as Pendle.

In Nelson, I met an impressive young man called Qadeer Ahmed, who works for an interfaith organisation called Building Bridges but, in his spare time, is also a youth worker. Nelson is fairly typical of the towns that are dotted across the hills and valleys of this area adjacent to the Pennines. Everything about it impresses upon you a sense of decline, of having been discarded by history. As you drive into Nelson, you notice the imposing but dour stone terraces. The shops are somewhat weary-looking, needing a facelift. Pubs, all of which seemed to have escaped the trend for gentrification, have kept the old style, and most look rather forbidding to non-regular patrons, the bar and saloon being sequestered behind opaque windows. Many shops are boarded over, and those that remain jostle with pizza and kebab outlets, some prominently bearing the word 'halal' to assure the town's Muslim residents.

The factories, once the town's *raison d'être*, look rather pathetic now. Some are clearly still operating, but others are derelict, and the sense of decay is evident everywhere. None of them are likely to be upholstered into modern luxury apartments in the near future. Elsewhere, the town is bisected into an historic civic quarter, with its town hall, library and main square, and a modern half that is a depressing display of 1960s and 1970s architectural brutality: angular concrete blocks and blunt modernist designs which have not weathered well in the rainy climate. Barely a street away from the civic centre, the old terraced housing is rather dilapidated. Entire streets are boarded up, although some look like they are being renovated – an indicator, perhaps, of the green shoots of recovery. Elsewhere, a smart new Indian restaurant and an upmarket flower shop also tentatively suggest some grounds for optimism.

Sitting in the offices of Building Bridges, which overlook the library and the main square, I asked Qadeer to tell me about the local young Muslims, some of whom I would meet later that day. He spoke about a split within the local Pakistani Muslim youth, one that has become increasingly polarised. One group, including him, had become more Islamically conscious, more Muslim in orientation and behaviour. The other group had, as he described it, gone 'off the rails'. As a youth worker, he had spent a lot of time looking into and after this latter group.

What did he mean by 'off the rails'?

'They're drinking, they're smoking pot, they're doing drugs,' he replied. The problem was made worse by the fact that there was a fear of even acknowledging it amongst Nelson's Muslims lest it dishonour the community. 'Acknowledging the problem was the first step towards solving it,' he added, 'but if you cannot even do that, then it just grows.'

About five years ago, he had stood for the council election as a Liberal Democrat, and at a function he spoke to a man who had been a social worker and then a police officer. At the time, the man was a police officer working in Bradford. Qadeer had been telling this man about the problem with drugs and alcohol in the community, but the police officer stopped him and said to him, 'Shall I tell you one of the biggest problems? It's prostitution. Pakistani Muslim girls, Pakistani Muslim clients, and the pimps are all Pakistani Muslims.'

'I was, like, whoa – totally blown away by that,' said Qadeer. 'Nowadays, if you go into Brierfield, and it's probably the same in Nelson – it's just heard about more in Brierfield – you've got a serious problem of excessive alcohol consumption amongst teenage Pakistani

Muslim girls and 40 percent of the abortions at Burnley are by Asian Muslims in Pendle.' Clearly, there was also a lot of extramarital sex going on too, which he said was 'previously unheard of'.

This, it seems, is in addition to the prostitution. 'The girls just do it for fun,' he said. They are doing it because, 'they've got nowt better to do and it's unheard of. I mean, guys do it as well obviously, but for whatever reason they don't get looked down upon, but if it's found out that, well, such and such a girl's been with someone, she's like an untouchable or bad news, bad news'.

It may be bad news, but clearly the threat of censure and dishonour is no longer exerting the kinds of pressure to conform expectations like it may once have done. No longer, it seems, are Muslim youth in places such as Pendle inhibited by the moral disapproval of the community, particularly its elders. Some young Muslim men and women clearly do not seem to be afraid of reproach and are undertaking many aspects of a lifestyle which they share with the non-Muslim youth who surround them. The community's system of moral self-regulation, which had hitherto prevented such behaviour, was now breaking down, and the older generation, in particular, were at a loss as to what to do. Perhaps that is why they do not seem willing to confront the fact that the problem exists in the first place: it speaks to them about the gradual erosion of their moral and social authority, and the norms and values that upheld it.

Qadeer's observations were corroborated by a story I heard from one of the young Muslim women I interviewed later that day. Amina, like many young Muslim women in the Pendle area, wore traditional Pakistani dress, a *shalwar kameez* – loose-fitting shirt-blouse and trousers – and on her head she wore the more traditional *dupatta*, a cloth worn loosely over the head that is common in South Asia, rather than a *hijab*, or headscarf. Although only 18 years old and still at college, she had been married to a Pakistani man for a few months. He, however, was still in Pakistan awaiting the visa that would enable him to join his wife and her family in England. Her family, like many of those that settled in the industrial towns of northern England, had roots in rural Kashmir, in an area known as Mirpur. Her father worked in a factory in Nelson but he had become ill through the hard work – a recurring motif in the family histories of many of those to whom I spoke in Pendle. He was also about to lose his job because the factory was closing and production was being moved abroad. The resignation in her voice as she told me this suggested that this is an aspect of globalisation to which many others in the area had already become acquainted – it was now her family's turn.

Amina's demeanour, her dress, her manner and her marriage, all suggested that she had slipped quite easily into the strong cultural traditions maintained by Mirpuri migrants to Britain. Although born and brought up in Britain, she speaks in a rather clipped, slangy English that, in its idiosyncratic grammar and pronunciation, in the range and choice of vocabulary, sounds like a strange hybrid of broad Lancastrian and South Asian English. She feels totally British but the strength of her attachment to her roots can easily be discerned. This cannot be said of all her friends, many of whom have 'gone western', as she put it.

What were these westernised Muslims doing? I asked. Were they drinking, doing drugs, going to nightclubs?

'Yeah, that's all they do,' she replied. 'Especially at college. I know a couple of girls, they go college [*sic*] but they don't go studying do they? They just go and meet their boyfriends – not even boyfriend, *boyfriends*.'

However, Amina had also noticed the increasing divergence within the community, with others 'going religion, they're *really* religious, into Islam and stuff'. Her emphasis let it be known that she does not feel part of either end of the spectrum but somewhere in between. Whilst she had thought that before the trend was towards increasing westernisation, now she feels that there is an equal impulse in the opposite direction.

It may well be that young Muslims are therefore turning to Islam not just in response to their parents' generation, nor just in response to 'western' secular culture and the lifestyles it promotes in general but, more specifically, in response to the behaviour of their *peers*, those young Muslims who have chosen that 'western' lifestyle and gone 'off the rails'. This is particularly likely to be true of close-knit communities such as those found in the small towns of northern England, which is precisely where a significant problem with drink and drugs amongst young British Muslims has been increasingly uncovered and documented. In the June 2007 edition of *Prospect* magazine, Shiv Malik writes how he had spent some time in Beeston in Leeds, investigating the backgrounds of three of the 7 July bombers – including the ringleader, Mohammed Siddique Khan. In due course, it emerged that Khan had begun his long journey towards terrorism in response to the growing drug problem in Beeston, becoming a leading member of a gang of local Pakistanis called the 'Mullah boys', who kidnapped young Pakistani drug addicts and subjected them to cold turkey until they were 'cleansed'. In the process, these young men became increasingly religious.[6]

I do not want to suggest, in any way, that this therefore means that scores of other young Muslims are potentially going to undertake the same journey. The other, more personal and psychological, factors that motivate someone to take their life as well as others' are much more likely to be important. However, it is nevertheless probably true that young British Muslims are responding to the social crises that they are seeing around them, crises that involve not just 'western society' in general but, much closer to home – and therefore much closer to the bone in such tightly knit communities and to *other* young Muslims who are likely to be acquaintances, friends and even members of their family.

However, some of those who had previously 'gone western' were now going in the opposite direction. 'I've seen a couple of people round here who were into a lot of western, like going out, getting drunk, doing drugs and stuff … but now they've really changed, really gone religious for some reason,' said Amina. She didn't particularly know why but she hazarded a few guesses, such as 'the bombs and stuff' and the 'veil controversy'.

A few days prior to that conversation, the Cabinet Minister and Labour MP for nearby Blackburn, Jack Straw, had made some comments about women visiting him in his constituency surgery wearing the full veil – the *niqab* – and he thought that such dress marked 'a visible statement of separation and difference', which in the current climate made relations between communities worse.[7] Amina noticed that after this a lot more women in the area began to wear the veil. 'I'm not sure if they want to wear a veil on 'cos that's what they [feel they] should be doing', she said, 'or they're wearing a veil on 'cos of that day – showing other people that "I'm wearing the veil on, you can't do nothing about it." '

One of her friends, in particular, typifies this trajectory away from a 'western' lifestyle to one more focussed on Islam. Like others, she began to smoke, drink and take drugs and eventually left home. To Amina, leaving home and parents almost seemed to be beyond belief, stretching liberty too far, 'I told her, you know, "there's no point doing it, you're not going to get anything out of it. The main people in your life's your parents, 'cos they've brought you up, they gave you everything" … She weren't living at home for a couple of months … she just walked out 'cos she weren't bothered with her parents – she were that bad she walked out.'

Where did she go? I asked.

'There are like children's houses round here so she lived in refuges and then she got her own flat 'cos she didn't have a job.'

In time, however, she noticed that her friend had begun to change. During the month of Ramadan, which had just passed, her friend began praying and then reading the Qu'ran and then spending more time at home and not going out. Eventually, she had returned home to her parents 'and she's really happy now'. For Amina, her friend's tale is clearly a parable of redemption and her return to religion a signifier of the verities of 'home' and the stability it affords (and there was undeniably a measure of self-satisfaction in her voice as she narrated the denouement): 'I told her that you're not going to get anything out of it but she goes, "Oh no, if I leave home I'll get more freedom and stuff," and I go to her, "What you gonna do with your freedom? You know, freedom is nothing, your parents are everything," and she was like, "no, no, freedom is better," ... Now she's always saying to me, "I'm really sorry that whatever you said to me I didn't follow it" ... Some people do learn their mistakes, some people don't.'

What is perhaps more interesting is not this 'happy ending' but rather the trajectory that this young woman followed, adopting a secular, 'western' lifestyle to the extent of taking the big step of leaving home but eventually returning to the comforts of 'tradition' via Islam.

Another of the young Muslims I spoke to in Lancashire admitted that he had followed the same course. Asif is 27 years old and lives in Blackburn where he was born and raised. Although he is now in his late twenties and a respectably married man with a child, living a few minutes away from his parents, he recalled that during his teenage years he was far from a model Muslim. 'I was the bad child of the family, I think,' he said with a slight grin.

Sometimes he used to tell his parents that he was going to a Tablighi Jamaat meeting when in fact he would be popping round to a flat he had managed to procure for himself and there he would 'sleep with a girl ... chill out, do other things like loafing around, never used to go to work, just get up to bad things'.[8] He also used to be part of a gang which would 'kick the shit out of everyone', and sometimes they would go to the mosque to cause trouble. He recalled that 'we used to go to the mosque sometimes and people used to cry, "*Namaz* [prayer] has started!" [to stop them entering the mosque] and they would think "let's keep an eye on him, let them start their *namaz* and then we'll start." That's what it used to be like and people used to think we were just loafers, and we're not gonna get anywhere in our lives … "they're gonna end up in jail" [they would say].' Again, there was a measure of satisfaction in his voice as he recounted how he and his friends have proved people wrong. All the gang members are now settled family men living respectable lives. One of them is a financial advisor, another a manager, and another runs his own business.

What made him change course? I asked.

'Just growing up, I suppose.'

During his rebellious phase, between about the ages of 13 and 20, he still prayed 'but was I praying my *namazes* properly? No, I don't think I was.' He liked to look at girls instead and see how many he could get, far preferring the life of a libertine to that of the dutiful and devout boy. One of his friends, like Amina's, also left home and, as if to verify the idea that younger Muslims are turning to Islam because of the relative lack of their parents' religiosity, Asif makes a point of saying that his friend's parents probably pushed him to do what he did, 'his family were really, really strict and I think the more stricter you are, in that sense, the more rebellious you become'.

Islam, for Asif, did not precipitate the change of direction, but rather it emerged strongly in him once he had settled down. Having met a woman with whom he gradually developed a serious relationship, he felt able to marry and 'the religion then came slightly after'. His sense of religion was a consequence rather than a cause of his eventual contentment. For others, such as Amina's friend, it was the other way round.

* * *

One evening in February 2007, I made my way to Canary Wharf. It was about five o'clock in the afternoon and the darkness was settling on London. The lights of the City stood bright in contrast to the dark, metallic blue of the twilight sky, the beacon atop the Canary Wharf tower blinking metronomically. I walked under the Docklands Light Railway and looked up at the cityscape, which, from my vantage point beneath the towering blocks, resembled the futuristic Los Angeles of *Blade Runner*. Above me, a train rattled its way towards the heart of London's financial district. In this labyrinth of modernity, about as far removed from the deprivation of Pendle as it is possible to imagine, I was making my way to interview a young Muslim civil servant, an encounter that would provide an insight into the complex processes and motivations which lie beneath religious awakening.

Zainab's story is, in many ways, similar to those of Asif and Amina's friend – and indeed, to many others. In many other ways, it is a deeply personal story. However, it is also a story which illuminates not just one young woman's spiritual, psychological and social journey but also some of the key factors behind the turn to Islam amongst many Muslim youth.

Zainab is in her mid-twenties and was born and raised in London. She met me in her office in one of Canary Wharf's vast tower blocks wearing a *hijab* and *jilbab*, a long garment which covers the body from the shoulders right down to the ankles. Her family migrated from Egypt in the 1970s and are solidly middle class. Her father is a doctor and she attended a nearby private school. Her parents are firmly Muslim in the sense that Islam forms the basis of their 'core values' and this is, she says, very important to them. However, in common with many of their generation, they were not very practising. Nevertheless, they insisted that she attend a Sunday school in a mosque, 'to further my Arabic language skills and then my [knowledge of the] Qu'ran and learn about my religion'. She was not really interested in religion so she didn't enjoy it, didn't learn very much and, when she got home, didn't practise at all – like her parents.

However, the contradiction between her parents' insistence that she attend the mosque school and their disinterest in religion confused the young Zainab. She recalled that she 'wasn't very religious at all when I was still at school and I don't think I knew whether I believed in God or not'. She even admitted that she went through an atheist phase but took care not to tell her parents.

During this period of adolescent confusion, Zainab focussed on her studies, 'I was a bit of nerd at school and I was constantly studying; even when my mum wanted to go out for a walk in the park or out for lunch or something like that I'd say no and stay at home and study so it was very much like I didn't have anything else on my mind.' Perhaps school gave her the external structure – and the certainty that comes from it – that she felt lacking within. 'It was always exams after exams and I felt that perhaps I didn't even have a personality.'

In her late teens, however, she began gradually to lose her single-minded focus on study and began to explore the possibilities of life in one of the world's greatest metropolises. In her final year at school, she began to go out nightclubbing but again kept this aspect of her life hidden from her parents. She then went to a prestigious college at the University of London and insisted that she move into student halls of residence even though her parents wished her to stay at home. 'I had a massive argument with my parents about moving into halls and they even tried to bribe me a bit and said, "You know, if you don't go into halls we'll give you the money that you would have paid in halls as a gift." ' Despite the temptation of the extra pocket money, Zainab stood firm and spent the first year in student halls, adopting the typical student lifestyle, going to bars and clubbing.

I asked her if she had felt under pressure to conform to such a lifestyle, but she categorically denied it. 'A lot of people think there's this peer pressure, but a lot of the time I think it's yourself that pressurises you more; so I don't remember other people saying, "Come on Zainab, let's do this, let's do that," – I remember completely *wanting* to do all these things and wanting to do them myself, for myself.'

In hindsight, it is clear that Zainab was, during this time, attempting to establish her identity, to move away from the sense of confusion that had attended her younger years. Her insistence on moving into halls despite her parents' opposition and her desire to sample what the ensuing freedom from parental supervision had to offer shows her exploring the limits of her new found 'self'.

For many, this period of efflorescence is a liberating experience but for Zainab it was far from that. Instead of release, the guilt, anxiety and confusion of her earlier life congealed within her just as she began to move in this new direction. 'I remember', she said looking down at her hands in the way people do when they recall something unpleasant, 'I didn't feel comfortable doing certain things like going to the pub and the whole social life thing. I felt I wanted to be a part of it but even if I tried to I didn't feel it was really me … I felt it was wrong, and I felt bad towards my parents.'

Soon afterwards, she developed quite severe depression and then, eventually, experienced a complete breakdown. It was at this point that she began to 'think about life more' and a religious impulse began to stir within her. 'So I had this breakdown', she said, 'because I was very overtaken by what was happening in my life; so whether it was my social life, or university or the pressure of exams, I sort of lost control.' At this point, she realised that 'the only thing that was going to pick me up out of this would be something outside anything human, really, so that's when I began to find out about religion and forgiveness and the only way I thought I could get out of this would be to ask for forgiveness from God'.

This religious awakening, which she likens to 'God knocking on your door', may have been influenced by her greater contact with Muslims. At school, she had been one of very few Muslims and, in any case, her friends did not talk about religion at all. At university, however, she was in contact with Muslims from all over the world. Soon after her awakening, she began to make more Muslim friends and go to the prayer room and she also joined the Islamic Society. For Zainab, this transformation was quite sudden, and in the space of a few months she had gone from living a lifestyle which involved things which are *haram* (prohibited) in Islam to a highly observant and religious state of being. 'My parents thought I was going from one extreme to another', she said, with a small smile.

Given the brisk change of direction, I asked her if there was any one thing that she could identify as having been the cause of it. 'No, I don't think so. I don't think it was anyone in particular or any particular book … I don't remember anyone having a conversation with me which made me think I'm going to become a Muslim. For me, it was a personal thing, what was happening in my life, and what I wasn't happy about.' Moreover, her spiritual awakening may not have been quite as sudden as it first appeared. Perhaps it stretched back to when she was attending Sunday school as a young girl. 'It was quite quick in terms of the time period from when I was living a non-religious life to when I changed and started praying, but gradual if you're looking at it from when I was younger.'

It was difficult for me to reconcile the young woman who sat in front of me that February evening with the diffident, anxious and confused younger self which she had described. By her own admission, she is a lot more confident as a person now and she feels as if she has grown enormously in terms of her personality; she exudes a sense of contentment that was only briefly disturbed when she recalled the difficulties of her earlier years. The importance of Islam in that process of self-development is clearly and manifestly signalled by her dress. But it is also surely significant that it would have been equally difficult for me to have looked beyond her *hijab* and *jilbab* to the past life secreted within her had she not told me about it, a life in which Islam has not been the only influence, one that is richer and more complicated than it might otherwise appear. How many other young Muslims share this tortuous negotiation of the conflicting demands, pressures and temptations of modern life behind their apparently comfortable Islamic identities? Quite a lot if those I spoke to are anything to go by.

* * *

Whilst Zainab seems to have successfully resolved the conflicting impulses and pressures within her, the same is not true of some of the other young Muslims I met. They might not admit it, and they may not even be aware of it, but beneath the veneer of their religiosity the conflict within them is still visible.

Razia is a British-Bangladeshi from Middlesex. She is currently a student, and although she says she has never been *too* religious, she has always been aware of her religion and 'what I'm supposed to be like'. It was during a family holiday back to Bangladesh in the late 1990s, when she was in her early teens, that she first began to be conscious of her Islamic identity and she began to cover her head. However, on returning to Britain, she removed the headscarf and did not wear one again until she returned to Bangladesh on another family holiday in 2006. This time she has continued to wear it; moreover, she has discarded the tight-fitting, fashionable western clothes that she used to wear and has also got into the habit of praying five times a day, 'except for the times when my alarm clock hasn't woken me up', she said, laughing. She added, though, that she always makes up for any missed prayers. Recently, she had gone even further and stopped listening to music, much to the chagrin of her elder brother who is, by all accounts, not very religious at all. Clearly, Razia believes that all these changes to her lifestyle have helped her to become a better Muslim.

'What has changed', I asked her, 'between the last time, when you temporarily discovered Islam, and this time, which seems to be more permanent?'

'My religion is far more important [now],' she said, but she admitted that whereas before she returned to a 'predominantly white secondary school' and her friends were not very 'open to new things', this time round she was at a university with a large Muslim student community and some of her friends were *hijabis*, whilst others just did not mind her wearing one. She thus felt far more comfortable.

What I found interesting about Razia's story was the way she could not completely repress her former non-religious lifestyle and the attitudes that accompanied it, no matter how much she tried to suggest otherwise.

Whilst, on the one hand, she would constantly emphasise the changes to her life – the wearing of the *hijab*, the praying, the discarding of tight-fitting clothes and no longer listening to music – and the way people around her have been surprised and even shocked by this transformation – 'I think a lot of my friends and family, they're really shocked with the changes I've made' – and although she made a point of criticising her sister for wearing a *hijab* whilst still 'misbehaving' with boys, drinking and smoking, on the other hand, another self keeps constantly slipping out from behind her outwardly devout Muslim identity.

As a child, Razia was, it seems, something of a tomboy and wild child. I would never have known it from the demure-looking, *hijabi*-clad young woman who insisted that one of her friends chaperone her during the interview, but in her younger days she would dream of being a car mechanic and loved watching *Top Gear*. In addition, she enjoyed playing and watching football. 'However, people don't like playing with me too much because if I get frustrated I tend to kick people in their shins,' she said, giggling at the recollection.

Then, without further prompting, she began to tell me about her love of fighting. She began fighting in response to a girl at school who had started to pick on her. She told her mum and then her teacher, who was indifferent, so she decided to take matters into her own hands, literally, 'and I know I shouldn't be happy about it but it was exhilarating and since then I've loved fighting. You know when you punch people you get that tingling feeling in your knuckles?'

Never having had a fight in my life, I had to confess that I didn't know.

'I love that', she continued, 'Which is why I think I have a bit of a temper now. Most of the time I am pretty calm and under control but when I get really annoyed about something I tend to say things I shouldn't and, if I'm really angry, I do tend to hit them, punch them, or whatever.'

Despite this rather disconcerting but interesting piece of information, I decided to risk probing a little further. 'Do you think you're constantly fighting this other self of yours which is less restrained?'

'Yeah. Definitely. It's like it's really hard to stay calm. Obviously, I'm trying to be all good now by covering my head and, you know, wearing clothes that cover up. It's hard because back in my younger days, you know, I used to be a bit of a tart. And I enjoyed that – and I still do, actually … well, obviously I have to stay covered up because, you know, this is what I want to do, I want to be good now. But yeah, I'm battling myself all the time. So, instead, what I do now is I just, like, wear my tarty clothes underneath and then wear my covered clothes on top, so other people don't know but at least I know what I look like.'

It gradually dawned on me that if clothing is, as is commonly assumed, a marker of identity, then her sartorial duplicity, as it were, is the perfect metaphor of her conflicted identity, one that she tries not to admit to herself. In a way, you could say that it is akin to Freudian displacement, the clothing being the means by which the unconscious conflict within her is manifested.

Later on, I asked her if she felt different now; had she left her older persona behind? 'I do feel different', she said, 'I feel better because I know I'm doing a good thing now. I do. But at the same time I kind of miss the older me, the one that used to get away with things. For example, my sisters, they've always had to wear long skirts. I was always allowed to wear little short skirts and little tops and stuff. I miss that, the way I used to get away with things. Before, my parents would let me do all this stuff but now it's me not letting myself do that. My mum, she doesn't mind me wearing my little outfits or whatever, but I myself won't let me do that, you know? And I miss that.'

The conflict raging within Razia between two different pathways in life is also manifested in other aspects of her life like, for example, her relationships with her friends. Since she became more religious, she has made friends with other quite religious people, and this has made her 'feel more comfortable because they help me to be more religious'. However, the friends she had from her schooldays, who are mainly white, are the friends she seems to cherish the most because 'whereas with my old friends I could make any crude comment and they wouldn't mind, with my new friends I feel worried how they might perceive me. They know I'm not perfect but I still do get a little worried.'

The same is apparently true with her relationships with boys – one self constantly struggling against impulses which lie beneath.

'I used to have guy mates but since I've become religious I've lost contact with them, because I don't want to…', she pauses for a while, as if thinking through the implications of what she is just about to let herself say, 'because I've always had a history where I'd be friends with a guy but then in the end – and I don't want to sound big-headed here because I really don't mean to be – but they almost always end up fancying me. So, since I've become more religious it's like I don't want to take that chance, which is why I haven't bothered. And recently I met my friend's boyfriend, and he liked me, you know, as a friend and he wanted my number and I was like, no, and my friend was like "Why not?" I said, "I don't know what's going to happen in the future," but she was like, "I don't think he fancies you, you know, he's going out with me." I was like, "I don't care," – what if I end up fancying him? Because I'm still a person, I'm still a girl at the end of the day, I can't help myself if I fancy someone or whatever. So I try to avoid anything which can put me off, you know?'

Which of these two selves is the 'authentic' Razia? As I look back on my conversation with her, I realise that it is her candour which is the redeeming aspect of her personality. Rather than condemning her as a hypocrite, her candour enables us to see right into the self-conflicted nature of her identity. Some people, when they think about identity, think of it as something that *is* rather than something that is *becoming*. They want to resolve it into a 'thing', one thing or another, rather than attempt to come to terms with the fact that identity is always a shifting scaffold on which we precariously build some semblance of ourselves. You could say that we inhabit or dwell within an identity rather than possess one. Some people, such as Zainab, do largely resolve their identities: for them, it is not always in such flux. Others never do. Perhaps one of Razia's selves will, in the long run, overcome the other – who knows? Which of them is her 'true' self right now? I find it difficult to understand why there are still so many who are reluctant to admit that the only honest answer is 'both'.

* * *

Young British Muslims are moving in several different directions at the same time. Some are becoming 'westernised', following a largely secular lifestyle in common with many of their non-Muslim peers. Others are becoming more religious and Islamically conscious. Many of those I spoke to had passed through a secular phase and then become more religious, and it seems possible, probable even, that there are others undertaking the opposite course. Some are struggling to reconcile the two trajectories in their own selves, oscillating between them or trying to keep one aspect of their identities under wraps – even from themselves.

What are we to make of this? Is there any explanation which might encompass the variety and heterogeneity of young, British Muslim experience today? Many have, of course, tried since it is the hot topic of the day, and figuring out the young Muslim predicament is considered a matter of political urgency. The authors of the Policy Exchange report, *Living Apart Together: British Muslims and the Paradox of Multiculturalism*, explain this 'contradictory trend towards growing secularisation and also greater religiosity' by putting forward Olivier Roy's argument that 'Islam in Europe is undergoing a profound change. While religion has become more important on an individual level, at the same time it has become less important in regulating the life of the community .... As Muslim elders have started to lose their grip on younger Muslims, this generation has developed a much more individuated, personalised approach to religion.'[9] Whilst this may indeed be the case, it does not actually explain why this generation may be turning to religion in the first place nor, for that matter, does it account for those who are taking the opposite course.

Others have turned to the old 'between two cultures' argument. The Australian Muslim psychologist Tanveer Ahmed, also cited by the Policy Exchange authors, avers that 'young Muslims growing up in the West may feel caught between two different cultural systems with competing values'. He argues that 'the turn towards a religious identity is partly a response to a sense of cultural alienation in the West .... According to this thesis, the Muslim is a "marginal man" [*sic*] who feels rejected by, and alienated from, one or both parents, wider family or school.' In Ahmed's words, 'In lay terms, they cannot carry their inconsistent selves through to adulthood … This often involves a dramatic shift to either side of the cultural divide, perhaps committing to an arranged marriage or seeking refuge in deep religiosity. Or it can occur in the opposite behaviour, such as eloping with a partner against their parents' wishes.'[10] Quite apart from the fact that very few – well, none, actually – young Muslims to whom I spoke exhibited any signs of 'alienation' (as we shall see in later chapters), what exactly might prompt one young Muslim to choose the religious path whilst another chooses the secular one? How might we account for the difference? Unsurprisingly, the psychologist ultimately must revert back to the psychological predilections of the individual. Is this an explanation or the lack of one?

I happen to think that this very notion of a 'contradiction' between secularisation (or westernisation) and Islamisation is at the root of the problem. It rests on the notion that a secular, 'western' lifestyle and an Islamic one are two antithetical alternatives in the manner represented by Hanif Kureishi in his novel *The Black Album*. The only option available to those who see the issue in these terms is to interpret the situation according to a choice that is available to the individual: adopt either the Islamic identity or the 'western' one. Like Kureishi, whose protagonist resolves his identity crisis by eventually rejecting Islam, many commentators implicitly favour the 'western' identity over and above the Islamic one. Some partially reconcile the two by advocating a liberal approach in which religion is acceptable as a privatised, apolitical identity.[11] But it is not self-evident why religion should be any less of a public identity than, say, race or ethnicity. In any case, why *should* identity be resolved and what are we to make of those young Muslims whose lives do not fall neatly into one or other camp but oscillate rather messily in between?

For my part, I think it is more helpful to think of 'westernisation' and Islamisation not as alternatives but as two sides of the same coin, two dimensions of the same phenomenon. If you listen carefully to what young Muslims actually have to say for themselves rather than what they say in response to someone else's agenda, the ways in which people frame their life stories, the figures of speech that they associate with particular episodes can often illuminate the choices they made and their understanding of them. This can often reveal processes within them that they are themselves only dimly aware of, if that.

The young Muslims to whom I spoke all narrated their personal histories in ways which emphasised a desire for self-empowerment. This motif is common to those who have turned self-consciously towards Islam *and* those who have followed the 'secular' approach. Amina's friend, for example, spoke of her desire for 'freedom'. Leaving her parents was, she thought, the only way she could achieve this 'freedom'. Asif's rebellious past, when he would hang around in gangs and sleep with girls in his flat, also seems to conform to this desire to sample 'freedom', as did his friend who, like Amina's friend, left home. But beneath 'freedom' lies another word: power. Most people interpret these rebellious behaviours in terms of the clash between secular, individualist – British? – values and Islamic values, but if we look beyond that we can see that these rebellions encompass a more fundamental desire to assert one's authority in the face of the disempowerment they feel within the parental home. That is why Asif's friend was more rebellious than he was – because his parents were stricter. And, as we have seen, the young men and women who have been engaging in extramarital sex in Pendle have done so despite the threat of disapproval and censure by their elders. Behind their lifestyle choices lies a statement of intent encoded in their disregard for the elders' authority.

The same desire for empowerment can be found in the stories of those who have adopted the Islamic approach, although in a much more nuanced and attenuated form. Zainab felt that she was 'forced into religion', because her parents sent her to mosque school, even though they were otherwise not very strict. The choice of words is significant because it emphasises her disempowerment. Against this, we can read her argument with her parents about living in student halls, and her insistence that she had not adopted the student clubbing lifestyle because of peer pressure, as examples of self-assertion, 'I remember *wanting* to do all these things and wanting to do them *myself for myself*' (italics added). On the other hand, her sense of her religious awakening in terms of a 'personal thing' that was not dependent on anyone or anything else also frames this crucial episode in her life in terms of her *own* self and not in relation to her parents or peers. Significantly, she described her turn towards Islam in relation to a psychological breakdown brought about by a loss of control over her life. 'I was very overtaken by what was happening in my life', she said, 'I sort of lost control.' In other words, she framed her turn to Islam in terms of self-empowerment – a restoration of 'control' over her life – and her subsequent success and confidence certainly corroborates that feeling in her own eyes.

Aisha in Slough also narrated her turn to Islam in the same way. Like Zainab, her parents were not very strict nor were they very practising. However, her parents would tell Islamic stories at the dinner table which, as a young girl, she imbibed, and this piqued her interest in Islam. This interest grew so that by the time she reached secondary school she had started wearing a *hijab*. 'It was my choice', she states categorically, 'my parents never forced it upon any of us sisters. It was solely my own decision, because I wanted to.' Again, the emphasis on one's own power to make these choices is apparent. Later she emphasised this again, just as unequivocally, 'to me, Islam is something I chose to do … It was something I did for myself not because someone else told me to do it.' Perhaps she was unconsciously responding to the stereotypical perception that *hijab* wearers are passive victims of oppressive Islamic patriarchy, in which case her assertion is directed not so much against her parents as against what she sees as the disempowering gaze of the western media and its unhelpful stereotypes.

This motif recurred throughout my conversations with these young British Muslims. Others have noticed it too. 'A common remark we heard from many Muslims we spoke to – religious and non-religious', say the Policy Exchange authors, 'was "everyone should have their own values", or "I don't mind people being religious as long as they don't force it down my throat." '[12] The word 'force' clearly operates as the flip side of 'freedom' and 'choice'. So whilst it is true to say that Islam for this generation is more individuated and personalised *á la* Olivier Roy, it is also true that both religious and non-religious young Muslims deploy the discourse of empowerment in exactly the same way. That is why we should see secularisation and Islamisation as two dimensions of the search for empowerment amongst the current generation of Muslim youth.

But what exactly is disempowering them? One answer can be gathered from Aisha's comments about her adoption of the *hijab*. Young Muslims clearly see the media as hostile to Islam, and everyday they see negative images of their religion and co-religionists reflected back to them.[13] Sughra Ahmed of the Islamic Foundation concurs. When young Muslims see stereotypically negative images of Islam and Muslims in the media, she says, it reinforces their belief – especially amongst the less educated and economically deprived – that 'they' were against them, 'they' did not understand them and 'they' are not interested in finding out. Fundamentally, it is interpreted as a symptom that 'they' don't care. This is dangerous, she says, because 'conspiracy theories are then bandied about to the effect that, "well, they don't like Muslims anyway so therefore there's no point in me getting involved, becoming engaged or anything like that, I'm fine as I am." This whole defeatist attitude starts to come in. And when it comes to things like education and working your way through the employment ladder, this whole negative attitude steps in, "well if those out there don't really understand who I am and don't want to understand who I am, are they really going to give me a job? Chances are no because all non-Muslims will hate Muslims because of what they're seeing and hearing." So it becomes a bit of a vicious cycle.' This cycle of desperation is, according to Sughra, what pushes some young Muslims 'off the rails' in places such as Pendle.

I agree up to a point, but if this is indeed the effect of the media then why would some young Muslims be pushed *towards* Islam and others *away* from it? This is why I think we need to see both religious and non-religious responses to disempowerment as part of the same picture.

Whilst on the one hand the media may indeed alienate some, it also fosters a climate in which it is taken for granted that 'youth' should be celebrated and empowered. The culture which is promoted by the media is one which celebrates individuality and originality and attacks authority. 'Youth' is associated with novelty, change and progress. There is no reason why the same Muslim youth who see negative images of Islam in the media should not, nevertheless, identify and associate with these other values and adhere to them. In other words, the turn to Islam is not therefore a turning *away* from the cultural climate of modern Britain – what people might call 'Britishness' – but in fact an *expression* of it.

Thus, none of the Muslims I spoke to actually felt alienated from British society. They were, like most people, dissatisfied in various ways and to varying degrees about many aspects of their lives, but there was nothing they said which might have led me to believe that they might be directing their antipathies towards a rather general and abstract culture from which they feel excluded. Indeed, on the basis of what they told me, their target is actually much closer to home. In fact, it *is* 'home'.

One of the main motifs that emerged from many of those I spoke to is the feeling of being stifled within a particular framework of life that they associate with the 'elders'.[14] Whilst they might not have specifically criticised their parents – although some did – I perceived that most felt in some way restricted by them. However, they do not feel restricted by their parents' religion, but rather by their 'culture'.

This distinction between 'Islam' and 'culture' resonated through many stories I heard. Islam and culture 'gets just automatically merged together a lot of the time', said Qadeer Ahmed, 'but there's a huge amount of differences.' He added that it is merged by people for their own gain, 'for example, arranged or forced marriages and stuff like that. Most families from the subcontinent will say it's a religious thing when actually it's a cultural thing for their own gain.'

This theme was taken up in great detail by Munizha from Slough. A constant thread running throughout her story was her implicit dissatisfaction with Pakistani 'culture' as opposed to the Islamic 'religion'. This perhaps explains why she felt the need to wear not only a *hijab* but also a *jilbab*. When she began to wear it, her parents disapproved, 'because my parents are from Pakistan and they're quite rooted in their cultural values. They just see it as like an Arab sort of dress and they don't see its religious significance.' In fact, they didn't

seem to see much religious significance in Munizha's turn to Islam as
a whole. Far from being pleased, they began to argue *more* with their
daughter when she became practising. 'At that point', she said, 'it was
very tense. … we argued about a lot of things, not just over the dress but
over praying as well. In Islam there's not just one set way of praying.
There's basic rules that everybody will follow but there's different things
you can do. With my parents, they always see prayer as like one set way.'

It is easy to miss, but isn't there a hint of implied criticism here –
that perhaps her parents don't really know Islam properly? This claim
to greater knowledge is obviously an assertion of authority. Warming
to her theme, Munizha elaborated how the main conflict was between
her mother and herself. As she became more practising, she would
begin to attend talks at universities, something which scared her mother
because she felt that the talks would radicalise her daughter and
prompt her 'to go against your parents'. 'The thing is', she said, with
passionate eloquence, 'for a Pakistani woman, it's not just about *taking
orders* from like a husband or whatever, it's about *taking orders from
the family*; it's a whole series of people. You have to match up to the
expectations of your mother-in-law, of your grandparents, of your
own mother, of your children, of your husband, so in that sense mum's
had a very different life…' (italics added). Here she tailed off, almost
as if coming to some sort of realisation.

Up to that point, Munizha had spoken about her religion and her
faith as a kind of journey, as an expression of her individuality. This was
common to many of her peers. But didn't the traditional family structure
as she had just described it stifle that individuality?

'It does stifle it, definitely!' she said, with typical forthrightness.

Suddenly, I realised the importance of the elders' relative lack of
religiosity. These young Muslims do not feel that it is Islam that has
disempowered them; instead, they believe it is their parents' 'culture' and
the restrictions it imposes on their individual and social development
that is to blame. That is the real target of their search for empowerment.
To be precise, it is the patriarchal culture of their parents' homelands
against which they are chafing, the restrictions on social and personal
freedom which such cultures impose upon these young Muslims – Razia
complained bitterly that she couldn't even go out and visit her friends
when her parents found out about her sister misbehaving at university;
Zainab noted that perhaps her parents' opposition to her living in halls
was rooted in 'a cultural thing because for us we don't really move out

until we get married' – were certainly disempowering or 'stifling', and they were designed to reinforce a patriarchal family and community structure that had become increasingly discredited in their eyes.

Precisely because Islam was the ground on which the elders established that patriarchal authority, younger Muslims have sought to challenge them on this ground. Becoming more devout, more knowledgeable about their religion is an implicit challenge to the authority of the elders. It is a way of authorising their personal life choices because it is justified *through* Islam and not against it. Without Islam as a bulwark, the elders' authority dissipates because they cannot challenge the basis of their children's choices.

So, I could begin to understand why young British Muslim women do not feel that Islam oppresses women but rather liberates them. Munizha said, 'I'm really criticising Pakistani culture today but that culture is very patriarchal in the sense that the woman has to stay in the home, has to cook and clean and whatever, whereas *in actual fact* if you look at the Muslim woman's identity, there is this big drive towards educating because, at the end of the day, if the Muslim woman is going to be the main educator of her children, she has to be educated herself. There is a drive towards knowledge, actually gaining knowledge as a Muslim woman and stuff and I think that's lost in the Pakistani community' (italics added).

I could also begin to understand why so many young Muslims – male and female – turn to their religion as a means of achieving greater personal and social freedom. In that sense, they are doing precisely what the other young Muslims have done by 'going western'. It is just a difference in tactics and strategy, but the objective is the same. And perhaps it is the religious Muslims who are being cannier. By tackling their parents' authority head on, the westernised Muslims seem, in many cases, to have to cut themselves off from their families. Perhaps this is why so many of them go 'off the rails', especially in close-knit communities where family support is the social oxygen that they have become accustomed to breathing. Perhaps, too, this is why so many who have tried the secular option have eventually rejected it in favour of the Islamic one. They are still heading in the same direction but along a different path. In such cases, Islam may in fact offer a *better* route to empowerment because it keeps intact those family and community support structures within which they have grown up and on which they rely. Consequently, the psychic disturbance of the struggle may be lessened.

This struggle for authority and power within the Muslim community between generations is a theme that recurs throughout this book. This struggle is also a struggle to establish a suitable identity in the conflicted environment within which they find themselves. Those who argue that the young British Muslim predicament is rooted in an identity crisis are not necessarily wrong. It is just that 'identity' must be defined in the widest possible sense, and its relationship to power – or the lack of it – must be borne in mind. It is not necessarily about the clash of cultural values. It is about becoming the authors of their own futures.

Chapter 2
Being Muslim

Young British Muslims are turning to Islam as part of a wider strategy of empowerment against the cultural restrictions imposed upon them by older generations of migrants from the Islamic world. Whilst such mores and practices may have offered a sense of comfort to earlier generations, they are increasingly seen by their offspring as an unnecessary and unacceptable suppression of their personal and social development. They have absorbed, and now take for granted, the freedoms that surround them in Britain, and they want to experience them for themselves.

However, they do not see Islam as part of that ensemble of restrictions. In that sense, turning to Islam does not mean, as so many think it does, a turning away from 'western' or 'British' values but rather an adaptation of them to suit their personal circumstances. For them, being a Muslim in Britain is not a matter of choosing one over the other; instead, it involves a profound negotiation of the different sets of ideas and values that swirl around them in their everyday lives. To put it another way, their journeys into and through Islam, how it shapes and affects their day-to-day existence, and what Islam actually *means* to them are all part of an effort to reconcile both 'sameness' and 'difference'. It can be seen as a quest and, indeed, many speak of it as such.

For many, the journey has involved a deep, spiritual experience precipitated by deeply personal crises or moments of heightened self-awareness. Zainab, as we have seen, began to move towards Islam in response to a nervous breakdown. Her experience is echoed by many others.

Aisha, 21 years old, from Slough, experienced something very similar even though her personal circumstances were very different to Zainab's. Whereas Zainab's family is solidly middle class, Aisha's hovers in a transitional space between working class and the ever-growing middle class. Her brother works for a large accountancy firm in the City, and all siblings have been to university and Aisha is looking forward to a career in teaching.

The aspirational aspect of her family life, however, was of a different sort to that experienced by Zainab, who felt the pressure to succeed early on. Zainab had to reconcile that success, and the lifestyle which accompanies it (relatively distanced from the kinds of close-knit communities that govern the lives of immigrants from further down the social scale, she would have had little contact with other Muslims and would have absorbed the attitudes and behaviours of her fellow middle-class pupils at a private school) with her parents' demands that she learn about their culture and religion (demands that were probably intensified by the insecurity that results from that same culturally anaemic middle-class lifestyle). Aisha's family environment, by contrast, was comparatively relaxed. Although she was taught the basics of her religion, there was little pressure to learn more about Islam. Instead, Islam surrounded her in a less obtrusive form, in the shape of stories told to her by her parents.

These stories fed an early interest in Islam and Aisha soon became a practising Muslim. By the time she entered secondary school, she had begun to wear the *hijab* but, in common with many others whose childhood fervour cools with the onset and distractions of adolescence, she soon began to drift away from her religion.

'I wasn't concentrating that much on my religion as I used to and, you know, my priorities changed a bit,' she said. She seemed a little embarrassed as she told me this, almost ashamed, as if recalling a lapse to which she really should not have succumbed. I felt like telling her not to worry, that this is just part of growing up, that most of us have in some way found that phase of our lives awkward to deal with as we struggle to define ourselves against the backdrop of an ever-expanding range of emotions, desires, experiences and expectations. But perhaps her embarrassment was not brought about by the memory of what had happened in the past; it may have been the anticipation of what she was about to tell me, the prelude to a moment of intimate candour.

'I remember, when I was doing my A-levels ...' she began, before pausing as if to reflect one last time before opening herself up. 'I've never really told anyone this but, during my A-levels, I came back home one day and I went upstairs and ... it sounds quite weird but it was like an out-of-body experience. I remember going up to my room and everything just seemed to close in on me. I don't know how to explain this, it's just one of those things you have to experience for yourself but I felt my soul had basically jumped out of my body and was looking back at me and I just felt this feeling of being forsaken and that was – oh gosh! – it was the worst feeling to have. Personally, I have never felt anything quite like that and in that particular moment I just felt like ... like being so alone, even though I was in a house full of people. I just felt that it was only me, you know?

'I think from that day on I felt a void within me. And then the next day, I remember getting up to pray and continuing my praying, doing it on a regular basis and slowly, slowly, I felt that the void was being filled up, and I felt whole, and I felt connected to my religion and I felt connected to God.'

In the silence that followed I found myself wondering about such life-changing moments – transfigurations, if you like – and whether it really is possible to account for them. Can we ever really explain how or why these events take place? Sometimes they might be brought about by factors which we can identify and which we can be reasonably certain were important but beyond that, in the kernel of the religious or spiritual experience, is there not something that is always beyond our grasp, beyond reason and language? One might even suggest that such moments are 'accidental' events in the sense that they come upon us unawares, without any conscious volition, and sometimes without any apparent unconscious motivation either.

This certainly seemed to be the case for Sameena, whom I met in Leicester. Sameena is a professional woman, currently working in social research but with a background in information technology (IT). She had been the only woman in an IT firm in the Midlands and one of two Muslims. At that time, she didn't really think much about her faith. Islam played a role in her life, like many others from the Pakistani community, during communal events such as Ramadan but she did not give it much thought beyond that.

This started to change, as it did for many others, after 11 September 2001. Munizha, in Slough, recalled that in the aftermath of the event she and her friends 'were confronted by our Islamic identity, and a lot of people started asking a lot of questions and it made you want to find out a bit more because we didn't know the answers'.

The same was true of Sameena. 'Everybody around me seemed to be talking about it,' she said. 'On the television, in the papers, and everyone seemed to have an opinion on what Muslims were. But the opinion that they had and what I was seeing portrayed just went completely against all the Muslims I knew. I mean, I didn't know a Muslim like that, this whole extremist fundamentalist type of Muslim they were talking about. I couldn't see that in my family, my friends, within my community. I thought, well maybe I should learn a little bit more about the faith.

And I guess it started like, well if somebody asks me about my faith what am I going to tell them? I certainly wanted to be able to tell them something substantial and not something that I think or I may believe. I actually wanted to know the facts.'

Sameena signed up for a ten-day residential course at the nearby Markfield Institute of Higher Education. Looking back, she realised that this pivotal decision came about more by accident than design. She had not even heard of the institute even though it was so close by, and she looked forward to the course as a kind of holiday, a way of getting out of the office for a few days. Her attitude was that of someone looking for a bit of a break during which time she might be able to learn something useful, not that of someone seeking a life-changing experience.

Then, the day before going on the course, she asked her sister if she had any headscarves.

Her sister was surprised. 'What do you want a scarf for?' she asked.

'Well, I'm going on an Islamic studies course, and I might learn a thing or two, but what if people are wearing scarves there?' said Sameena.

None of her family or friends had ever worn the *hijab* so perhaps it was a surprising question to ask of them but a scarf was, somehow, conjured up and Sameena went to the course 'as if I was going on a training course for work'.

'Anyway, just before I went into the first session', she said, 'I put the scarf on, thinking, well if all the girls have got it then at least I won't stand out like a sore thumb. Yet before this period I'd always thought that the girls who were wearing it sort of judged me, that they looked down on me and in turn I looked down on them thinking what a successful career woman I was, not oppressed by a scarf on my head.'

When she put the scarf on Sameena was surprised to find that she felt quite comfortable in it but she thought to herself that she would wear it only for the duration of the course and not afterwards. It transpired that her guess was correct – most of the women there were wearing the *hijab*, so she felt glad that she had too.

The course was anything but relaxing.

'It was very intensive and it basically opened my eyes up to the fact that Islam was very, very accessible, easily accessible; it was for everybody to understand. It wasn't just for the scholars or the intellectuals, it was for everybody right up from the most lay people to the scholars. And it really brought it home to me that in many ways I was already practising Islam in terms of the fact that I tried to be honest, and that's a big thing in Islam, especially when dealing with money and business deals and things like that. It's very easy to get carried away with myself and I made it a point of principle not to, and I didn't realise that this was Islamic too. I am quite a friendly character and always try to smile at people and say hello in the street, and when I moved into my new house I went to see my neighbours, that kind of thing. All, again, very Islamic behaviour. And I was very surprised to see just how much of Islam was already within me without me even realising it. And that led me to the conclusion that Islam was for everybody.'

What Sameena was trying to get across was that, for her, Islam emphasises an ethics of everyday life that it is not specifically about observing particular rituals and practices or about holding certain beliefs but rather it is a means of regulating one's relationship with others, a way of living based around being good to others.

For Sameena, the result was a spiritual experience. It was not brought about by the course, which she felt was very academic and rather dry, but rather by the peaceful surroundings of the Markfield campus. The way she described her awakening is interesting precisely because of the contrast it affords with Aisha's.

'A couple of days into the course I just felt that I had to start again, that everything I thought I knew – and I thought I knew where I was – had to be rethought. There was a whole new world I hadn't even discovered, that I hadn't even thought about and now it was here and I really liked this world. I enjoyed my faith, and I still do. I mean, a lot of people see Islam as a chore and quite a sort of rigid faith, but once you sort of get involved in it and learn more about it you realise just how flexible it is, and I wanted to continue on this path. I felt an overwhelming sensation that this is where I wanted to be, this is what I wanted to do.'

Whereas Aisha's spiritual epiphany made her aware of a void within, and her journey into Islam has involved a progressive filling of this lack, Sameena's moment looked outward onto an expanding horizon filled with a new sense of possibility. For both of them, it was a widening of perception and a moment of self-knowledge. Whereas for Aisha it remained within a personal dimension, for Sameena it represented a moment of revelation about the world beyond her 'self'.

And this is perhaps something important. As Sameena describes it, the acquisition of faith, the choice of a particular path in life, is not seen as a restriction or a narrowing of possibility. Instead, it represents an expansion of possibility. Conversely, the secular way of life that she had been living before is retrospectively assigned as being relatively constricted.

Whereas for Aisha, Islam made her 'feel secure', because she knew at last that she had 'a meaning, a purpose in life', that same feeling in Sameena is directed outwards so that the world is invested with meanings that she never knew existed. I am not suggesting that hers was a more 'positive' experience; it is not for me, or anyone else for that matter, to make that value judgment. What I am saying, however, is that the paths into and through Islam are incredibly heterogeneous even when they superficially look similar. Therefore, it is important for us to consider carefully how we speak about such experiences and the motivations that we assume lie behind them. When we speak of young, British Muslims pursuing a more 'personal' or individuated Islam, for example, what is it that we are, in fact, saying? Are we, as usual, circumscribing the variety and range of lived experience with the skeletal categories of our analysis, flattening out the elasticity of a living force into the rigid vacuity of an inadequate concept?

* * *

Not all young Muslims have come to Islam later rather than sooner, of course. Some have been devout and practising Muslims since their childhood, their faith constant throughout their lives. In Lancashire I met Omar, whose journey began when he started to memorise the Qu'ran aged just eight years old. He completed this task at the age of 12 and has continued his Islamic studies ever since.

'At first I just read it and memorised it parrot fashion,' he said. 'But once you've studied the Qu'ran, once you've gone into deep research of what the Qu'ran is, and when you've put that into practice, when you're actually reciting the Qu'ran, it's an amazing feeling and, you know, you feel as if you're having a conversation with God Almighty.'

As he said this, I thought of Muhammad Iqbal, the great Urdu poet-philosopher, who believed that a reader should approach the Qu'ran as if it was *they* who were the recipient of the revelation. Such a thought – that of being literally in the direct presence of God – must be incredibly powerful for those who believe in it. There is an immediacy about it that is difficult to grasp for non-believers. No wonder, then, that it captured the young Omar's imagination and has stayed with him throughout his life. No wonder, too, that he thinks of the Qu'ran as 'my next best friend, as part of me'.

Soon he was teaching rather than being taught. Aged just 13, he began to tutor in the local *madrassas*, the Islamic schools attached to mosques, instructing young children in Arabic and Islamic history and helping them to recite the Qu'ran. At the age of 16, Omar had the honour of leading the Friday prayers during Ramadan in his local mosque in Blackburn, with a congregation of 500 people behind him.

'It was a great feeling that I could actually lead a prayer,' he told me.

Was he nervous?

'At first. Your body becomes stiff and your legs tremble, and you think, what if I get stuck? What if something goes wrong, what then? What are people gonna say?'

But these nerves were soon banished by the thought that what he was doing was no different to when he would pray by himself in his house. 'I thought that there was only myself and God overlooking me. Obviously, there were other people there but I just thought there was no-one behind me. Just me and God.'

His desire to learn more about Islam soon brought him opportunities to travel abroad. 'I had an option to study Islam further, either here in the so-called *dar al-ulums* or universities – or Islamic colleges, if you like – in England, or to go further afield – to South Africa, or India. I pondered this and thought my heart said I needed to go out somewhere, to explore other avenues, other countries.'

Eventually, he opted for South Africa, because he had close relatives there. So, in 1995, aged 16, he left home for another continent. 'I was very nervous. Very vulnerable, scared,' he said. 'I mean, I had been travelling before with my father but not on my own and after hearing of such things as apartheid and the racial tensions in South Africa, I didn't know what to expect. When someone says to you, "Africa" or you see something on the news, your mind suddenly clicks – a lion, or an elephant, or the wild jungle – so I made a firm intention, my heart said, "Let's go to South Africa", and I made this special journey there to study Islam in depth, and I made a promise to my parents that I wouldn't come back before the year finished so that no matter what happened – if I don't like the course, say, within the first few weeks or the first few months – I wouldn't turn back and say, you know, "I haven't fitted in well here", and come back. So I completed my first year, and I made a lot of friends, met new people, met new faces, young people, young children from far and wide around the world, from America, from other parts of Africa, from Europe, from Palestine etc. When I came back home, I told my parents I had made the right decision.'

He studied in South Africa for a further four years and has since been to India, Pakistan, Bangladesh, Zimbabwe, Mozambique and the United States, which he has visited a number of times, leading prayers during the month of Ramadan. Listening to Omar, I realised that Islam was at the root of all the opportunities he has had to explore the world beyond his immediate frame of experience, beyond his family, his community and the local area. Just as Sameena found her religious awakening actually expanded rather than narrowed her vision of the world around her, so too has Islam enabled Omar to look beyond some of the restrictions of day-to-day life. Whilst for Sameena this manifested itself in a new way of looking at the world, for Omar it has broadened his horizons more literally. For a child raised in the industrial north-west of Britain, a social landscape that has been in steep decline for some time, one can imagine this represented a liberation, which he might have once thought unimaginable.

Unsurprisingly, Omar said that his religion 'does come first and foremost'. Other young Muslims, whilst often being very fastidious in the practice of Islam, are not quite so single-minded. Aisha, from Slough, echoed many others to whom I spoke when she said, 'People think that, you know, Muslims, they just pray and worship and nothing else but it's not true. I mean, I have found a balance. You know, I do my regular prayers, but at the same time I go out and socialise with my friends, and watch a bit of TV now and again, and make time for family, and obviously if I've got homework to do and university essays to write I'll make time for that. In that sense, you have to find a balance, really. I mean, Islam doesn't always say pray, pray, pray and that's it; it realises that you have to make sacrifices as well, that you've got other priorities as well that you need to attend to.'

Thus, when we hear the common view articulated by many Muslims that Islam is a 'whole way of life', we need to understand that although this is true it does not mean that it is an all-encompassing, all-devouring, totalitarian presence in people's lives. In fact, behind the term 'way of life' lies the messy complexity of lived realities in which Islam is lived in relation to other aspects of people's lives which have very little to do with faith. Indeed, even though Islam may be central to the day-to-day living experience of Muslims, the nature of its importance differs markedly amongst individuals.

Whilst many – probably most – do attempt to perform as many of the ritual obligations of Islam as steadfastly as possible, others take a more flexible view without believing that this in any way compromises their faith or its importance to them. The young artist Yara el-Sherbini, who is the author of a highly amusing and wonderfully satirical book of jokes called *Sheikh 'n' Vac*, said that 'I find it difficult to define the word devout, or practising, because yes I am practising in my practical, everyday thinking but it doesn't mean I follow the rituals of Islam. Unfortunately, I don't follow the rituals that *man* has put down and assigned to Islam; no, I don't follow those.'

Likewise, Leila, a 32-year-old solicitor in south-east England, argued, 'It depends on how you look at worship. Some people look at worship and think, oh my God, I have to get up at dawn and do my *namaz*, you know, I'm so tired and what have you. I've been taught to look at it as, well, you're going to have a chat with God … and I think that's where worship comes into it for me, as in, well, God doesn't really need me, I need him, so if I don't get up at 5.30 to do my *namaz* in the morning *I* feel bad, not because I haven't done it but because I know I need to do it and I feel a void for not doing it. So for me it's a form of comfort.'

In other words, Leila believes that performance of Islam's ritual obligations is not necessary for the sake of it but rather because they help to keep one's peace of mind. 'People and life events generally can only do so much for you and I think the more dependent you are on people the more worldly you get,' she said. This increasing worldliness is, for Leila, not necessarily a good thing. 'It's quite hard to keep a balance between the spiritual world and the worldly world so I think, for me, I need prayer to keep me in balance.' Interestingly, this interpretation actually reverses the usual sense of where the pressure to practise one's religious obligations comes from. Customarily, in a secular society, we believe that the pressure to practise comes from religion. Leila, however, seems to be suggesting that in actual fact, it comes from the daily pressures of everyday life and, in that sense, prayer is the necessary counterweight which helps keep her life in balance. It is not life that balances Islam but rather Islam that balances life; the emphasis is turned on its head.

Lest we should imagine that this flexibility towards the daily prescriptions of Islamic practice is exhibited only by students, intellectuals and artists, and middle-class professionals, these same sentiments were articulated by the working-class young Muslims I met. Asif, for instance, now displays all the exterior signs of his increasing religiosity having discarded his wayward youth. The shallow fuzz of a nascent beard had gathered around his chin and lower face, and he was wearing a skullcap. He is determined to live by his religion now and make up for past sins. 'Islam at the moment, it is important. I want to do everything what Islam says, try to act upon it. That doesn't mean you can't do this, you can't do that. I'll still go to the pictures, still go out for dinner, but I want to pray all my *namazes*, I want to keep a beard, I want to follow the similar way of the Prophet. If I embrace Islam fully, it doesn't mean I'll become one way, one-sided, restricted. You can still be yourself.'

The point was reinforced by a 28-year-old graffiti artist from Birmingham called Mohammed Ali, who is beginning to create a stir in the art world and amongst other young Muslims. 'Islam isn't about restrictions, prohibitions,' he told me in his lilting Brummie brogue. 'One might think from reading the *hadith* that it's about restrictions and prohibitions, but it isn't – it's a guidance for life and there's plenty of good, there's time for celebration. Islam isn't about doom and gloom and we're all destined for the hellfire because there's so much that we can be happy about. We should enjoy life and there's clear evidence of that in the Qu'ran.'

Qadeer Ahmed, of Building Bridges in Nelson, admitted that he tries to pray five times a day but 'there's days when I do and days when I don't and that's largely due to laziness and a bad sleeping pattern'. Actually, his candour about not being able to pray is, in fact, because he believes that falling short in such observances is less important than the other ways in which he feels himself to be an imperfect Muslim. For him, what is going on inside him is what counts and it is in this area that he finds himself lacking.

'A lot of it is the internal thing. Ill feelings towards people, jealousy, things like that. If you think you've been hard done by someone you'll have ill feeling toward them and that shouldn't be there. You should be, well, it's happened, you get on with it kind of thing. That's what affects me and my feelings towards others. I don't like being hard done by, because if I feel hard done by then I tend to keep that feeling within me for a while and I think that can affect you in many ways. It can affect your praying, it can affect your dealings with people because you get a bit wary of each and everyone you meet. I feel like if I could get rid of that then things would be a lot easier for me. That's the way it should be – you shouldn't really care what people think about you or say about you. I mean, scholars or pastors say "don't worry about what people think about you, just be good to others and it shouldn't really matter".'

This sense that being a good Muslim is, fundamentally, about being good to others and it is at the core of Qadeer's view of life, as it is for Sameena. 'For me, Islam is about just quietly getting on with it, trying to improve myself in my everyday life, in my dealings with Muslims, with non-Muslims, the world, everyone.' It was not much of a surprise, then, to find out that Qadeer, in his spare time, works as a youth worker helping Muslim and non-Muslim youths confront the many social and personal problems that are endemic in deprived communities.

In fact, this sense of Islam being about becoming a better person by being good to others is something that I found to be common to nearly all the young Muslims I met. Omar also shared this view. Dressed in a skullcap and caftan, and sporting a long, rather shaggy beard, Omar looks very much like the 'typical' Muslim as imagined by many non-Muslims. His message, however, is not typical of those radicals who seem to be making all the noise.

'I'm not trying to propagate the message of Islam across to people', he said, 'but I want to be a good role model for other people around me. I know there's a lot of misconceptions around, you know, that people with beards are terrorists, those sorts of stereotypes, but I don't see it that way. I see it that I, as a British Muslim, must try to be a role model for other people no matter what faith they're from, no matter if they haven't got a faith and if they're not practising Muslims as well.'

As such, there was a great desire on his part to 'give something back to the community', and judging by his comments, I take 'community' to mean something wider than just the Muslim community. By getting involved in community work, he also hoped to shed the rather forbidding image many young people have about religious teachers – the *maulvis* and *maulanas*. Instead, by working with the community at grass-roots level, he was hoping to be able to 'engage and discuss issues which surround young people today', thereby helping them to prosper.

I found it truly remarkable how many young Muslims spent their spare time doing community work. Many young professional Muslims I interviewed in London, for example, would finish a long working week on Friday but still rise early on Saturday mornings to teach in a school run by the organisation, City Circle. Zainab was typical of these committed young men and women. She attends talks every week on Thursdays and Fridays and teaches English at a Saturday school; she is also heavily involved in a number of projects in the East End: a foster

awareness project trying to educate the Muslim population there about
the importance of fostering 'because there's all sorts of misconceptions
about whether fostering is allowed or not in Islam'; there is also a drugs
awareness project, and she has been a co-ordinator of a youth leadership
project. On top of all that, she had recently signed up for the Tower
Hamlets mentoring scheme, a scheme run not for Muslims but for youth
from all communities and social groups.

Such energy, commitment and selflessness were found not only among
the professionals but also among many non-professional Muslims
I encountered. Qadeer, as we have seen, spends virtually all his spare
time working with the community, as does Asif. This sense of social
responsibility has many sources, of course, but much of it is drawn from
their understanding of Islam and its relevance to everyday life. As Aisha
said, 'Islam is all about changing yourself for the better, I would say. And
for me it did change me for the better. And in changing yourself, you
change the way that people perceive you as well and then it becomes a
community thing as well as on an individual basis. You do need to look
out for your community – you have a social responsibility towards
yourself, towards your parents, towards everyone else as well whether
they're Muslims or non-Muslims.'

It is a point reiterated by Raihan Alfaradhi, a young man who works
as an auditor in the City and another who spends much of his spare time
working for various community and religious organisations. Having
been heavily involved in student politics during his time at university,
both in the London School of Economics (LSE) student union and as an
executive officer of its Islamic Society, he is now on the executive of the
Young Muslim Organisation UK. 'In all honesty', he says, 'I actually
think it's the fact that I'm Muslim that I can contribute so much to this
country. It's pretty much because I am a Muslim that I feel a debt to the
communities that I live in, the society in general. You have to contribute
back, you have to give something back.' In the context of our present
concern with alienated and radicalised young Muslims who feel as if they
have nothing to contribute and who would not get the recognition they
deserved even if they did, it is worthwhile bearing this other trend in
mind. There are plenty of other young Muslims in Britain for whom
Islam is not a badge of alienation but the very basis of integration and
social engagement.

* * *

The particular ways in which young Muslims in Britain today have turned to Islam varies enormously. Within this kaleidoscopic reality, however, some patterns are evident. Another common feature is the openness of their journey into and through Islam. Islam, for them, is not marked by a sense of closure but rather of incompletion; for many of those to whom I spoke, it is less a final destination than a departure point. Many commentators have suggested that an Islamic identity affords a sense of stability for a generation who are caught between conflicting cultural values. If this is so – and it may well be – it is also the case that this search for stability co-exists in many with a refusal to settle into complacency.

Qadeer Ahmed, for instance, spoke of his relationship to Islam in a manner which accentuated the way his faith constantly acts as a spur to become an even better person. 'If you're at a level at which you think you're doing well [with your religion], then you might as well be as far back as possible,' he said. 'The world's not going to stop, the world keeps moving and so Islam should keep moving with you or you should keep moving with it. We should be doing more and more and not thinking, "Well, I'm doing really well with this."'

This emphasis on movement echoes all the others who openly talked of 'pathways', 'journeys' and 'discovery' in relation to their faith. There is a sense that Islam requires an active pursuit rather than a passive acceptance.[1] 'When I started researching into Islam', said Munizha from Slough, 'I wasn't sure which was the right route for me.' She thus began to enquire into ways of practising Islam that lay beyond her own Pakistani Sunni tradition. Shi'ism, for example, was a path that attracted her for a time even though she eventually declined it. Perhaps this openness was a consequence of the lack of religiosity which surrounded her as a child. In common with many of her friends, she believed that she 'wasn't fully grounded' in Islam and so she felt she had to actively look into things, and as a result she began to look deeper than she might otherwise have done if she had just blindly followed the Islam of her parents. This pursuit of Islam led to many conflicts with her parents precisely because she would not settle for their kind of Islam.

The point was reiterated by the graffiti artist Mohammed Ali. Like nearly all his peers, he had been sent to a mosque school to learn the Qu'ran and that gave him a certain identity as a Muslim. Then, as his family went up in the world, they moved out of the tightly knit Muslim community of Sparkbrook and into a largely white, middle-class suburb close to King Edward's Grammar School, which he attended from the age of 11. By his own admission, it was during his time at grammar school that he 'started to kind of lose myself a little bit'. Islam faded from his life until he began to 'rediscover' it during his time as a student at DeMontfort University in Leicester.

'You had this understanding from what your parents taught you and then, at university, you have a look yourself and then you think, "Hang on, the *hadith* is actually quite specific about this and that", and during that phase, when you discover the *real* Islam, that for me was probably the biggest eye-opener because it made me *think*. It's interesting, all these things that you kind of blindly accepted in life, it's so much more beneficial, so much nicer, when you actually read it and think, "well, actually Islam is very clear and it's something that we can all appreciate and we can go out and find out directly and we don't have to rely on other people – you can go and read it and research it yourself".'

The ubiquity of terms such as 'journey' and 'discovery' in young Muslims' descriptions of their movement into and through Islam is also paralleled by the propinquity of words such as 'learning' or 'research' and 'reading'. Munizha spoke very forthrightly about taking the time 'to actually take the holy book out, read it, and research about the religion and understand what my responsibilities were as a Muslim woman'. A 21-year-old woman called Nazma, whom I met in Lancashire, had established a community group that seeks to raise awareness of Islam within the local community. Significantly, this group is called *Ikra*, which is Arabic for the verb 'to read' (and is also, just as significantly, the very first word of the Qu'ran).

In the minds of many of these young Muslims, then, the nature of their quest – the active pursuit of Islam and the open-endedness of their 'journey' into and through it – is closely associated with the acquisition and expansion of knowledge. Islam acts as a resource in much the same way that secular forms of knowledge do in modern, secular societies. Indeed, many secularists rather blithely assume that religious knowledge is something of an oxymoron, that knowledge is only knowledge as such if it is modern, 'secular' knowledge such as 'history' or 'science'. Young Muslims, however, do not share this allergy to other forms of knowledge. Moreover, they insist on knowledge as being the basis of Islam.

A 30-year-old Muslim professional that I met in London, Abdur-rahman, recalled that during his university days in the late 1990s, the American Sufi scholar Hamza Yusuf made a great impression on many students. 'He was very popular on the campuses', he said, 'and he had a big impact on a lot of people. He basically brought [Islam] back to being a knowledge-based religion. You have to know about your religion; you have to learn Arabic; you have to understand the Qu'ran for yourself, directly; you have to respect qualified scholarship and not just any man who thinks can just print off a leaflet. That takes dedication, that takes years, and when we heard people like Hamza at that time, who would articulate our religion in a very academic, very intelligent way, bringing together traditional Islamic roots with modern social sciences and history, that sort of thing – well, that had a lot of impact on people because it made you a little bit more comfortable that you could be an intelligent Muslim, that a Muslim wasn't necessarily the man in the mosque who's got a beard blindly following what he's been told.'

But there is an ambivalence here that Abdur-rahman has, perhaps unwittingly, revealed – one that has been a feature of Islamic history since the death of the Prophet. It centres on the issue of who possesses the authority to interpret Islamic knowledge. There are some, like Abdur-rahman, who believe that authority must rest with trained scholars who have undergone rigorous training. And yet, the appeal of Islam for people such as Munizha, Mohammed Ali and, indeed, many, many others is that there is no official priesthood or clerisy that stand as guardians over the 'correct' interpretation. In that respect, every single Muslim has the right to directly interpret Islamic knowledge – of which the Qu'ran and the *hadith* are the main sources – for themselves and in the light of their needs.

It bears repeating that this problem, known as the problem of *ijtihad* or free interpretation, is a systemic feature of Islam, which is in fact the most individualistic of the three Abrahamic monotheisms. Indeed, for all the talk of a need for an Islamic reformation, the parallels with Christianity should not be followed too closely; the struggles over interpretation which lay at the root of the Reformation in Christian Europe are, and always have been, an endemic feature of Islamic history. If you do not like some particular group's interpretation then there is nothing stopping you from looking for your own. The chronic instability this bequeathed to Islamic politics and society eventually necessitated limits on *ijtihad*, leading to the infamous 'closing of the doors of *ijtihad*' in the twelfth century CE.

Many speculate that this is the reason why Islamic societies, which, until the Renaissance, had been so far ahead of their Christian counterparts in terms of science, technological sophistication and scholarly accomplishment, fell behind to a newly energised, post-Reformation Europe unleashed from its thraldom to the Vatican. Perhaps it instilled the habit of 'blind acceptance' against which many of today's young Muslims now fight. There is probably more than a pinch of truth to this. What is of most concern to us here is that in the face of modern Europe's relentless subordination of the world during the colonial period, the gates of *ijtihad* were slowly prised open and now stand fully ajar.

The return of *ijtihad* paved the way for Muslim reformists and modernisers to tackle the unprecedented problems that they had to contend with, problems not anticipated or adequately addressed by the extant interpretations. It has also, incidentally, multiplied the ideological and doctrinal differences within Islam at a vertiginous rate. The same freedom of interpretation that might allow 'moderate' reformers to come to some *modus vivendi* with western norms and values also affords the room for 'radicals' to push for a totally different agenda. This is the double bind which Muslims currently face, because even if they were to accept that only qualified scholars should be allowed to interpret Islam and not anyone who, in Abdur-rahman's words, 'can print off a leaflet', this would not, in itself, resolve the issue because there is no guarantee of consensus.

Take the question of music, for example, which is one of the most vexing issues facing young Muslims in Britain today. There was much disagreement amongst the young men and women I spoke to about whether listening to music is permissible. The problem is, this is not likely to be resolved by turning to the qualified scholars. No less an authority than Professor Tariq Ramadan, for example, believes that listening to music is completely permissible.[2] And yet there are many whom I spoke to who think it is *haram* – forbidden. It is not likely that they came to this conclusion themselves; instead, they would have drawn upon available 'scholarship' which attests to that view. How does one arbitrate between these two points of view? Currently, there is no way of doing so. If one scholar issues a *fatwa* – a legal opinion (note: opinion, not ruling or edict) – another can easily issue a counter-*fatwa*.

The consequence is that modern Islam is a seething hive of argument and counter-argument; as in the early decades and centuries following the Prophet's death, twenty-first-century Islam is riven by internal conflict, debate and dissension. There is a dizzying proliferation of groups, subgroups and sects, each with a distinct ideological profile, although certain broad patterns can be detected. Those non-Muslims who cling to the naïve belief in a clash of civilisations are simply ignorant – or choose to remain ignorant – of modern Islam's polychrome texture. Modern Muslims do not blindly follow one particular group, leader or opinion. They contest and argue their points of view.

In this context, the insistence by many of today's young Muslims that one should not 'blindly accept' what one has been told is a kind of rhetorical device, distinguishing their own interpretation of Islam and affirming their right to hold it. Implicitly, they accept the reality of diversity and difference of opinion as an endemic – even systemic – condition. Moreover, even as they differentiate themselves from those they see as blindly accepting old-fashioned interpretations, this implicit acceptance of difference of opinion testifies to the fact that they are aware of plenty of others who, like themselves, are actively interpreting and pursuing their own path through Islam. The question of who is to resolve or arbitrate between these different paths is left open.

This is why the question of authority and leadership is such a critical one at this juncture. In a later chapter, we will examine what young British Muslims feel about those who claim that authority and who seek to represent them. Mostly, these men (usually men) are older, and thus this important question is yet another dimension of the generational conflict that is such a defining feature of British Muslim life. But there are emergent leaders amongst the younger generation, and their views on the whole matter of what Islam actually is about and what it should mean to Muslims in this day and age could be important signposts for the future.

* * *

Edgware Road, one of London's most important thoroughfares, is the heart of the capital's Arab community. This long street, which heads north from Marble Arch, is lined with cafes and restaurants. At any given moment in the day, clusters of men idly pass the time smoking charcoal *hookahs*, reading the Arabic papers or watching the traffic and people. The women, who move unhurriedly up and down the street, sport a variety of costumes, from the latest western designer outfits to full *burka*. The entire range of Arab culture is to be found here, and here too one can see the ideological differences that mark out the Middle East in full view, condensed by proximity in this important centre of the Arab diaspora.

On a warm spring day in March 2007, I ventured behind Edgware Road into the warren of streets that lie behind it – streets lined with mansion block apartments and elegant townhouses. And yet, behind the façade, many of these apartment blocks are surprisingly shabby; not dilapidated by any means but still rather down at heel, without the wealthy stolidity to be found just across Oxford Street in Mayfair. One receives the impression that the super-rich London Arabs of popular legend may indeed visit Edgware Road but they would prefer not to live here, retreating instead to their Kensington and Knightsbridge abodes once the daily round of shopping and socialising is done.

It is precisely because the Arabs who live on or around Edgware Road span the social spectrum, from the upper middle-class business families at the top to the working-class small shopkeepers, waiters and service personnel at the bottom, that the area retains its role as the beating heart of the British Arab community. And it is for this reason, too, that we must look here for signs of development in the formation of British Islam because whilst many assume that British Islam is South Asian in timbre – and indeed the vast majority of British Muslims are from that region – there are nevertheless many other Muslims from other regions whose voices have and will shape the kinds of Islam that will emerge. Perhaps the most significant among these is the British Arab community, for a number of reasons.

First, as the historical homeland of Islam, Arabia has held a symbolic authority throughout Islamic history. That authority is visible today in the patronage of Islamic organisations all over the world by the Saudi Arabian government. Secondly, increasing numbers of young, British Muslims whose families originate from South Asia are turning to Islamic models that have emerged from the Middle East, particularly Wahabbi-style organisations that have received funding and support from the Saudis, Wahabbism being the official Islam of that kingdom. In doing so, they are turning their back on their parents' Islam, with its rich tapestry of hybrid influences from South and South-East Asia. This appeal has undoubtedly been bolstered by the political attention on the Arab world. However, there is also a simultaneous movement *away* from Arab models of Islam amongst many young Muslims towards a more polycentric view of Islam adapted to local environments. Many commentators suggest that, in future, the most important strains of Islam will emerge in the peripheries of the Muslim world, in Europe, in South-East Asia and even in America.

Edgware Road lies at the confluence of all these conflicting currents. In which way is it heading? It is difficult to tell right now in the turmoil that has engulfed the world since the late 1990s. Whilst political events in the Middle East are undoubtedly providing a platform that is enhancing the appeal of certain radical Islamist organisations – however much the British government might protest otherwise – a generation of British Arab Muslims is emerging which is also perhaps looking to forge another path, one that is attuned more to the specifics of living in contemporary Britain.

I met Ayman in his small council flat just off Edgware Road. He showed me into his living room, and as I waited for him to bring some refreshments, I scanned the shelves which were lined with books on Islam, mainly in Arabic but a few in English – copies of the Qu'ran and volumes of the *hadith*. The impression was of a man in search of as much knowledge as he could gather about his religion, and yet, unlike Omar who had began his Islamic scholarship at a tender age, Ayman told me that he became religious only some three years beforehand.

He had lived all his twenty-three years in this area. His father had moved to London in 1973 and established an import business, selling foodstuffs and other groceries to the Arab stores on Edgware Road. Like many young Muslims, his childhood was not particularly religious – in fact, it was not religious at all. He was, he told me, 'very naughty' at school and he did not do very well in his examinations. He lived the life of a typical teenager in many ways but soon he began to realise that he had not achieved his potential. He began to reflect upon his life and took steps to improve it. At first, this did not involve religion. He was determined to pursue further studies and gain some qualifications. This he did, and he is now pursuing a master's in management studies at the University of Westminster because 'in the future I want to do a project in the form of an institute or an organisation, and you obviously need the management side of things'. It is clear that his ambitions run high; the institute he would like to establish will, he said, 'benefit the religion and benefit the spread of the proper teachings of it'.

Even though he began to reflect upon his life, and began to question the purpose of his life and the other existential questions that we all at some point consider, religion was not the first thing he turned to. Partly, this was because of how he perceived religion and religious people. 'I never thought that religion would be the answer of why I'm here and this is the path I should be following because as a youngster, and especially as an Arabic youngster, we always used to look at religion by looking at the examples of religious people – they would be wearing long dress-like outfits, long beards, and they would look at you as if they wanted to strangle you for not having a beard, or they'll want to strangle you for not being religious.'

This rather forbidding image of religion meant that he and his friends 'never ever thought of religion as being the mercy and the kindness and the smile and the brotherhood and the sisterhood. Personally, I never thought of it like that until I started listening to some tapes by an Arabic scholar called Wagdy Ghoneim, and there was laughing going on. When he preaches he adds jokes to real life situations which tend to convey the message of happiness to mankind in this life and the hereafter.' This new, light-hearted style of preaching was a breath of fresh air for Ayman but even still he admitted that 'I used to listen to it for a laugh but I never used to relate it to religion in that sense.' Nevertheless, when the religious trigger did occur, it was this benign approach to Islam which helped define his belief. He talks with open admiration about preachers who preach with a 'smile on their face and who really want to hold your hand and say, "I'm here for your good, let's do it together", as opposed to, "I'm going to be opposed to you because you're not religious."'

The ideas he has absorbed from his masters course are another key influence on Ayman; this secular knowledge sits alongside, and often intersects, the religious knowledge he has acquired. His language is suffused with terms such as 'objectives' and 'goals' and 'strategy' and 'aims'. 'I asked myself', he said, 'if there is an objective behind everything I do in life – I go to college and there's an objective behind it, I get married for an objective, then I have children and all the rest of it, then how about all of this in the context of what I am actually doing here in this life?' For Ayman, his religion is a way of meeting this objective – the meaning and purpose of life. Looking at it this way, he believes, helps him to analyse the world around him, and his 'objective' is to help create an Islam that is 'fit for purpose' – he did not, in fact, use this term, but I can imagine him doing so. It is an approach that has led him to become something of a presence in the community, and he often gives sermons in his local mosque.

What exactly are the objectives in this respect?

'My objective is for Muslims to come back to the proper teachings of Islam', he replied, 'to take everything in our religion, not just what they want, what they desire, or what suits them or what may not come in line with politicians, or the police, or intelligence, or whatever.' This was quite some opening gambit, and quite a radical formulation in many ways, not totally dissimilar to the 'fundamentalist' approach. In historical terms, this idea of 'going back' to the 'proper teachings of Islam' has been a characteristic of modern Islam ever since the gates of *ijtihad* were prised open again in the late nineteenth century. This appeal to the first generation of Islam – the *salaf* – is typical of both reformist and radical interpretations of Islam in the modern world. The term *salafi* applies as much to Osama bin Laden as it does to historical figures such as the 'liberal' Muhammad Abduh, the late nineteenth-century *mufti* of Cairo who was admired by, amongst others, Lord Cromer.

Salafism is therefore not an adequate term, in and of itself, to distinguish between competing interpretations of what Islam is 'really about', the problem being that there are conflicting definitions and descriptions of the period of the *salaf*. In essence, it boils down to a rejection of what are perceived to be some of the cultural 'accretions' that have latched onto Islam in the course of its history as it has spread across the globe and encountered different traditions in different contexts. However, precisely what those accretions are and which should be rejected are a matter of debate and, as usual, much disagreement.

The Islamic scholar Tariq Ramadan suggests that we should look at the divisions within *salafism* as being between 'reformist' *salafism* and 'literal' *salafism*. He says that the 'literalist' *salafis*, like the Wahabbis, should not be allowed to hijack the concept of *salafism*. Instead, 'reformist' *salafis* should return to the first generation of Islam, to its sources, 'to find the spirit, the objectives' of the Prophet's teachings.

That Ayman's language is so close to Ramadan's is not coincidental. It soon became clear that he is a 'reformist' *salafi* in the mould advocated by Ramadan. 'One area I really concentrate on', he said, 'is, I always say, "guys, we cannot pick up the Holy Qu'ran and read the Holy Qu'ran and think we can understand it the same way that Allah revealed it to our Prophet." Because, in essence, if I believed that then I am saying that I have a mind at the same level as my God, which is absolutely ridiculous.' Echoing Abdur-rahman's insistence on the importance of qualified scholarship and learning, he went on, 'that's why we have sheikhs, that's why we have imams, they've gone through years of studying and analysing areas where the Prophet has not said, "OK, 1+1=2". There's the explicit and there's the tacit texts in our religion and the reason we have this is because the explicit is, ok, these are the principles of our religion but the tacit part is because our religion is for every day and age, so you can't have 1+1=2 in every aspect of our life if life changes … that's where the tacit part comes in.'

The 'tacit' is where, in other words, *ijtihad* comes in and this, argues Ayman, must be left to scholars. It is scholarship that is the means of combating the naïve appeal of literalism. Instead of reading the text 'as it is', one must read it in context and with due attention to the 'principles' that lie behind a particular episode as well as the historically specific context within which that episode took place. Literalism is unable to do this and simplistically seeks to 'copy' the original – the *salaf* – and 'paste' it into modern society without any awareness of the changing context.

'One serious problem we come across is what I call the "copy–paste" problem that some Muslim schools are going through now. It's this: what we read in the books about the life of the Prophet we have to see exactly the same now. And this is something I just can't believe. I'll give you a short example: you'll find some Muslims who wear trousers or their garments above their ankle because they say there's a saying of the Prophet – and there is this saying – which says that anyone who walks with their clothes below their ankle will go to hell. Now they've taken this literally by reading it and taking it as it is. They've all gone out now and they're all wearing their trousers above their ankle. Now one thing we need to bear in mind when we read the Qur'an or the sayings of the Prophet, and this is why I say we need to revert to our scholars, is: where was it said? How was it said? Was it said in a situation that can be generalised, where the meaning can be generalised? Or was it unique to some situation or some person? You need to ask these questions.'

'Now, the meaning of this saying is, at the time of the Prophet, what many people used to do is walk with clothes dragging behind them to show people that they're rich and that they're better than other people because they have so much money they can drag their clothes in the dirt behind them. Now the Prophet says that anyone who does that will not go to heaven, meaning that this big-headedness and this lack of consideration for the poor who are going to see them walking past, when they do not even have enough food to feed their children, then ok, if you're going to act like this then you're not going to go to heaven because part of our religion is to have consideration for others. So, the meaning behind this is not to be big-headed and to have consideration for others. But the literal meaning which people have taken is, ok, I now am going to walk the streets with my trousers above my ankle. And this is what I mean by copy–paste.'

This attention to the specific contexts in which the sources of Islamic knowledge were originally articulated extends, according to Ayman, to their application. In other words, different geographical and social contexts demand different interpretations of Islamic teachings. One cannot just 'paste' the solutions appropriate for one country into another just as one cannot paste the *salaf* literally into the twenty-first century. This is a rebuke to many 'fundamentalist' approaches to Islam, from the Taliban to the Wahabbis. The one-size-fits-all Islam to which they aspire is fundamentally flawed.

One cannot help but be impressed by the passion of his conviction, and I agree substantially with his analysis. It is a message that has been articulated by the generation above him, by scholars such as Tariq Ramadan and Hamza Yusuf. Perhaps what he has absorbed of this tradition can be passed onto his contemporaries in due course. However, the ghosts of past battles between 'reformists' and 'literalists' still haunt the scene. Those of us with a knowledge of the struggles within Islam since the nineteenth century will recognise that these are precisely the terms over which literalists and reformists have staked their respective positions ever since, and successive generations of literalists and reformists have laid claim to the true meaning of Islam without resolving the issue. The problem is that it ultimately rests on interpretation, argument and persuasion.[3] The two sides can find 'scholars' willing to testify for one side or the other and neither can definitively nor conclusively prove that they are right. Therein lies the limitation of *salafism*.

* * *

Are there other avenues which young British Muslims might pursue that might avoid the *impasse* faced by reformist *salafis*? Some days prior to my meeting with Ayman, I found myself on the other side of London, in the East End, where the largest community of British Bangladeshis have settled since the 1970s, although some pioneers migrated here in search of work in London's dockyards as long ago as the mid-nineteenth century. Today, what is known as 'Banglatown' encompasses not just Spitalfields and the iconic Brick Lane, with its curry houses, *sari* shops and grocery stores, but also the neighbouring wards in Tower Hamlets: Whitechapel, Mile End, Stepney Green and Bethnal Green. Densely clustered in apartment blocks and older terraces, the Bangladeshis are just the latest in a long line of immigrant communities that have disembarked in London's dockyards and made it home: Huguenots, Jews, Italians and Irish have all preceded them.

Raihan Alfaradhi was born in Stepney Green in the mid-1980s. He lived for seven years in Stepney before the family moved eastwards, first to Poplar and then even further out to Redbridge. Despite growing up in one of the most impoverished boroughs of London, Raihan's family can be said to be middle class, at least in terms of their values and aspirations. His father and mother were both teachers; his mother in a primary school and his father, who originally came to take up a post teaching religious education in a state school, has subsequently risen to become a head teacher. Education is thus embedded into the family mindset. His father had been taught, like most rural boys in Bangladesh, in a traditional *madrassa*, but he then made a name for himself by becoming one of the top graduates in his year from Dhaka University. Raihan was able to take advantage of the assisted places scheme, which enabled some poorer children to be sent to private school, to attend the City of London School and from there went on to study at the LSE. When I met him, he was working as an auditor in one of the City's top financial companies.

Raihan's credentials as a future leader within Britain's Muslim communities – and certainly within the Bangladeshi community – are perhaps a little more clear-cut and established than Ayman's. His father was the president of Islamic Forum Europe for many years alongside the current head of the Muslim Council of Britain, Dr Abdul Bari. Raihan grew up calling Dr Abdul Bari 'uncle'. In addition to this, his own efforts have marked Raihan out as someone with the dynamism and determination to take a leading role in shaping the future. He was heavily involved in student politics at the LSE, becoming a representative of the student union, and he participated in the running of its Islamic Society and soon became the London co-ordinator of university Islamic societies. He has also been on the youth committee of the Muslim Council of Britain and is on the executive of Young Muslim Organisation UK, which he describes as 'the youth organisation of the Islamic Forum Europe'.

He acknowledges that his view of Islam has been influenced by his father but, at the same time, admits that 'there are only a handful of people' who look at it the way he does, which is 'different from the majority of people'. It is a view which has been determined by the fact that he has 'reconciled the fact that I'm British as well, I was born here, everything about me is British'.

What, then, is Raihan's vision of Islam?

'I've lived my life in a kind of moral-ethical way, and the way I've chosen is through principles that Islam has laid down. You obviously have to have some kind of principles – everyone has principles – but in society you have slightly different sets and the way I look at religion or Islam in particular is that it provides you with a handful of things that you can live your life by. So, for example, not hurting others, and not doing harm to yourself. There's maybe only about four or five of these big principles and everything else stems from those. For example, not harming others – a lot of things come from that; not harming yourself: with alcohol, smoking, drugs, all that stuff, you know? Anything which happens in my life, I have to judge it by those principles … the whole point is that if you do something which someone says is part of your religion but it contradicts those principles then it can't be part of it. The principles wouldn't have led you to it. So, for example, suicide can't be allowed.

'The reason why I think very differently from the majority of Muslims is that they look at it in almost the completely opposite direction. So, it's like, okay, I can do this or that, I can pray five times a day, I can fast, I can do all these things because someone told me to go and do this, but they don't think about if what they're doing contradicts what they hold true of Islam as a religion and its principles. So, for example, some people go around swearing this that and the other to non-Muslims, that they're going to go to hell and all that stuff, you know, and that completely contradicts the whole point of being nice to people and being friendly. If you want to tell people about your religion, fine, but do it in a way which is nice, do it in a way which is convincing but you must leave the decision up to them. At the end of the day, you can't force people, you know. I couldn't force religion on anyone, for example. Unfortunately, the problem I find with most Muslims now is that they look at it in completely the opposite way and because of that they naturally contradict themselves at some stage or another, they become extreme in some form or another.'

Is that because they have not worked out *why* they are following Islam? I asked.

'Yeah, because they haven't fully understood the whole point, the principles behind the religion, why you do those things. The fact that I pray five times a day, the fact that I fast, and all the other things I have to do, the kind of rites, or rituals, or whatever you want to call them – those things come as a natural consequence of the fact that you believe there is a higher purpose, not because you were just told to do it.'

For Raihan, then, the principles lie behind the actions, which are derived from them, and if one commits an action that contradicts those principles then that action cannot be justified.

'The truth can't be said for the converse', he continues, 'because you might do all the "right" things you're supposed to do in your life, well fine, you've done those things but you might also do something which is really wrong, which you don't realise is wrong, or you don't see it.' Without working out what principles are guiding your actions, he argues, you are not able to judge, to discriminate between good and bad actions. Hence, as he says, at some point you may contradict yourself or commit bad actions without realising it – or become extreme in your actions because there is no ethical core guiding your behaviour.

'The majority of Muslims only *do* the right thing' he says, by which he means what they have been told to do, to perform, out of obligation; however, because they have not thought about why they must do those things, 'they almost always stop there. I wanted to go the opposite way because if you do, then you'll end up with both the principles *and* you have the rituals. If you do it the other way, there's no guarantee you will ever reach the whole point of the religion. It almost becomes like a hollow shell.'

Raihan has quite firmly, and self-consciously, set himself against the grain but his view of Islam may not be quite so idiosyncratic as he imagines. The emphasis on 'active pursuit' amongst many young Muslims I encountered suggests that they too might be following the ethical route he espouses, trying to work out for themselves the basis of their religion, the principles that they feel should guide their actions. There are lot of overlaps, for instance, with Ayman's *salafist* position, which seeks to find the 'fundamental' principles that might guide Muslims today. Nevertheless, the emphasis there on establishing the original context of a 'tacit' text does suggest that, for Ayman, these principles are a little less open-ended than they are for Raihan. For him, the 'active pursuit' could mean a search for the right 'answers' in the extant literature and knowledge of Islam. This is slightly different to what I think Raihan is trying to suggest. If I interpret him correctly, the 'answers' are not to be found by establishing what the 'original' context was but by constantly measuring one's own behaviour against the set of principles from which such behaviour is derived. It is not really a *salafi* position but rather an ethical one that is more sanguine about discarding some of the sources. As such, it is perhaps a little more forward-looking than even the most reformist *salafi* position, which inevitably 'looks back' in some way to that founding generation even as it does so to look forwards. The more ethical position concerns itself less with that original moment.

However, this does not necessarily resolve any of the problems faced by reformist *salafis*, not least because it also cannot overcome the problem of differences in interpretation. If the ethical position espoused by Raihan might be content to overlook some of the more troublesome verses and *hadith* which might contradict the ethical principles they have worked out for themselves, they nevertheless must always confront others who are not willing to do so. On what basis would they say such verses do not matter? Similarly, the reformist *salafi* must constantly confront alternative interpretations and descriptions of the *salaf* itself.

Incidentally, all this highlights just how problematic and inadequate the term 'fundamentalism' is. Ayman, for example, believes that 'the fundamentals of the religion will stay the same' for all time but the contexts in which they are applied will differ. By this, he means something akin to (but not quite the same as) Raihan's point about finding the principles to live by from which all else is derived. In common parlance, however, 'fundamentalism' refers to the literal reading of the foundational text – the copy–paste school – which both Raihan and Ayman reject. The fact that it can apply to all three of these renders it literally meaningless. Any devout believer of whatever ideological hue or persuasion believes in what they take to be the 'fundamentals' of their religion. Of course, Raihan and Ayman might disagree on what these fundamental principles are but this further highlights the problem with the term 'fundamentalism'.

What is interesting is that both Ayman and Raihan accept differences of opinion as intrinsic to the practice of Islam. Raihan's ethically oriented, open-ended notion of living by certain broad principles derived from Islam implicitly accepts that, within such broad categories, there is room for many different interpretations of how to live according to them. Similarly, Ayman admitted, 'There are many different interpretations of our religion out there now, so what am I to do? I want my religion but which is the right – I'm not going to say the right way because there are different ways of practising our religion – which is the right path for me?' Once again, the metaphor of the journey is indicative of the kinds of Islam that young British Muslims are imagining for themselves. Not only does it suggest an active, forward-looking, constantly evolving and dynamic Islam – progressive, might be another word for it – but also one that recognises that there is no single pathway through life, no single religious road. Some of these roads may be less travelled than others but there is an implied acceptance that they are equally valid. This is hopeful when we consider not just the pathways in Islam but those outside it too and the implications for relations with non-Muslims. It would be naïve, however, to imagine that such differences – both within Islam and between Muslims and non-Muslims – would not lead, in other contexts (especially in relation to politics), between other groups and individuals, to problems of other kinds. Equally, it would be obtusely pessimistic not to acknowledge the possibility this might help us find ways of living together more harmoniously.

* * *

Raihan and Ayman, like most others I met, are self-avowedly Muslim and committed to their faith. There are, however, some who are less sure, whose journeys are just beginning or who are faced by doubts and hesitations. They are perhaps the ones who are seeking the hardest but, precisely because of that, are not able to find what they are looking for. Many believe such people to be without foundation, looking at them somewhat condescendingly as being without principles, but sometimes theirs are the most interesting journeys of all, their tracks criss-crossing the frontier between belief and doubt, their explorations marked by fascinating detours and interesting *cul-de-sacs*.

The City of London is perhaps one of the unlikeliest locations to find someone on a spiritual odyssey. Its monuments to Mammon sit awkwardly in the mind alongside the strict monotheism of the Abrahamic faiths. Nevertheless, it was here, amongst the towering temples to global capitalism, that I encountered one of my most interesting interlocutors. Shaheen met me in the gleaming lobby of one of the City's largest accountancy firms. As she led me to the meeting room where the interview would be conducted, I noticed immediately that her dress and her manner were unlike most other young Muslims I had met. Instead of a *hijab* or *dupatta* and loose-fitting, full-flowing Islamic forms of dress, Shaheen's head was uncovered and she was elegantly attired in a close-fitting sweater, a full-length skirt and leather boots. Her clothes were not revealing by any means, but they were an immediate indicator that she preferred to follow other standards of propriety in her public persona. Although this may have been unusual in comparison with the other young women I had spoken to, it does not mean that she is in any way unique. Wearing demure western-style clothing and leaving the head uncovered is common amongst women of a certain class and background. It was, however, the first hint that her story would not follow quite the same pattern as the others.

Having said that, in many respects her life story does follow a trajectory roughly similar to many of my respondents. Shaheen was born in Pakistan in the late 1970s, the youngest of three children. Her father was an airline pilot and they led the comfortable, glamorous lifestyle of the elite in that country. There were parties at which alcohol would be served; her mother wore the best, most fashionable clothing, and they kept company with significant and important people. Unfortunately, when she was still very young, her father developed a serious medical condition that terminated his flying career. After that, he attempted to start a business in the north-west of England, in Manchester; the business failed but he had bought some property and this sustained the family and has done ever since. Nevertheless, the business failure may have contributed to her father's worsening drink problem and eventually her father and mother separated, her father moving to London whilst the rest of the family stayed behind in Manchester.

Bringing up a family on her own, her mother secluded herself from the other Asians in Manchester (the sense of shame at her family breaking down may have contributed to this) and, in any case, their class background meant that when they first arrived in the United Kingdom, they remained distant from the working-class and formerly peasant Asian communities that congregated in Britain's northern conurbations. This sense of apartness from Asian and Muslim communities was reinforced by the area in which they chose to live – an affluent town just outside Manchester. It was further reinforced by her attending the local grammar school, which was heavily populated by white, middle-class pupils. Muslims were conspicuous by their absence at that time.

This isolation from Britain's Muslim communities, this secluded insistence on doing it alone in the face of the many troubles in their lives, has perhaps had a formative impact on Shaheen's life as has the turbulence that lay beneath the surface of their respectable, middle-class lives. On the one hand, it led her to identify completely with the secular, British lifestyle she shared with her friends at grammar school and, when

she eventually started attending Manchester University, she firmly
and decisively rejected the overtures of the Islamic Society during
'freshers week'.

'My life literally was my mum, my brothers, and my aunt always lived
with us, my mum's sister. And my friends, that was literally it. All my
friends were white, Christian or not practising at all. At school we never
really talked about religion either. I mean we'd celebrate Christmas,
we always have Christmas to this day, we have like Christmas tea, we'll
have a turkey. We didn't really celebrate *Eid* because literally my mum
wouldn't know when it was. We'd find out maybe a week later, "Oh, it
was *Eid* last week." There was nobody to kind of tell us, we were very
isolated in that respect. When I became a little more open minded and
actually talked to Muslims, I found it really strange that they wouldn't
celebrate Christmas, and they found it really strange that I would.'

She only began to be aware of her difference from her friends as a
teenager when 'all my friends were able to do things that I wasn't able to
do'. For instance, she and her friends were very keen fans of the 'grunge'
music scene that was then emerging with bands such as Nirvana and
Pearl Jam. Since Manchester had developed into a capital for the
music scene in the 1990s, her friends would often go to concerts and
she would want to go too. Her mother only relented when Shaheen
accepted that her elder brother would have to chaperone her, despite the
embarrassment this would cause. Even as a student, she lived at home
and would drive in for classes, perhaps meet her friends for coffee and
a bit of shopping and then drive home again.

It was not really because she held Islam in some way responsible for
these restrictions that she rejected the Islamic Society during freshers
week but rather because she found she had nothing in common with such
Muslims, 'I remember just passing the Muslim stand, they were lovely,
there were these girls in *hijab* and everything else saying "Here's some
cassettes, go and listen to this … here's some leaflets, go and read this",
and I just remembered looking at it and just being quite shocked at what
I read. It was probably just some stuff about fulfilling your obligations to
pray, etc. but I just thought, "I'm not going to do this. That's not me. I'm
not them." And I completely dismissed it.'

On the other hand, the isolation and turbulence has led to – and I
mean this in the most positive sense – an unsettling of her mind such that
there seems to be a permanent need to question herself, to interrogate
the basis of her beliefs, feelings and attitudes. She is not confused; she is,

however, uncertain and this uncertainty has pervaded her intellectual and spiritual development, a process which began not with Islam but with existentialism and the philosophies of Nietzsche and Sartre, with the plays of Beckett and Stoppard.

'The A-Levels I did were Philosophy, French and English. It was the happiest time of my life, happiest because I was so into the subjects I was studying,' she said. That period of her life began with a rather surprising twist. 'It was really strange', she went on, 'when I began to do Philosophy, when I was 17 or so, I did form a belief in God and I really believed in God. I don't know where it came from, it didn't come from my family, it just came from within. And I remember in Philosophy we did some arguments which were like for and against the existence of God. Studying them – and it was only A-levels so it was quite basic – gave me a reasoned appreciation and I had enough faith in my own mind to resist the arguments against God, and I felt, "No, I really believe in this." '

This fledgling faith was nipped in the bud by two crucial life events. First, her father, with whom she and the rest of the family had begun to re-establish a relationship, suddenly died; then, she failed to get into Oxford. These twin blows shook her faith and, at the same time, she was exposed to new, more sceptical and pessimistic philosophies and encountered new forms of literature that would dramatically change her outlook.

'Have you heard of absurdist plays? Like Samuel Beckett and Tom Stoppard?' she asked.

I nodded, the English lecturer in me utterly delighted by this new turn in the narrative.

'In English, we did *Hamlet* and then we contrasted that with *Rosencrantz and Guildenstern are Dead*. So that's how I got into absurdism. In philosophy, we did existentialism with Nietzsche, and in French we studied Sartre as part of understanding French culture. It all welded together, and I developed a really good understanding of absurdism, and I guess at the time, when I was feeling quite pessimistic about everything, I started reading more absurdism and it really started making sense. I just thought religion was a bit of a farce like in *Waiting for Godot*, where basically two hikers have nothing, but they've given themselves meaning and they're putting their faith and their hope in something, in the hope that things might change tomorrow. And I was thinking that's what religion is, that's exactly what it is, where you're giving yourself patience, you're giving yourself strength, you're asking yourself to hold on until tomorrow, yet you're actually in the same place, if not worse.'

And yet here she was, a self-confessed Muslim. What changed her mind? I asked. Her reply was particularly illuminating.

'My awareness of Islam was very poor, like, limited to: Being a Muslim you should pray five times a day. Being a Muslim you play a certain type of music. Being a Muslim means you don't drink or do any of that stuff. And that was kind of it. At that time I wasn't really interested in spirituality, and even as a university student I guess I wasn't. So rather than attributing it to some kind of search for something spiritual.... .'

She paused, taking stock, trying to find the right words. Then she changed tack. 'I think back to how narrow minded I was', she said at last, 'I completely dismissed it. And I guess it was from some of the people I met during my Masters that just told me, basically, I was the one who was narrow minded not them [the Muslims she had dismissed] because I was dismissing something without knowing anything about it. And it was from that point on that I just started taking different steps to try and open up my own mind a little.'

Looking back, I find it significant that Shaheen is reluctant to name spirituality as the reason for her change of direction and instead prefers to interpret it as a kind of intellectual turning, an opening of the *mind*. But intellectual awakenings, like spiritual ones, can be rooted in or triggered by things which have very little to do with either the intellect or the spirit. What exactly made her see her narrow-mindedness for what it was?

'Quite honestly, a boy. There was a guy that I met, he was on my Masters course, and he was obviously interested in me and he made some attempts and I was completely not interested in him at first. I just didn't like him, his mannerisms. I found him too forthcoming, too presumptuous. Then, after a while, I started giving him a chance and started meeting him. He was religious, he was very practising. I'm not like him, and I never became like him. He was quite – I wouldn't say, radical but … you know, he would pray five times a day and had quite extreme opinions on things like … everything that's happened on the news recently, he'd say it was a conspiracy, it was this, it was that, so he was quite … well, in my mind that's radical. But he got me a book, Charles Le Gai Eaton's *Islam and the Destiny of Man*, and I never finished it', she laughed, 'but I read the first two chapters. And it just talked about the Muslim civilisation, you know, and when Islam was first born and the great things that have come to Islam. And I started thinking, this is more than just women covering their heads, there's a lot more behind here, and that kind of opened my mind a little bit.'

This young man – whom I shall name Haroun – had also read philosophy and was able to engage with her and 'he had a very good mind for discussions like that. It was really fascinating to be able to talk to someone about absurdism and existentialism and be very negative and say, "Well, Sartre said this ... and Beckett says this, now what do you have to say?" and he was still able to give me answers, he was like, "Well maybe this is how Islam would explain it" you know, or "I acknowledge your argument but this is how I respond." So that kind of helped me.'

The ghosts of Sartre and Nietzsche, of Beckett and Ionesco, would not be so easily vanquished, however. 'I've learned absurdism and I've been and watched absurdist plays, and to this day I still see deep meaning in it, and often when I feel negative, or things aren't going right, I'll go back to that line of thinking and I'll think this isn't absolute truth, it's just blind faith. But through Haroun I did see a way out of it and that was part of the reason why I started giving Islam more importance.'

This residue of absurdism and existentialism still gnawing away at the insides of her mind has profoundly shaped her view of what Islam means to her, and I realised that what I was listening to was a quite remarkable, and unusual, juxtaposition of two traditions in a very supple and active mind.

'This might sound really strange', she continued, 'but often I say to people that I think Islam is a beautiful religion and I feel I'm a Muslim but I don't know if I believe in God. Which is perhaps a really stupid thing to say but I guess it's my reliance on the kind of absurdist line of thought, when I often say to myself, "How can we believe in that? How can we? There's no proof, there's nothing. It's simply that, by believing in God it makes my life easier because I think everything I'm facing now, any trials and tribulations, there is actually a meaning to it and things will get better, and if I'm not rewarded in this life I'll be rewarded in the hereafter." I can't help but have that cynicism. But forgetting the existence of God or not, there are many things in Islam which I actually have a deep regard for.'

I began to wonder why, despite these moments of pessimism, when one side of her is telling her that there is no meaning to it, there is no God and it is all an illusion we prefer to the actual void of existence, she does not end up rejecting Islam and why she keeps returning to it.

'I've just read Martin Lings's *Life of the Prophet* and it was just incredible.[4] And it's a difficult book to read, I found it very difficult, but I stuck at it. It's written with such simplicity, you have to stop and think, and it brought tears to my eyes, it was so moving, and I couldn't understand why because it was written so simply, it's not like it was written in beautiful poetic language. And I just … you know, when you find out about the Prophet's life, you just think there is more than … that this is not coincidence. This man and what he went through and how he handled things, and the kind of parallels between what was happening to the Prophet and what was happening to the first group of Muslims and the revelations that came in the Qu'ran, many of which are in direct response to the trials and tribulations that they were facing. It was only when I read that book that I realised that there were lots of verses in the Qu'ran that don't directly reject the disbelievers, talking about disbelievers that he was then currently communicating with or coming across. It's just too strong and powerful for this all to be made up. How can it be? How can it not be real?'

It is, of course, not uncommon for faith to be kindled by the example of outstanding individuals, which is why in Islam the example of the Prophet – as the greatest of men – is followed so assiduously and so revered (and, of course, why many Muslims are so egregiously offended when that life is besmirched in any way). The same is true of Christianity, with its hagiographical traditions, and many other religions that put their most significant figures up on pedestals, seeking from their exemplary lives the clues to unlock the mysteries of faith. Sceptics, of course, respond that this is all propaganda, that such lives are cooked up or airbrushed; they are pedagogical instruments, not real lives at all. In this instance, they might suggest that the rational interpretation for why the revelations responded to real crises in the Prophet's life is because God was merely the justification for his responses to those events and crises. In other words, they stipulate that these correlations are just too convenient and conclude that it merely proves that God does not exist. On the other hand, Muslims would counter by saying that this in fact *proves* that God exists; it demonstrates his ability to intervene and guide the faithful in the secular world.

It all comes down, at last, to the question of faith but what I find interesting about Shaheen is the flickering shade of an argument that seems to bypass these two incommensurable alternatives. It is this: for a Muslim who is not really sure if God exists perhaps what Shaheen finds moving and convincing is the power of *belief* itself, which enables such responses to particular situations. To put it another way, the ethical or the political response to a given situation can be enabled not just by 'reason' but also by 'belief' – in a meaning, a purpose, an entity and a figure of speech or thought, which goes by the name of 'God'. This is an argument which not only accepts the role of reason in human circumstances but also accepts its limitations. It is an argument which seeks to push *through* reason to that which lies beyond it and which is perhaps equally important. Freud might have called it the *id*; religious people call it 'God'. They are not, of course, the same thing, but then the two can be nothing more than mere figures of speech because they are beyond language.[5]

I am not sure if Shaheen would see it in these terms, but I am certain she knows that what she is grappling with is doubt. She performs that doubt in virtually every sentence she utters on the subject. 'I don't know', she continued, 'I don't know why I can't … I almost can't grasp it fully, I can't reject it fully. I don't know why. I do … I have a phase where I'll pray – I never … I don't think I've ever prayed five prayers in one day but there'll be a month or two weeks where I've prayed Isha [the final prayer of the day, performed at night] every night. But then, like now, I don't think I've prayed for a couple of months, a few months. It all depends on how my life is going.'

Paradoxically, she is certain that doubt is a part of faith. 'It is about doubt. I think it's quite beautiful in its own way. That's what faith is, it's the not knowing. And that's what makes it so … not tragic, but you think, if I see a woman who … I can look at my mother, and she believes, and now she actually prays, but she has this absolute belief and I don't admire that as much as someone who tells me, "I'm a Muslim, I pray, I've got beliefs, but I know there might not be anything at the end of it, but this is my chore and I'm putting all my faith in this." And there's something very rich about that. And then there's a part of me that almost thinks that I would be very naïve if I was to do that, if I was to put my faith in something.'

It was dark by the time I left Shaheen's office and shuffled out into the London streets. Above me a train rumbled by and soon I would be on another one making my way home after another long day in this most secular of cities. Looking out of the window at Big Ben, and the twinkling pods of the London Eye, I reflected on Shaheen and her faith, her doubt and her inability – refusal – to resolve the two. She was right; there is a richness in it. We are accustomed to believe that faith is a belief *in* something. But perhaps faith is about the difference between knowing and belief. It is not necessarily one thing or the other but about a co-existence which admits that you know this much but you do not quite know for certain if there is anything more. Is there anyone, religious or non-religious, who is content to accept only what they know for sure? Do we not all believe in something else, something beyond what we actually know? Is faith not, then, part of all our lives in some way whether or not what we believe in is a God? 'There are more things in heaven and earth than are dreamt of in your philosophy,' says the old prince, and I find myself nodding assent on behalf of all of us who can never make our minds up.

This I do know for sure: Shaheen is not very representative of most young Muslims. What I am less sure about is how unrepresentative she is. How many young believers wrestle with the doubt within them and are either unwilling or unable to articulate it in the way she did? There must be many who cross the line from faith to doubt just as there are those who have gone the other way, and there must be many others who shuttle back and forth during the course of their lives. For these people too, faith and doubt co-exist though perhaps not in the kind of intimate proximity they do within Shaheen. Most of those I talked to spoke about their faith, their living faith, not as a static object but as a moving force. It moves them to live their lives according to certain principles; it moves them to practise those principles in a certain way; it moves them to look out into the world; and it moves them to search deep within. I believe – though I cannot be certain about this – that Britain's young Muslims will keep moving.

Chapter 3
Identity

Since the terrorist attacks in London on 7 and 21 July 2005, British Muslim communities have come under especially severe scrutiny. A slew of opinion polls have probed into their sympathies and motivations, their attachment or otherwise to their country and their position on many fundamental political issues of the day. All these have collectively gathered under the rubric, in some quarters, of the 'problem' of Islam's relationship to the West. The realisation that the bombers of July 2005 were not foreign radicals but young Muslims born and nurtured within Britain at first was received with shock and then, as the shock receded, was replaced by a growing suspicion that the putative loyalty of British Muslims was open to question – that they might constitute a potential fifth column within the context of the so-called war on terror.

The identity of young British Muslims has thus been at the centre of public discussion. Do they consider themselves to be British and feel allegiance to the British state as committed citizens willing to play their part in eradicating the threat to Britain from terrorists? Or do they feel no particular attachment to Britain but rather conceive of themselves as belonging to another orbit of loyalty, to a global Muslim community that is increasingly seen by some as being engaged in a 'clash of civilisations' with the West? If so, are they potential recruits to terrorist movements, willing to take up arms against the states in which they live for the cause of a religion which they believe to be antithetical to 'western' values?

The initial polls were relatively reassuring. A Market & Opinion Research International (MORI) poll commissioned by *The Sun* in the immediate aftermath of the first terrorist strikes in July 2005 indicated that 86 percent of British Muslims felt 'very strongly' or 'fairly strongly' that they belonged to Britain. MORI conducted a more-detailed survey for the British Broadcasting Corporation (BBC) in August 2005 which showed, amongst other things, that 76 percent of Muslims felt that immigrants should pledge their primary loyalty to Britain (as compared to 73 percent of the total British population), that 91 percent of Muslims felt that immigrants should accept the authority of British institutions (compared to 93 percent nationally) and that 88 percent felt proud when

British teams did well in international competitions (90 percent of the general population felt this way). Another poll conducted by ICM Research in February 2006 demonstrated that 91 percent of Muslims felt loyalty towards Britain.

Nevertheless, the suspicion has lingered that there is, in fact, some inevitable tension, if not outright conflict, between competing claims on the loyalties of British Muslims.[1] Younger British Muslims in particular are seen as being particularly prone to this identity conflict and therefore a cause for some concern since they are more likely to be attracted to the radical political Islam of those groups who encourage or espouse terrorism.[2]

The argument in the first two chapters of this book has been that the turn to Islam amongst the younger generation of British Muslims is not in fact a turning away from Britain and Britishness but in fact represents an attempt to find their place within British society. Unsurprisingly, nearly all the young Muslims to whom I spoke felt comfortable with their British identity. 'I am a 100 percent British and still a 100 percent Muslim', said Raihan Alfaradhi, 'I don't see why you should have to choose between one or the other.' This was echoed by the others, although they spoke about their identity in slightly different ways, with slight variations in emphasis.

Shahid, a 22-year-old accountant who was born in Bangladesh but grew up in north London, said, 'I think it's a bit ignorant of those Muslims who say "We're not British" because I think there are certain things of British identity that Muslims can take. I'll give you an example. If you compare going for a job interview in New York and London, the American will be completely arrogant in emphasis – even the way they ask the questions like, "Tell me what you're good at", and the American will say, "I'm great at this, I'm great at that", but I have found the British are a lot more modest in the way they think and the way they talk. I think it's because they have a lot of respect for each other. Even when you go on the Tube a lot of people might say that everyone is cold and so uptight, they never look at each other, but I think in a strange sort of way they are also very respectful of other people's privacy. I think there's a lot of values there that Muslims can take, definitely.'

He adds, however, that 'it's definitely a two-way process; it's not a matter of "am I Muslim first or British first?" I don't think that's the question. I think Islam is quite flexible in the sense that there is definitely a flexibility there for us to have some sort of Islamic thinking that's relevant to the Middle East, one that's relevant to Europe, and one that's relevant to Africa, or wherever.'

So did he believe that for British Muslims their Britishness and Muslimness are in contradiction, or in tension?

'Never. I mean Islam never came to contradict any region.'

Soumaya, a 23-year-old administration officer in Lancashire, was equally unequivocal when I asked her the same question, but she put it in a more practical way. She saw no contradiction 'because we've got the freedom to practise freely over here – there's no restrictions on that. I mean, in terms of going to your mosques, in what you wear, in what you believe, there's no restrictions on it, so I don't think there's really any clashes with being British. I don't think it's affecting your faith in any way. You can call yourself British and yet you can practise your religion freely too.'

Did she feel quite strongly that she was British?

'Yeah.'

Had she ever thought of herself, or felt herself, to be slightly alienated from Britain at all?

'Not really, no. I'm quite comfortable with it,' she said, quite matter-of-factly.

There were others who did differentiate between the elements which make up their sense of selfhood. Abdur-rahman, a very intelligent and articulate young man who works for one of the major public transport organisations, was aware that his identity was a moveable feast, shifting according to the context within which he was called upon to think about it, 'I'm quite clear. If anyone asks, "Are you British?" I'd say yes, but then if anybody asked me if I was a British Muslim I'd say yes as well. But if anyone just asked me, "What are you?" I'd say, "I'm a Muslim." So, I don't know what you want to take from that,' he said laughing. But he finished by saying, 'I think you can hold dual identities, it's not a problem, it really isn't.'

Munizha, from Slough, acknowledged that she felt very comfortable with her Britishness because she had never known anything else. 'I have friends and their parents are from Pakistan and they feel like they are Pakistani and it is very much a part of them. I don't have that sense of having a Pakistani identity as part of me, but they were people who, when we were younger, they went to Pakistan a lot … whereas for me the first and only time I've ever been to Pakistan was when I was sixteen and my sister had just got married, but I never knew anything about Pakistan as a country, like as a direct experience of it, before that. And so, by the time you're sixteen you're quite well grounded aren't you?'

But wasn't she brought up within a Pakistani culture even though this was located in Britain?

'I mean, obviously, we wore traditional Pakistani clothes, ate Pakistani food and things like that and my parents spoke to us in their mother tongue but I am not fluent in it anyway, so I didn't have that sense of a big Pakistani identity. So when you say I feel comfortable in my British identity I would just say that there is nothing really else – there's nothing apart from my Muslim-British identity – I put Muslim first because obviously my Islamic identity is more a part of me than the British society and culture – but this is where I've been brought up and this is what I've known.'

Others also felt that Islam was the more fundamental aspect of their identity. I shall return to this prioritising of aspects of identity, and what that might actually mean, in due course. However, at this stage, Shaheen's voice insists on making an entrance because she was, in fact, the only one of my interlocutors who did not respond by affirming her Britishness. This was something of a surprise because Shaheen was firmly middle class, works for an international and highly cosmopolitan City firm, grew up in an affluent, and predominantly white, suburb of Manchester and was educated at a grammar school where she was the only Muslim pupil. Unlike Munizha, therefore, she was not surrounded by Pakistanis, nor was she immersed in the social patterns of the Pakistani community. Although she was born in Pakistan, she left when she was just two years old.

Nevertheless, when I asked her about her identity, she replied, 'I'm Pakistani, I always make a point of saying that I am a Pakistani.'

She must have registered the surprise on my face because she quickly added, 'When people ask me "Are you British?" I say, well, it's a hard one. I'm British because I live here and … but if I move to Australia I'm not Australian, am I? If I move to China I wouldn't be Chinese.'

Quite typically, she began to think the question through, aloud, her sentences marked by hesitations, doubts and inconsistencies – symptoms of a mind wrestling with a problem that remains just elusive enough to slip through the established patterns of her thought.

'I don't know what Britishness is, it's very hard, but I don't … it's very difficult, but I always am a Pakistani. But I'm very grateful to Britain because I'm the person that I am. I am not a pure Pakistani, I don't think

I have to be one or the other. I'm a growing … I'm a changing person, I'm constantly changing. There's Britishness in me, there's Pakistani … very, a lot of Pakistani in me. Because…I guess it is questioned, maybe it's rightly questioned, because if I had to pick an allegiance between Pakistan and Britain I'd probably pick … ' and here she paused, 'I'd probably pick Pakistan. But that might be as a result of feeling some alienation from the political policies of this country.'

Did she think she could never be properly accepted as British because of the colour of her skin or her religion?

'Maybe recently. Never felt it before. When I have felt it I've tried to compare it to countries like Pakistan where people are quite openly racist, they make comments about white people, they make comments about black people, and I think a lot of the people who accuse Britain of being racist or whatever – which might be the case, or it might not … I mean, I think we do need to look at ourselves. My own parents make comments about people of other races, you know, so I think Britain is a fairly tolerant country if you compare it to places like where we're from.'

Again she paused, for longer this time as if gathering her thoughts once more to have another crack at the question. 'It's hard', she said, finally, 'because I don't … I always used to think I was Pakistani, always. From the age of 17 when I really started forming opinions for myself, before this whole race thing [i.e. loyalty] was ever questioned, I was always a Pakistani. From the age of about maybe 16 onwards I started going every year – I go every year back to Pakistan. And in the past few years I realise, well actually, I say I'm Pakistani yet I don't … when I'm there, after like two weeks I feel very frustrated by aspects of Pakistan which are very diffusive [sic]. I can only communicate to people to a certain extent. You know, people there are amazing, they're very warm, you know, very witty, very intelligent, but there are some things you just can't talk about. And that's maybe my Britishness, the sense of humour's very different. There are similarities but there are some things they just don't get, you know? We put copies of The Office on, you know; here, it's hilarious and I love it, but I put it on over there and they'll be like "What's going on?" These are quite important things and that makes me question, am I Pakistani? I don't know if I am.'

In the end, Shaheen concluded by turning the question around, 'Isn't this like an artificial discussion? You can't look at any of these things [i.e. the different dimensions of one's identity] in isolation, and if you look at them all together, it's a huge jumbled mix.'

In much the same way as she performed her doubt about her religious faith, I look back, and in hindsight, I can see how Shaheen performed not only her doubt about her identity but also her identity itself – slipping back and forth, *across* identities, never resting for long and never settled. Her Britishness, which is never consciously affirmed, is nevertheless present throughout, emerging at crucial points such as when her appreciation of *The Office* makes it apparent just how firmly embedded in the British cultural milieu she is.

Herein lies a certain truth about Britishness which is overlooked by the shrill anxieties of our time. All these stories about young British Muslims' identities demonstrate one salient fact: the gravitational 'pull' of a common British culture that exists in the ebb and flow of daily life; a multi-layered, somewhat impalpable, but nevertheless firm ground that exists without the need for official sanction, without some top-down bureaucratic attempt to instil Britishness and British values. This common culture – made up of so many strands and so many different dimensions – penetrates and shapes the lives of all communities in Britain sooner or later, even when it might not seem outwardly apparent; it does so especially amongst the young who absorb it much as a sponge absorbs water or trees absorb carbon dioxide – imperceptibly, without fuss or fanfare.[3]

* * *

Young British Muslims testify to the many different ways of 'being' British. Nevertheless, some common patterns do emerge. One of the most apparent is that their sense of belonging to Britain coexists, to a greater or lesser extent, with a sense of exclusion from it. The consequence is an ambivalence which signals less comfort with Britishness than is perhaps outwardly apparent, not so much with being British *per se* but with their place in Britain.

Fahmida, a 22-year-old student from Uxbridge, thinks of herself as British, but this is sometimes confounded and confused when she hears Muslims being spoken about in the media as 'they'. 'You always hear, "this is a Christian country and 'they' should do this and that" and it's like, excuse me, they? – who's they? Or, "all we ask them to do is … " Who's them? I think of myself as British and when you say Muslims as "they", well, am I a "they" as well? I mean, why isn't it just "us" altogether?'

Aisha, from Slough, also spoke in similar terms.

'When people ask you, "What are you?"' she said, 'and you say "I'm British" they then say something like, "But what are you really?" meaning "where do you really come from?" And I'm thinking, "I'm from here, I was born and bred here. If you wanna know where my parents come from, they're from Pakistan." If you tell them that – I think sometimes there isn't even any point in me answering that question because even if I say that I'm British they'll never really accept me for being British because of the way I look, the colour of my skin and all the rest of it.'

Likewise, the artist Yara el-Sherbini told me a story about her recent return to her native Pontefract in West Yorkshire.

'I grew up in Pontefract, and I sound like I'm from Pontefract, I don't sound like I'm from anywhere else – but in Pontefract people would still sort of say little subtle things like, "Where are you from?" and of course, when they ask that they don't mean you're from Pontefract, they mean where are your parents from. I'll never forget a couple of years ago I went into a pub and ordered a drink and they said, "Oh, well in Ponty … " Basically, they served me orange cordial instead of orange juice but I said I wanted orange juice not cordial and the barmaid said, "Well, in Pontefract, when you want orange juice you say 'Orange juice'." It's like, where do you think I'm from? What do you mean, "in Pontefract"? I've grown up here, I'm from Pontefract! If I was white, you would never have said "In Pontefract … " So these little statements still make you feel that, even though you're *in* Pontefract and have grown up in Pontefract, you're not *from* Pontefract.'

When asked about their experiences of growing up in Britain, many fondly recalled memories of their neighbourhood, their school, their friends and the myriad things that contribute to a life. But most of them also recalled less-savoury experiences. These mainly involved direct experience of racism.

In Lancashire, Qadeer Ahmed recalled that his was the first Asian family in the neighbourhood in which he continues to live. 'It was quite a racist area at the time. We couldn't play in our back garden. We had a pretty back garden and it led to garages, behind the gardens, and we used to get lads a lot older than us coming round and swearing at us and throwing stones at us and stuff. So we just wouldn't want to play in our back garden because we were afraid. And there's loads of graffiti on our back fence as well.'

Fortunately, the area has improved. 'Times have changed', said Qadeer, 'and people too. There's a lot more Asian families there as well.

And over the years, obviously, racism isn't as open so we don't get any racist abuse now.'

At the other end of the country, Raihan Alfaradhi was growing up in Poplar, in the East End of London. It too was 'quite a racist area', and the Alfaradhis, like all the Bangladeshi families that had moved into the area from other parts of the East End, encountered racial abuse.[4] 'We had a few problems with kids, you know, just like throwing eggs at your windows and all these kinds of things,' said Raihan. However, unlike Qadeer's neighbourhood, the improvement in race relations does not seem to have been quite so marked. Even in the more upmarket Essex suburb of Redbridge, where many wealthier middle-class Bangladeshis have recently settled, there have been racially motivated incidents. 'I mean just the last year we were driving around in Redbridge', continued Raihan, 'me and my dad were in the car and – yeah, it was summer, last summer – and some kids came around the bend in a car and there were four – there must have been four white guys in the car, they can't have been that old, they must have been 18 to 20 year olds, and one guy had some eggs in his hand and he just threw them into our car. It was summer so obviously we had the windows down and everything and it like hit my dad and it went on the back seat and stuff, and that was in Redbridge and you wouldn't expect that in that area.'

Likewise, the Birmingham-based artist Mohammed Ali recalled how his grammar school, King Edward's – one of the top schools in the country – was located in an area that was notoriously racist. 'And I don't just say that because there were loads of white people around or whatever, I know from experience because I've caught the buses there and I've been spat at by National Front guys; I used to see on the bus seats stickers for the NF, so I know that area, and I've had skinheads looking at me, spitting at me. Two little kids, I remember, shouted at me, "Oi, you Paki!"'

He went on, 'I was with my friend, Martin Barlow, and he's dead now, but I still remember that day them kids shouted "Oi, you Paki!" – he was like, he chased them – I remember that, I'll never forget that, especially because he's not around no more as well … but the guy, kind of, he was affected by that.'

He stopped, caught short by the memory, perhaps by the sense of loss, of an old friendship that now, from out of the depths of time, reveals something about one's past.

'It's weird … with Martin Barlow … everyone used to tell racist jokes about Pakis and Sikhs, you know like you do? Even I used to tell them! It's weird – I dunno, man, I think at that grammar school I kind of lost myself a little bit, you know, everyone's around you and your mate jokes about Asians and stuff or whoever – black kids, 'cos there was a black kid there, and we'd joke about his lips and stuff, and he'd laugh about it, we'd laugh, they'd take the pee out of him, out of me, you know, Paki – smells or whatever – and you'd laugh it off and it was kind of kiddish racist jokes but you kind of laughed it off. Now obviously … when you're young … I dunno … I was probably feeling insecure at that time, and I thought maybe I could just be like everybody else or something [by laughing it off].

'Martin was like that as well. You know, he was probably one of the most to be like, whatever, "Pakis, Pakis", you know, and I'd be with him. Now when I look back at myself I think what an idiot I must have been! Those kids, they probably saw me as some kind of coconut or something … like, what an idiot![5] If I'd have seen myself back in those days, I would have probably thought the same, what an idiot! How come he's going round with this guy and he's taking the piss out of Asians and he's [referring to his younger self] kind of laughing with him?

'That day, I still remember – and it was later on in school when I was kind of more grown up a bit, Martin Barlow, one of those kids you'd imagine to be racist, when he chased those kids – I still remember that day because it affected me, because I thought, that's interesting, that made me see the human side to him – and how he'd … it wasn't just a joke, then, these kids from the local area – the racist kids – they shouted "oi, you Paki" and they'd meant it, it wasn't a joke, and his instinct was to just chase them. It made me think, "yeah, he's sound he is" and I used to always defend him when he got into trouble because I'd seen another side to him. "I know he's not racist, he's just trying to attract attention, and trying to fit into the clan".'

Like Mohammed Ali, Yara el-Sherbini also noted how her experience of racism was complicated and nuanced by the other side of the coin, 'I had a lot of racism from day one', she said, 'really horrible – BNP, abuse, someone burnt my arm, little silly things, but *all* the time. But more importantly, you felt it everyday even if it wasn't everyday, you felt it because you'd become accustomed to feeling like you were the outsider. You feel like going into the pub and everyone's looking at you and – you know what? – half the time they are; half the time they're not but still that feeling's already there, which was very inhibiting and very uncomfortable, and very damaging in many ways but, on the other hand, I had amazing friends who never even noticed the colour of my skin – it wasn't ever an issue, it was just who I was and that was fine. There are people for whom it really didn't matter, and their parents never said don't play with her – an absolute acceptance.'

It is perhaps the doubleness of their experience that is most unsettling. If they had merely encountered nothing but racism throughout their lives they might never have seen themselves as British but, on the other hand, might have felt more existentially stable. All these young Muslims not only possess plural identities; these identities are radically unstable because they continually have to negotiate swirling cross-currents of influence, the attractions and repulsions of several sets of cultural values and ideas. This is no doubt the case for all of us to a greater or lesser extent, but those who find themselves at the centre of such intense cultural anxieties must feel particularly vulnerable to the contradictory pressures of our times.

These pressures are intensified by the numerous forms of social, cultural and economic exclusion which they continue to experience. These days such exclusions have assumed new, more-focussed forms. Racism in its old form – biological, based on skin colour – may not be quite so apparent (and it is unarguable that there has been much progress over the last twenty years on this score) but, as the sociologist Tariq Modood has argued, its new guise is predominantly cultural. Cultural racism establishes forms of hierarchy based on cultural differences rather than skin colour, 'on the "natural" preference of human beings for their own cultural group, and on the incompatibility between different cultures'.[6] Moreover, Modood notes that it is Muslims who are currently feeling the brunt of both the new emphasis on cultural racism and the residual effects of the old biological racism because most British Muslims are racially different. The mutation in the ideology of the far-right British National Party (BNP) perhaps exemplifies this best – they have modulated their stance on Black Britons, but the new Other is the Muslim who can never be reconciled, so they believe, to Britishness.

The vast majority of British Muslims give the lie to this absurd ideological caricature. Nevertheless, the BNP's hostility towards Islam and Muslims is perhaps only an extreme example of a phenomenon that is widespread in more attenuated form: Islamophobia. There is still debate about whether Islamophobia actually exists, and even if it does, there is disagreement as to what it actually is.[7] Nevertheless, two things are not in doubt. First, there has been a notable rise in anti-Muslim hostility and suspicion in some quarters; secondly, that British Muslims are aware of it and many have experienced it.

Shaheen said she had never felt any anti-Muslim hostility directly. 'I've never, you know, had any kind of abuse or comments or anything like that,' she told me. However, she did say that she knew people who had – something that was echoed by many of the others. 'My mum's cited a few incidents where she and my aunt have received racist slurs on the street', she continued, 'and I think they're more prone to it because I guess I blend in more.'

Likewise, Razia noted that her brother is afraid that her wearing of the *hijab* will mark her out. 'One of his major problems about me covering my head is that, you know, you're standing out, you're different and that's provoking hostility. I was like, don't be so stupid, and true enough nobody has ever done anything to me, nobody's made comments about me. I don't really sense much of a tension like just going out in the street or shopping or whatever.'

She did agree, however, that Muslims were subject to a climate of prejudice but that she had never felt it in her life. 'It's only when I watch the news or any kind of show, you know, and then I get a real sense of it all. It's horrible.'

Soumaya, in fact, had a much more positive tale to tell. In Nelson, she said, the community had really pulled around each other. After 9/11, for instance, 'people became even more caring and protective towards each other. I've seen a lot of whites who, even though they wouldn't talk to you before, have been more friendly just to show that they do appreciate that not everyone's the same, and I've never personally faced any problems in that sense.' Nevertheless, she did concede that 'on the TV and in the newspapers you do see that it is a problem in the bigger cities'. Citing the recent incident when two young Asian men were told to disembark from their flight back from Spain because the other passengers would not travel with them on board merely because they looked 'dodgy' (i.e. Muslim) and spoke 'Arabic' (in fact, Urdu), Soumaya did admit that non-Muslims had become afraid of Muslims but that she had not encountered this in Nelson.

However, just as many young Muslims to whom I spoke *had* experienced anti-Muslim hostility themselves. Aisha in Slough, for instance, noticed that the atmosphere around her changed after 9/11 but in total contrast to the manner described by Soumaya. 'Before that', she said, 'I don't actually recall having been abused in any sense. It's only after that I noticed that people were giving me stares as I walked down the high street and this one person actually came and swore at me. Everything around me was starting to change and I didn't like the feeling because, you know, I'm feeling scrutinised here because of something I hadn't even done.'

In Nelson, another young Muslim woman I spoke to suggested that the rosier picture portrayed by Soumaya was not felt by everyone to be entirely accurate. Amina had noticed that relations between Muslims and non-Muslims were 'getting worse and worse'. For her the pivotal moment was not 9/11 or even 7/7 but the recent controversy surrounding the veil that had been initiated by Jack Straw's comments in a local newspaper. She said she had experienced 'vicious abuse' in certain areas, directed both at her race and at her religion 'because I do wear a scarf on'. She now has a markedly different relationship to the environment within which she lives and works. 'Before all this', she said, 'I was comfortable walking around alone in the town centre, going to my cousins, going to family friends, but now I do take someone with me 'cos I don't feel comfortable after all this.'

It was not only in the street that some Muslims had felt hostility towards them. Munizha recalled her experiences during college when anti-Muslim feeling was expressed quite forthrightly in the more sedate setting of the classroom. 'At A-levels I did Government and Politics so there was a lot of debate going on there. We had Muslims and non-Muslims there, and there were people who were non-Muslims and they were very anti-Islam, very anti-Islamic faith and Islamic law, and I think that sort of built up a bit of resistance, 'cos obviously in Politics you have constant debates.' Being quite a forthright person, I could imagine Munizha getting as good as she got during her turbulent classroom arguments.

Many young Muslims I spoke to did not really know what the term *Islamophobia* meant or were only dimly aware of it. Many others, however, did and they were firmly of the opinion that it exists. Abdur-rahman, for instance, identified two strands of Islamophobia. 'One is the uneducated, irrational fear, which is just built on a lack of knowledge, lack of context, lack of understanding about what Muslims do, what Muslims are about – we're just people at the end of the day. The other is … it's more, how do you put it? It's more malevolent. It's like the

Melanie Phillips brand, if I could put it like that. […] So, yeah, there are two levels there. I mean you can do something about people being ignorant – you just have to talk to them. I try to do that by talking to people I work with. I mean, when you're at work, you work. You don't want to preach to people, but if people ask you a question then you have to give them a direct answer. You know, I've invited people back to my house to show how we live and stuff – that's the only way around that sort of prejudice, it's personal contact. But the other one, I don't know what you can do about that. It's just there – and in people of quite high positions of authority, like, you know the Richard Perles of the world.'[8]

Does he think that a lot of people just don't know anything about Islam and Muslims?

'Yeah. It's true. They know a lot more than they used to, but they're picking up on the wrong things. Things like, Muslim men can have four wives – I mean, there's conditions and other things that have to happen for that. They pick up on that Muslims don't like homosexuals and they throw them off a cliff and that sort of stuff and that's what they're picking up on and that's being fed by the malevolent strand of the Islamophobic brigade.'

I observed that therefore, perhaps, if people have more contact with each other, have conversations, ask questions and find out more about Muslims and Islam, then over time that sort of Islamophobia will eventually recede.

He nodded his head in assent but added, 'you've got to remember Muslims are different people as well so they have different views so you can get contradictory and conflicting views about Islam from Muslims. Here's a common one: I don't drink; I don't really like to go to the pub – in fact, I don't go to the pub. But then you'll hear people say, "Ah but my friend, he's Muslim and he goes to the pub and he drinks," so even on a personal level you can get these contradictory messages.'

The belief that Islamophobia arises out of ignorance was echoed by many. Zainab put a slightly different emphasis on the matter compared to Abdur-rahman. She felt that non-Muslims knew quite a lot about Islam in some respects. 'I think in comparison to other religions … a lot of our activities are so outward like you have to tell people "Oh, I'm going to pray" or like the *hijab*, or going on *hajj* … so they're quite aware of these things because they're so outward, but I think in terms of … – obviously they know what our core values are – I think it's all the other stuff in between that they don't know about.'

What sort of things? I asked.

'What it really means to be Muslim. I don't think they know, for example, the importance of having pure intentions, or how all aspects of our life are worship – those really core things that you have to keep reminding yourself about as a Muslim and they keep you going, like forgiveness, for example, patience, I don't think they know about – and these really fit into everything else.'

I was not convinced that non-Muslims in Britain *do* know much about Islam's core values, but the point Zainab seemed to be making was, I felt, a deeper one. She was suggesting that although non-Muslims see the visible 'signs' of Islam – and Islamic practices are highly visible in some parts these days: the headscarf/veil, the appearance of mosques and minarets, the cultivation of beards, etc. – they are not able to work out the 'meaning' behind these signs. The significance of such signs for practising Muslims eludes them and so quite a lot of what Muslims believe is never articulated in the wider coverage of Islam in the media. Instead, those signs are misconstrued because they are placed in the context not of Islam's 'core values' but within the frame of a set of misconceptions and prejudices.

It is perhaps unsurprising, therefore, that across the board young Muslims feel resentful and suspicious of the media. Even those who were not particularly aware of the term Islamophobia or did not use it nevertheless concurred that it was the media that contributed most to the climate of hostility towards Muslims.

Sughra Ahmed of the Policy Research Unit at the Islamic Foundation explained that many young Muslims today are much more aware of the media, much more conscious of the ways in which their faith is portrayed. They 'read the papers and are conscious of what goes on on television and they understand the language that's being used and why it's being used and they understand the whole machine, the mechanism that's going on behind it'. What they see is a 'stereotypical image of Islam and Muslims'. She cites the BBC television drama *Spooks* as an example. '*Spooks* first started showing Muslims as terrorists a few years back, and there was a ripple, a significant ripple, that went through the community because it was adhering to old stereotypes and it was a popular programme shown at a popular time.'

All the young Muslims I spoke to cited instances when they felt the media represented Muslims and Islam unfairly but two of these can perhaps be used to illustrate Sughra's more general point, not only about the media representations but also about young Muslims' increased self-awareness of the 'mechanism' behind them.

My visit to Lancashire coincided with Jack Straw's infamous remarks about the veil, and many comments were made about this, but another story had also recently emerged about which they felt more strongly. On 28 September 2006, police raided a house in Colne, the town next to Nelson, and found several types of chemicals which could be used to make explosives. They also found a copy of the infamous *Anarchy Cookbook*, a guide for bomb making that is usually found on the Internet. Ball bearings, which could be used for shrapnel in any exploding device (thus maximising casualties), were also found. Two men were arrested, one of whom had stood as the BNP candidate for Pendle Council in the May 2005 elections. Despite being one of the largest hauls of potentially lethal explosive-making equipment, the raid and arrest of the two men went unnoticed in the national press. Even the local press devoted little attention to it; a brief mention in the local Colne newspaper being the sum of it. One can only imagine that life in Colne is so dramatic that a major police action of this sort no longer meets the priorities of local journalists.[9]

Some six weeks later I visited Colne, Nelson and other towns in Pendle to speak to the young Muslims who live and work there. Coming from London, I was ignorant of these recent events but I would not remain so for long. The sense of indignation was palpable and widespread. 'Is it not important, or is it because they're not Muslim?' asked Qadeer incredulously. 'If it was a Muslim, anyone, anyone with common sense would say it'd be in every single paper, it'd be on Sky news, you'd know about it, every single person would know about it', he continued, and it would have been obtuse not to agree. These sentiments were often echoed throughout Pendle but, in a dramatic example of how media exposure (or lack of it) can either help people to make connections or keep them ignorant about events outside their own experience, residents in more distant Lancashire towns remained unaware of the episode.

Interestingly, neither of the men was charged using any anti-terror legislation, which may have led some to suspect that the police have come to see such legislation as being relevant for certain groups of people and not for others. This seems to be a conclusion that young Muslims in Pendle have reached. In the same breath as they spoke about the BNP story, they contrasted it with the police raids in Forest Gate on two

Muslim brothers, in which one was shot and wounded, and which turned out to be based on faulty evidence.

'All these other innocent people, like them brothers in London [referring to Forest Gate], they went into their house thinking they've got something to do with terrorism but they had nothing to do with it, and then there's this other case [the BNP one], right on our doorstep ... ' said 26-year-old Saiqa, who works for the Pendle Women's Forum.

'Right outside our house!' added her friend Nazma.

'... and no-one even knows about it'.

Qadeer Ahmed, in his usual, informed manner, thought the issue was not just about the double standards and silences of the media but also about the basis of much of the recent anti-terrorism legislation itself. 'We've made so many arrests over the last three years, through anti-terrorism laws and stuff, and what they fail to say is how many of these people have been charged – and not just charged, then proven – to have had terrorist links.' Qadeer's instincts have since been proven correct by a study of the effectiveness of stop and search.[10] He did not say so explicitly, but I took him to be making the point that the media coverage of Muslim affairs and an anti-terrorism legislation that seems to be specifically targeted at Muslims both emerge from the double standards of an Islamophobic attitude that permeates contemporary British society.

Some months before, on a bright February afternoon, I had spoken at length to the young British artist Yara el-Sherbini in the aftermath of the Danish cartoon row which had engulfed many parts of the Muslim world and which had been covered extensively in the media as a conflict between Islam and freedom of speech. Yara had herself recently published a book of cartoons, or rather an illustrated joke book called *Sheikh 'n' Vac* – actually, to call it a joke book is to do it a disservice; *Sheikh 'n' Vac* uses both verbal and visual humour to explore some of the dilemmas surrounding Islam and Muslims in the contemporary world and, in particular, subjects some of the lazy stereotypes and clichéd representations of Islam and Muslims to serious scrutiny.[11] What were her thoughts on the controversy?

'I remember being not so annoyed with the actual Danish man who drew the cartoons. No, I was more annoyed with the way the press *created* the situation. I mean, of course, yes it was meant to cause offence, and the newspaper must have known, and that gentleman must have known it would cause offence but they did that openly and willingly because they wanted to rattle someone's boat, let's say, they wanted to cause a problem. My problem was with the way the media created a thing, created all of this, and created a drama, and of course, unfortunately Muslims *again* around the world decided to take up that baton and say, "Oh, let's all fight" and make a big deal out of – I wouldn't say nothing – but something that could have been … '.

She paused, as if reflecting on a change of tack, moving from defence to offence.

'… oh my God, there's so many ways that could have been challenged, and more subtly discussed and talked about in an intellectual way, and I know there were intellectuals that said, "Come on, we object to that, but come on, what are you doing fighting and burning down the Danish embassy, this isn't the way." Of course, as we know, the media wouldn't really allow that voice to be heard except a little voice in *The Guardian* and the left every now and again. So my frustration was with the mechanism that allowed this to be created.

'So my problem was not with the gentleman [who drew the cartoon] necessarily – okay, he was a bit of an idiot – but my problem was with the way it was used, and I'm really sad that people didn't challenge that. I wish Muslims had challenged that in a really playful, humorous way and said, "OK, brilliant cartoon, here let's draw some more, let's do a cartoon drawing session" – or something a little bit more innovative. But I think that even if that voice was present, it wouldn't have been heard anyway because the mechanisms for starting this drama would not have invited that kind of voice.'

She picked up a copy of *Sheikh 'n' Vac* and continued, 'I remember also feeling, on a personal level, because this was already published [pointing to her book] and here there are cartoons, not of Muhammad because I wouldn't draw cartoons of Muhammad because I know that I would cause offence, I know that. And that's not going to be beneficial to any kind of dialogue or debate because offence doesn't create a sense of dialogue or debate. But I remember thinking "Oh, am I going to get into a little bit of a drama here because of my cartoons and doodles, and will that be quite negative because it won't allow my actual voice to be heard, and am I going to be put in a little categorised box as a 'Muslim artist', and how come a Muslim artist is allowed to do this [and others aren't etc.]?" So I was very aware of that.'

Was she apprehensive about that?

'I was very apprehensive about that, I have to be honest because my … the fundamental reason I'm making my art is to create a space for debate and dialogue particularly about being a British Muslim now, which is why I made this book, and I'm not just going to sit back, I'm going to talk about it. "Come on, let's have a platform"; and I always think that the reason for me making work is to create that platform and inviting debate, but there are very different ways in which that can be framed and I don't think that cartoon drama would have allowed my voice or my work to be framed in a productive way. I was apprehensive about the way in which the media could have used that to frame it in a way that said, or took the position that, "Well how come a Muslim can say that and we can't?" – that sort of position, even though what I'm doing is so fundamentally different from what he was doing. I'm questioning those ideas and he was creating those ideas – it was the antithesis, but the problem was I knew it could have been framed [as part of the same thing].'

Her training as an artist had clearly enabled Yara to see that no story is ever reported by the media neutrally. The framing of a story is crucial because it sets certain limits on the responses (counter-arguments, say, or dissenting voices) to the perspective established by the terms of the story (in this instance, for example, the limits or otherwise of freedom of speech was the determining perspective around which all discussion of the controversy could be gathered). Perspectives that lie outside this frame find it difficult to establish themselves as valid counter-arguments.

It is for this reason that so many young Muslims are suspicious of a media which they believe to be hostile to their perspectives. They feel they have to fit into the existing media agenda or they will remain forever outside it. That agenda might, for instance, allocate resources to cover a terror raid on a Muslim household in East London whilst not even registering a raid on a bomb-making factory in a non-Muslim household in Lancashire. Such exclusions may not be consciously motivated or attributable to individual antipathies; rather, they are part of the system – the 'mechanism' – by which the media helps to establish one picture of reality over others. Unsurprisingly, such exclusions contribute to the sense of exclusion felt by many young British Muslims. In other words, it is not only about discrimination in the workplace or poverty or lack of opportunity. It is about a lack of recognition and a feeling of being an Other in their own country and of being unsure about their place in society.[12]

* * *

It is only fair, at this point, to emphasise that such uncertainty does not in any way undermine the strong sense of Britishness that is so typical of the young Muslims I met. Instead, it would be more accurate to say that it qualifies it. It is how they experience their Britishness at present. Their commitment to Britain coexists with their lingering sense of exclusion, but it is by no means overwhelmed by it.

One indicator of this is an awareness amongst them that it is relatively easier to be a Muslim in Britain than almost anywhere else in the 'West'. Echoing Soumaya, who saw no contradiction between her Muslim identity and British one because in Britain Muslims have the freedom to practise their religion without restriction, Abdur-rahman agreed that 'it's easier to be a Muslim in this country than in some other countries'.

'Being a Muslim you can do almost 100 percent of what you need to do to become religious', he continued, 'you know, practising, without any problem or effort. I've not missed a Friday prayer in about 10 years, because I always know where the mosques are, I've always made it a condition – or let my employer know – that 1 till 2 on a Friday is blocked out because I go to the mosque. I've not had a problem as long as I do my hours and deliver. I'm lucky because I work in a professional environment where they don't really care how you do the work so long as you do it. It'd be different if you were a train driver, where you have set work shifts and patterns – you can't just leave your train!'

For Shahid, his experiences in Europe had reinforced his impression that Britain is 'the best place in Europe' to be a Muslim. 'I went to Paris a couple of years ago and I was around a couple of Muslim friends, and there was a general feeling, not necessarily that people knew they were Muslims but a general feeling that they didn't look French. I mean obviously, at this time, it's not great because of the anti-terror laws and a lot of people are going through a reaction, but I think at present we should be content that we're not in the situation in which some European Muslims are.'

Did he feel that there was a danger that Britain might be sliding that way? I asked.

He paused for a second before replying. 'Yeah, there is, although I don't think … we are sliding that way, yes, but I don't think it will ever be to the intensity that it is in France, where they will ban the headscarf and things like that. Obviously, the foundations of France as a nation-state, it was all based on like a secular state, but I don't think Britain – although I would say that most of the people are not practising in Britain – the foundations of the state are not based on secularism – they're based on having a God. So, I don't see [Britain] losing those foundations; although the people might lose it in their personal life, I can't see the state losing it.'

Although all the young Muslims I spoke to noted this darkening horizon and did express concern about it, it did seem to me that without exception they also felt genuine satisfaction with life in Britain, that they enjoy living here. In fact, nearly all of them compared Britain favourably to Muslim countries as well.

'Even when you compare Britain to a lot of the Muslim countries, a lot of the time Muslims may not appreciate how well off they are here,' said Shahid. 'I was in Tunisia this summer and whenever they see a guy with a beard or anything the police are straight onto it because Tunisia went through this secular revolution a few years ago.'

Others elaborated upon their preference for Britain over Muslim countries even more forcefully. Fahmida had only been to one other Muslim country, Saudi Arabia, to perform what is known as the *umrah* or the minor pilgrimage. Her experience there left her with no illusions about what some Muslim societies can be like.

'I find that over there the Arabs are quite hostile,' she said.

Really? I asked.

She nodded, 'Very hostile to non-Arabs. Because I think it's one of those things that they feel that basically they're at the top, they're the top Muslims; even though within the *haram* [the sacred precinct surrounding Mecca] there's no violence or anything like that, but you know tone-wise, when you go shopping or something, it's like ... you definitely feel the hostility and it's not just with Bengalis, it's Pakistanis as well; the Arabs are just really hostile towards non-Arabs.'

Had she been put off ever going back there?

'When you're in contact with Arabs, yeah. Even Saudi Arabia is quite diverse now – in Medina, you've got a large Bangladeshi community, you've got a large Pakistani community as well – so when you actually ... – it's a bit like, you know how Luton's turned into now or like East London's turned into now? – you don't need to go into an Arab shop; when you're in that area you can always get it from a Bangladeshi shop or that shop or that shop, so I suppose when you're around your own community, it's fine, it's really peaceful, you wouldn't want to go anywhere else, but it's like when you have an odd encounter with an Arab, you know, it's just like, "Oh god!"'

She drew this last phrase out to heighten the effect of her exasperation, so I was left in no doubt as to her feelings. But I thought I would press her a bit more. Some Muslims, I said, say that they would prefer to live in a Muslim country rather than in Britain. What about her?

'It would be a good experience – like one of my Bengali friends, she graduated last year and she went out to Egypt for a job and she's saying that it's brilliant over there because like, you know, the whole Islamic environment, you get to hear the *azzan* [the call to prayer] in the morning and that's refreshing, that's enlightening in its own kind of way, just listening without praying; but then again, she says she misses Britain. She says sometimes it gets a bit boring, there's nothing to do – like during Ramadan, most things are closed, there's nothing to do afterwards; or like for *Eid*, they did *Eid* on Tuesday – yesterday – and it lasts for three days in Egypt and then it's the weekend, and so you've got a whole week off doing nothing, so in that sense … it would be a good experience, but I don't think I'd be comfortable outside Bangladesh or England.'

The way she said this made me feel that it would be a 'good experience' in much the same way many a young Briton believes travel to be an 'experience' – as an opportunity to learn more about the world and perhaps about themselves; but, ultimately, this travel is, for most, grounded in the knowledge that one day they will return home. I did not receive the impression that she yearned to live amongst Muslims, to be surrounded by them always; it might be nice for a while but that was the extent of it.

Fahmida's views were amplified by Qadeer. 'I love living in England', he told me, 'because generally I think it's an awesome, awesome place to live. Someone once said to me, you know [Britain's] like this, it's like that and its not Islamic blah-de-blah; I tell you, it's a lot more Islamic than Saudi. I mean, I've been to Saudi, to Makkah [Mecca] and Medina, for *umrah*, I won't go anywhere else; if it weren't for those two places I wouldn't even think about going to Saudi. I wouldn't think about it.'

It sounded like he had no desire to move to a Muslim country, I said.

'No, no, why? We've got more here as British citizens than we'd ever have [over there]. First of all, in most Arab nations up until recently you couldn't buy a property there and the Asian community, they're treated like shit, they have the worst jobs. I mean, I'll give you an example, a couple of us together after we'd completed *umrah* we were in Medina and we went into a shop because the guy who was with me wanted to ask about a ring, and he asked [the shopkeeper] "how much is this?" and he said, "It's too much." He said [again], "How much is it?" He [the shopkeeper] goes, "It's too much for you." And things like that get to me, 'cause I knew what he meant, he meant 'cause we're Pakistanis, so [my friend] said, "What do you mean by that?" And he [the shopkeeper] said, "It's too much for you 'cause – ," and I said, "What do you mean?" And it's all because we were Pakistani, "Oh it's too much for you," – you know, saying we're cheapskates, kind of thing, basically.

'And that's just a little thing. You don't get no rights in those Arab countries; if you were to be tried … I would hate to be tried in an Arab country, you're up shit creek if you're going to be tried for something in an Arab country 'cause you're gonna get … more likely than not they're gonna punish you for something you haven't done. Here, at least you've got quite a fair judicial system, so I'd never want to go and I … I wouldn't want to leave this country, no chance.'

* * *

This self-awareness about the benefits of living as a Muslim in Britain even extends to a critical scrutiny over their assumptions about themselves and their experiences of exclusion – an indication that some young Muslims at least will not succumb to bitterness and rancour in response to what they perceive to be an increasingly Islamophobic atmosphere.

Raihan Alfaradhi, for instance, was very reluctant to pin the blame on racism or Islamophobia for the troubles facing the Muslim communities, even though he constantly acknowledges that such forces of exclusion do exist and do exert a pressure on the situation. He would speak of racist incidents (such as having eggs thrown at their windows or into their car) that had happened to him during his childhood, or even very recently, but he would then explain the behaviour of those who perpetrated the incidents in other terms. 'It's what kids do, isn't it? It's not necessarily for any particular reason. I think there's nothing to do there obviously … as a family growing up you obviously feel it and think ok, it's not pleasant at the time, but looking back at it it's not something you can say that they were picking on you for any particular reason.'

I observed that for many people it would in fact be straightforward to say that these incidents were indeed motivated by a particular reason. Why was he so reluctant to suggest that it was because of racism?

He agreed that other people might be quicker to come to that judgment, but he felt that would be too simplistic. He spoke of his time at the London School of Economics (LSE) where he was a student union officer, elected to tackle the anti-racism brief. It was during that time he realised that racism was a complex phenomenon and that what appeared on the surface to be racism might in fact be merely a symptom of deeper social and other issues. Moreover, he also realised that people had many dimensions to their personalities and that one side may not in fact represent them as a whole.

'I wouldn't like to call it anti-racism, even', he said of his work, 'I would change the name to pro-diversity, or whatever. I'd like to be pro something rather than anti- something else.'

For Raihan, then, the charge of racism too quickly obscured other more fundamental problems, which remain unresolved because people are too intent to look only at the racism. I asked him if he thought that just as some might be sometimes too quick to blame racism, Muslims are too quick to blame Islamophobia.

'Yeah, I would agree. I mean, Muslims are sometimes a bit too quick [to blame Islamophobia] and I think there needs to be a lot more work done [within the Muslim communities],' he said. However, being politically astute, he also realised there was a context within which such accusations are being made at the moment.

'The problem is that then you've got a flipside, which is what happened for example after 7 July, where, you know, the government or whoever absolve themselves of any blame and then kind of put it down to the communities and stuff. I think people do need to do their own thing [i.e. look to themselves] and I think we've realised that as Muslims. Most Muslims have realised that, you know, some years ago, but the fact is that you can't really go out and say that because as soon as you do the government are going to say, "OK, do you accept that it's all your fault? Now off you go and deal with it," kind of thing.' This situation is ultimately counter-productive because not only does it obstruct Muslims from admitting to problems within their own communities but also, in fact, encourages them to blame others too quickly. Moreover, it isolates the Muslim community as being solely responsible for such problems. The two sides therefore reduce a complex phenomenon to a simplistic diagnosis.

Sughra Ahmed also felt that things were more complex than they appeared. Whilst insisting very firmly that Islamophobia does exist and that young Muslims 'are more conscious of the discrimination that goes on', she nevertheless told me of a recent experience which suggests that she is aware that this same increased awareness might in fact also lead some to hasty judgements.

'My friend and I were in Barcelona recently on holiday and we came across an Italian restaurant and it was lunchtime so I said let's go in. Now when we went in, there was a set of steps to go down to the actual main part of the restaurant where you're seated, so you wait at the top of the steps before somebody comes and gets you. So we waited and the waiter turned around, looked at us and nodded, in other words, "I've acknowledged you, I will be with you." Five minutes later, which is a long time waiting when everybody else is eating, I'm obviously visibly wearing the *hijab*, I am Muslim, my friend was also doing the same thing, she was wearing *hijab*, so people were looking. And we found that quite common in Barcelona, people were staring. I mean normally on the Tube you get that – you don't get that as much but you do get that – and I smile at the people and return it, because they're not going to know me unless I actually give them something to understand me by. So again I did the same thing in Barcelona, but in this restaurant it was quite sinister, you know, people were actually staring like, "I don't like you being in my space." And it was funny how I interpreted that very, very quickly and I felt uncomfortable. I didn't let on to my friend because I already knew that she was uncomfortable.

'And then ten minutes passed and she said, "Shall we decide on somewhere else?" And I became quite determined, thinking I want to know why this has happened. I'm not too concerned about eating here now, I want to know why that particular person has not come to us. And they were rushed off their feet in this place, really, really busy. And in the end the waiter looked in my direction and I didn't look very happy. So he spoke in Spanish and said something, and I wasn't very happy so I didn't smile and I said, "Do you speak English?" And he sort of said a very Italian type gesture as in, "Oh, you don't speak Spanish", and said "Please bear with me, we are very, very busy, we will find you a table, just give me a couple of minutes." And I thought, is he genuine? Anyway, he found us a table, we sat down, started our meal, and as we were eating a woman came in, a Spanish woman with three children, and she asked for a table. And they made her wait five minutes and then said to her, "I'm sorry we don't have a table." And I turned around, and it really made me think, I said to my friend, "If we had come now, when she has come, like twenty minutes later, and we had been made to wait five minutes and then they tell us that there's no room, what would we have thought?"

We would have thought because visibly we are wearing the *hijab*, that he is not happy with us being Muslim and in this restaurant. And some of the time we can be a bit quick to judge, because there is a sensitivity around you know, "well of course they're going to perceive me like this because that's what the world is telling them, why should they think anything different?" '

There is no doubt that Muslim communities in Britain and elsewhere in Europe are facing a dramatic rise in anti-Muslim sentiment and hostility. Young Muslims in Britain are clearly aware of this and can feel it, and they, unsurprisingly, share the temptation to blame others for their problems. But it also does seem that many of them are aware that such temptations may also be a convenient diversion from having to confront problems closer to home.

Qadeer Ahmed summed it up quite nicely. 'In football I get sent off a lot', he said, 'because I get quite angry and frustrated and stuff, and I always blame the referee or I'll blame the other player, and he [my coach] said "when you're pointing your finger at someone remember there's always three fingers pointing back at you". So I think that's the way Muslims are – I think that a lot of the times they like pointing fingers but those fingers that are pointing back at them, they don't think about them. If we were doing everything the way it's supposed to be done in Islam then I don't think anyone would have any problems with us and we wouldn't have any problems with anyone else, but more often than not we like to blame, to point fingers – it's the media's fault or it's Tony Blair's fault, it's the Government's fault, it's this, it's that. I'm in no doubt that things like the media and the Government don't help, but it's like anything, if you aren't going to help yourself don't expect any help from anyone else.'

Such attitudes suggest that many young Muslims within the 'moderate' majority from whom we hear so little have the necessary awareness (and desire) to shake off the 'victim' mentality that pitches some others into a *cul-de-sac* of resentment. Self-scrutiny is a necessary part of engaging in dialogue with others as equals, without the defensive mentality that indicates insecurity. To be fair, this defensiveness and lack of self-awareness is not monopolised by Muslims, even though many in the media might think so. Positions are hardening on all sides as the turbulence of our times takes its toll on our sense of identity and on our relationships with others who are different from us. The search for a common ground – for a common culture which we can all make and remake together – in such conditions of conflicted intimacy requires courage and fortitude from all parties, but most of all it requires the capacity to examine ourselves critically.

* * *

The search for a common culture is rendered difficult, however, by the current models and ways of talking about identity, which restrict the possibilities open to us in re-imagining ourselves and our relationships with others. We usually speak of identity as something that we 'possess', a thing that we 'have' which in turn defines who we 'are'. Perhaps this is not surprising given the commodification of nearly all aspects of our lives. When the market is seen as a solution to nearly everything, it is inevitable perhaps that we talk about ourselves in terms of things that can be possessed. Thus we say we 'are' British if we possess something called 'Britishness' – or that people can become British only if they acquire this thing called 'Britishness'.

It would be better to speak of identity – as I have done in chapter 1 – not as something we possess but as something we inhabit. This accounts for the *collective* nature of identity (which, even when it is intensely personal and particular to ourselves, is always also *social* because we can only define our 'own' identity in relation to others) because others can inhabit that identity too, even though they might not inhabit it in the same way. 'Belonging' might therefore be seen not in terms of 'being' British by 'possessing' Britishness but rather in terms of whether we feel 'at home' in such an identity. Identity can thus be compared to dwelling, and the more capacious the dwelling, the more people can be accommodated within it. In conditions of 'super-diversity', we can begin to start talking about ourselves not as being one 'thing' or another but rather of 'accommodating' difference. For the possessive model of identity, however, difference is invariably a problem.

Such a notion of being 'at home' in an identity liberates us from the nationalist fixation with a culture we may or may not have. Such a fixation renders both the 'culture' and the 'identity' which expresses and adheres to it rather flat (and boring). This 'flat', one-dimensional sense of identity is incapable of encompassing the many different dimensions of identity, the rich profusion of selves which we all inhabit in our everyday lives: our sense of locality, the environment that surrounds us, the buildings we see and dwell in, our work, the institutions with whom we interact, the people we encounter, the social spaces we gather in, the groups we relate to and so on. It is when we feel 'at home' in the many contexts of our lives that we feel most truly ourselves.

One way, then, of gauging the identities of people is to listen to them speaking about 'home'. Migrants – and most Muslims in Britain are either migrants or children of migrants – often have an unstable sense of home, usually talking about both the place from which they migrated and their destination as 'home' – an indication of their multiple sense of belonging and identity. When they return to their country of origin, they talk about 'going home' but, at the same time, when they return they also speak of 'coming home'. As Sughra Ahmed pointed out, this was especially the case for the older generation who never really felt 'at home' in Britain, 'quite a few years ago, it used to be the case of, well, we came here for work, let's do that and let's go back "home" in inverted commas. And now they've settled their minds to the fact that their children, their grandchildren are here and everything's here, and they don't really have a lot back home apart from the fact that they can go there on holidays and visit relatives and things like that, and it's quite nice to do, but to live there long term would actually be quite difficult now.'

Their children, the current generation of young British Muslims, speak of 'home' differently, with different emphases. Mohammed Ali, for instance, recalled the impact of his first trip back to Bangladesh. 'Back in the day, I was forced to go, you know, to learn about my roots', he said, 'and I think definitely that woke me up a little bit as well. Seeing poverty helps you appreciate what you have here today and I think that's important, to learn about your identity, and who I am today it's partly because of my parents, and they were brought up over there, and some of the customs and the things – the way I am today is because of that. So I think it's important to go back, go back "home" as they call it – I wouldn't call it my home; my parents call it "home". Some people say "I'm going back home" – No. That's not my home but it's important to discover where my parents came from and it opens your eyes and surely learning about other cultures benefits you as human being?'

Likewise, Shahid told me, 'I love where I come from, I love Bangla culture even though I consider myself to be thoroughly British now. I can't imagine myself – although the lifestyle is quite attractive there – I can't imagine myself living there because I have a totally different background. When I go there, people can tell I'm British even though I'm not white – I don't know how. But yeah I do feel there's a bit of me left there when I'm here. Even at home it shows because I can't remember the last time when I've been watching English TV at home – it's always Bangla TV in the house: my parents are quite obsessed with the latest news and politics there. Plus, I've never spoken English to my parents, never ever, which has helped develop my Bangla a bit, so I mean, I think at home it's a completely different experience from when I step out of the house.'

Shahid shows how it is possible to 'possess' a culture – he speaks Bengali, he watches Bangladeshi TV and so on – but still not feel 'at home' in that culture. He speaks of Britain as 'home' instead; even though within the actual four walls of his physical home the culture he expresses is not British, the culture he inhabits outside those four walls is, and thus he is able to speak of it as 'home' in a way he cannot speak about Bangladesh.

All the young Muslims I spoke to had access to – or inhabit – two or more cultures but, judging by the way they talked about 'home', they feel 'at home' in Britain and British culture more than they feel 'at home' in their other cultures. This shows us why opinion poll questions such as the infamous one that suggested that only 61 percent of Muslims feel that Britain is 'their country' are so misleading.[13] The most 'alarming' so-called fact to have been reported from this survey was that the younger generation felt less strongly attached to Britain than those aged 45 or over (44 percent of those aged under 45 felt that Britain was 'my country' compared with 55 percent of those aged over 45). This is because the question is framed in precisely those 'possessive' terms which I think are so unhelpful and does not take account of how a sense of disempowerment (as suggested in chapter 1) might affect the response. If, on the other hand, they had asked if Britain was their home, I would wager that the results would have been completely different.

Another way of assessing young Muslims' sense of belonging is to look at the way they speak about the environments they dwell in: their neighbourhood, their locality and their town. This may, of course, be affected by several factors: lack of facilities, job opportunities, things to do and so on may all attenuate their feelings about their surroundings. Nevertheless, I was completely surprised to find that even in the deprived northern towns the young Muslims I encountered were overwhelmingly positive about their local area.

I asked Qadeer how he felt about growing up in Burnley. 'It's good, I love the place,' he said without hesitation.

He must have noticed my involuntary scepticism because he felt compelled to reiterate the point, 'No really, I really like the place. I'd say home sweet home, never really had any problems.'

Actually, during his childhood, the racism was so bad that he and his siblings could not even play in their back garden, but despite this, Qadeer's enthusiasm for his hometown had not diminished. In fact, if anything, it had grown.

Likewise, Soumaya felt the same way about nearby Nelson. 'I like Nelson', she said to me, 'I think it's really tight-knit. I do have friends who are living in other cities and they hardly ever get to meet each other. Being in Nelson, you're just so close to everyone, and you know a lot of people around – a lot of caring people, so I wouldn't want to move out.'

Were there any circumstances which would make her consider leaving Britain?

'No,' she said with a smile. 'I did go back home to Pakistan just like for holidays and my brother has got married back home, so I've been then. Because I've been brought up in a different atmosphere and a different culture over here it would be really difficult to adjust yourself to the culture over there and for that reason I don't think I could really settle down there.'

'You don't want to leave Nelson anyway!' I said.

'No. Never mind UK!' she said, bursting out into laughter.

These sentiments were often repeated. A couple of hundred miles south of Nelson's dilapidated terraces, but in some ways a world apart, Zainab echoed Soumaya in her love of London, 'I love it here. I feel very comfortable here, all my family is here, all my friends live here. I have these activities which I do regularly, I do lots of voluntary work so I'm very much acclimatised to living here. I wouldn't really move unless I met the right person – nothing else would encourage me to migrate really.'

At other times, though they might not have spoken explicitly about their sense of attachment to their locality or neighbourhood, their commitment could be discerned through their depth of engagement in local activities – local politics, volunteering and charity work, social work and suchlike.

Munizha's commitment to her local community in Slough was expressed strongly by a story she told me about the local elections, which had taken place a few months before. This politician – she did not name the party – was from the Pakistani community, and one day he visited their home canvassing for votes. They had a debate on the doorstep and

Munizha recalled how, in response to her scepticism about his promises, 'he ended up turning it all around and started talking about things that are going on in the Muslim world and stuff, trying to make it out as if, you know, if you vote for us we're united as a Muslim community basically, and none of it was about what we're going to do for you in the local community; and this is the problem, you know, they don't actually talk about their policies and what they're going to do for your community, for your children, to actually improve your community and stuff and what services they're gonna offer and, you know, if you've got a problem what they're gonna do to address the grievance. I found it really strange that he was going off on one about what was going on globally rather than what's going on locally.'

In Lancashire, Omar embodied this spirit of community engagement in a different form, working at the grass-roots level to bring communities together into a shared sense of mutual commitment to one another. Working outwards from the smallest of units, he talked about working towards a more encompassing and capacious affirmation of neighbourliness.

'You know, in the work that I do for the citizenship programme within schools, there's a lot of separation, segregation, amongst people from the Muslim community to the white community. I mean, no-one's saying you have to be them, no-one's saying that you have to have a close relationship with each other, but it's about trying to work together and bring stability, first of all, into that classroom and then in that year group and then in the environment of the school and then within the whole community.

'It's about getting them involved in the right actions, the right frame of mind, getting them to actually engage, not just integrate but also interacting with their peers of faith or no faith and actually engaging in dialogue and actually, you know, having debate,' he said.

Such commitment to one's immediate locality, to one's local community, surely must make us pause before we begin uttering clichés about loyalty and belonging. As Zainab rather forcefully puts it, 'I would never say that British Muslims are more loyal to their religion than their country but obviously it depends on what you define your country to be. If you define your country as your community, your local community or even the wider community, there's no need to even say something like that, do you see what I mean? Like, I don't think I really need to be asked that because I contribute to society, I have a regular job, I do lots of things in the community, I have friendships with Muslims and non-Muslims – ok, I do lots of things in the Muslim community but that has an effect on the wider community.'

She paused as if searching for the right formulation to express what she was trying to get across. Then, when she had put her finger on it, she concluded, 'I think a lot of times you get asked lots of questions that don't actually need answering or don't actually mean anything in themselves.'

This in turn must also make us think again about how we talk about one of the shibboleths of current political discourse, namely 'integration'. It is a word mouthed promiscuously by politicians and media pundits, a valuable coin in the currency of the commentariat, but it is invariably spoken of in empty abstractions, and I suspect that most people who pontificate on the matter do not *really* know what they mean when they use the term. Often it seems to boil down to a rather banal belief that *they* should mix socially with *us*, the so-called majority community. And yet, one opinion poll statistic that is seldom discussed shows that British Muslims are doing exactly this. In a poll published by *The Times* and ITN News in July 2006, 87 percent of Muslims said that they had a close personal friend who was non-Muslim, whereas only 33 percent of the general population said that they had one who is Muslim.[14] Notwithstanding the obvious statistical distortions inherent in the comparison (since there are far fewer Muslims, it is of course likely that the proportion of the general population who are friendly with a Muslim is bound to be less), this does perhaps show that at the very least Muslims *are* mixing socially with other communities. So, even when measured by such vague criteria, it does not seem that Muslims are not integrating.

What, then, does 'integration' actually mean in terms of lived practice? It seems self-evident to me that people who display a commitment to living and working in a particular locality, who take an interest in local politics or who participate in voluntary activities and/or social work and have friends from other social groups – as all these young British Muslims do – are in fact integrated into British society. Why, then, do people still continue to speak of their failure to integrate? Again, I suspect it is because most people conceive of 'integration' in terms as flat and one-dimensional as the models of culture and identity they usually have in mind to accompany it. Ultimately, it seems to rest on a wish that *they* should be less culturally different from 'us'.

If we are to understand how integrated Britain's Muslim communities truly are, we need to speak about 'integration' differently. We need to be more precise and capacious in our thinking about what it involves. But on top of that, we also need to frame it differently. Currently, 'integration' is often invoked as a demand, implying a one-way process in which *they* come closer, culturally, to *us*. Instead, integration is surely a two-way process involving dialogue, give and take, and mutual accommodation.

Raihan, for instance, acknowledges that migrant communities like his, the Bangladeshis of East London, need to do more 'in terms of what we're doing to bring up our kids … to make sure that our kids have a level playing field' with others more established in British society. Working in the City, he has seen at first hand how his peers from a middle-class English background have been brought up with the social skills and etiquette necessary to make them feel at ease in the kind of social environments required to succeed in the workplace. 'Now that some of us have been through the system', he continued, 'we realise how it is.' Bangladeshis, he felt, had not acquired these skills and so were unable to deal with these situations. Such skills are vital for 'integration' because then children of migrant communities are able to relate to and operate in their social environments, be it in the workplace or elsewhere in the public sphere. However, once they have them, then integration is more straightforward, 'and then obviously no-one in government can say we're not contributing or we're not doing that or we're not, you know, pulling our weight. I think the only reason they can say that now is because we're not even coming from the same starting place' – because, in other words, the playing field is *not* level. 'That's not realised enough by the kind of people who matter,' he said.

On the other hand, the 'majority' community also need to adapt. They need to think and talk about minority communities differently. If integration is about contributing to British society then the contributions of migrants need to be acknowledged and affirmed – and not just in economic terms. Such an acknowledgment might be the first step in dismantling the exclusive notions of Britishness that perpetuate the division between 'them' and 'us'. The building of mosques, the arrival of *halal* butchers and Asian grocery stores and the gradual transformation of some neighbourhoods into an 'ethnic' area – all this is, in fact, evidence of Muslim integration and commitment to Britain. In the current climate, however, they are interpreted as signs of 'separatism' and 'segregation'.[15]

'What about the people in this country who are just sitting here, purely by virtue of the fact that they were born here?' asked Raihan, 'they've not contributed anything, in fact all they do is sit on some kind of benefit, commit some benefit fraud as well on the way, you hear all this kind of stuff and *they're* not contributing anything back. I think people coming over to the country have difficulty enough, because they are contributing so much, because most of the time they are going to do stuff that we don't want to do anyhow, like cleaners, dustbin men, whatever, you know, those kind of jobs anyway. So they are contributing in even more profound a way by the fact that they're doing something which no one else wants to do. It might not be such a big contribution but why don't you take the dustbin people away for a while, one week, the whole country will, you know, probably come to a standstill. If all the ethnic minorities left the country the country would collapse completely, and people don't realise that; they're still kind of f'ing and blinding until they're blue in the face about how they've been disadvantaged and all that kind of stuff.'

Integration is complex and multidimensional. Perhaps nothing illustrates the point better than a story Abdur-rahman told me about his school, a top public school in south London that is one of the pillars of the British establishment. He had come down from Manchester, where he had grown up, and did his GCSEs and A levels at this public school. 'I got put in a class which happened to – well, the whole class was dedicated to becoming doctors and dentists and they happened to – be Asian! Apart from one guy, a class of about fifteen people, doing maths, all looking to be doctors and dentists – apart from one person, they were all Asian,' he said.

I find myself thinking that this is somewhat ironic. We are being told that British society is 'sleepwalking into segregation' by no less an authority than the then Chairman of the Commission for Racial Equality, Trevor Phillips. It is a theme that is being reprised continually. When this is said, it is usually in reference to the impoverished 'ghetto' communities in the inner cities. And yet, here was a virtually segregated class in one of the top public schools in the country, which merely goes to show that just as our conceptualisation of integration is too narrow, so too is our picture of 'segregation'. It is true that there are many neighbourhoods which seem exclusively composed of a particular ethnic or religious group – many Muslims I spoke to confirmed that the areas they grew up in had become increasingly less 'mixed' over the years. But you could also look at 'segregation' in different ways. Is not a school that is entirely composed of wealthy or middle-class children as segregated in its own way as one comprising, say, only Muslim children? Why privilege only ethnicity and/or religion as markers of segregation (or integration)?

On top of that, all these young men and women were studying to become doctors and dentists. The next time we need a tooth extracted or a surgical operation – and, indeed, the next time our rubbish is cleared or our streets are swept – we might want to think about this and what 'integration' might actually mean at the level of ordinary life. What is *our* contribution to society, to Britain? As Raihan said to me, 'The point is, everyone needs to be moving forward, everyone needs to be contributing in one way or another, everyone needs to move this country forward and that's the only way we're going to, you know, keep on benefiting each other at the end of the day.'

* * *

'Flat' notions of culture and identity severely restrict the ways in which we can think about who we are and our place in the world. Precisely because culture is the vehicle through which we do this, it is important to work out new ways of conceptualising it so that we move beyond 'them' and 'us', 'insider/outsider' scenarios. Young British Muslims and youth from other migrant communities are, I think, leading the way in rethinking culture, identity and belonging. Perhaps it is because they have to live with visible and palpable differences every day – within themselves and between them and their immediate environment, their families, their peers and so on – that they have started to see difference as something that is not necessarily problematic but, in fact, enabling and enriching, opening up possibilities that monocultural perspectives might foreclose. For most, this is not an intellectual or aesthetic exercise but an existential fact of their lives, and it demands a response at every level even though they may not be aware of it.

It soon became clear to me that the caricature of British Muslims as inward looking and self-absorbed is grossly misleading. All the young British Muslims I met were comfortable with living in a pluralistic, multicultural society and, in fact, cherished being surrounded by people different from them. Whilst many noted that the neighbourhoods in which they grew up have become less culturally diverse in recent years, and some admitted there was little, if any, interaction between different communities in some places, they nevertheless had friends, acquaintances and colleagues who were non-Muslim. This was, they felt, a very important aspect of their lives.

Aisha grew up in Slough. The neighbourhood, she recalled, 'was quite multicultural but I think now it's more Asian populated now …. I don't really recall any tensions at the time; my brother, he went to the same school as me and all his friends were from the same street, from that same neighbourhood, who were from different races and I grew up with that as well. I've noticed that in the last couple of years more and more Asians, particularly Pakistani Muslims, are moving into where we're living.'

What did she think of that?

She felt ambivalent about it because 'you tend to feel at home but at the same time … the thing is, our family – well, me and my siblings – we never really had that cultural pull. I mean, my parents have been very liberal in that sense. I don't know how you've been brought up but, you know, back "home" you always have to be aware of what other people think. We had to be aware of that as well, because we know that our problems will be everyone's problems, and I really, really hate that and so do my sisters and my brothers as well. So mum and dad are always telling us to be a bit wary of what we do, and, you know, who we're walking down the street with – it's horrible.'

Was that less of a concern when the area was more mixed?

'Yeah – before it was less of a concern. But you know how these aunties, when they get together, they tend to talk about "so, did you see so and so's daughter with this and that and the other?" and I really hate it. The thing is my family, we've never really been brought up in that sense – we don't really sit at the dinner table and talk about his and her daughter or anything like that. I really do hate it because I'm thinking "why should we care about what other people think?" '

Listening to Aisha saying this made me realise once more just how little surface appearances can tell us about a person's identity. Aisha was wearing a full *hijab*, showing only her face, and a long, loose all-in-one robe similar to a *jilbab* but not quite so baggy. Many might think of her as firmly embedded in a Pakistani Muslim identity, that her clothes signalled an acceptance of its norms and mores. But Aisha's clothes offered little indication of her true feelings, her real sense of who she was and what she believed, what values she held dear and what social practices she felt were acceptable. Her response to the cultural life of the

Pakistani community was, in fact, more 'British' than Pakistani, with an emphasis on individuality and autonomy.

However, being 'British' for Aisha involves more than expressing a greater sense of individuality. It also involves a recognition and affirmation of *difference* in society. 'When I was doing A-levels I made friends with people from different backgrounds and we did have conversations about religion as well and that made me a bit happy because they were asking me questions, and they were questions about religion as well, so it was really nice when we were actually getting together and we were talking about religion and we were finding a common ground. I think that's one thing that you need to establish as well: if you're living in a multicultural society, the best way to approach it is to find a common ground to you all and start building the society from there and that is, to a certain extent, how our friendship grew as well. I mean, I was friends with a Sikh so obviously we had some conversations about religion, and we both believed in God, so that was one way of taking it from there.'

At the same time, she was aware of the dangers of emphasising differences to the point of divisiveness, 'I mean, some of these people – these guys that you see – if you start pointing out the differences [like they do] and say "well you do this and we do this" well obviously you're going to discourage people and you're going to make them hate you even more and that's not the way to approach things. I accept the fact that there are going to be some people who are going to be racist, or who are going to be anti-Islamic but, then again, there are going to be people who actually want to find out more about you and if that's the case, then I'm ok with that. I'm not prepared to convert the whole world because Islam is about your own personal journey – if you find it, then great, if not, then that's up to you.'

Likewise, Soumaya cherished her friendships with non-Muslims because 'it's good to know each other in a way because then you can understand your differences and you can understand *why* you're different and appreciate it. With having Christian friends, you've been brought up with them from the start, from when you went to nursery, through to school and college, and as you are working and meeting them day-to-day you get to learn about their basic beliefs and stuff, and just like they want to know about our festivals, in a similar way we can ask them as well and I've been quite happy to learn things about them as well. I've had some Hindu friends as well at university, and from them I got to know about their beliefs and they've understood my beliefs.'

Had her interactions with non-Muslims ever made her feel unsure about her own identity as a Muslim?

'No,' she replied.

Had it strengthened it?

'It has, actually, yeah. Because, I mean, Islam doesn't really rule out anyone, and it doesn't say that if a person is not a Muslim you can't speak to them, you can't be friends with them.'

Soumaya's point was echoed by Sameena from Leicester, who only began to take notice of diversity in society after she became a practising Muslim. 'Since I've become a practising Muslim', she said, 'I'd say yes, I've become very much more conscious of Islam playing a role in a wider community full of other cultures and faiths, and it's really helped me realise that there are … as a nation we are so diverse that we can't even begin to explain it. Within a culture there's diversity, within a faith there's diversity, within a community there's diversity. Even in a secular sort of society there's diversity. So it's really opened up my eyes to that. But beforehand I think I was completely oblivious, I just took people for who they were as people, not of a certain faith, not of a certain culture, colour or anything, just people. If I clicked with them, great. If I didn't, perhaps not so great but no big deal. And that's one of the things that I was thinking of when I was talking about university, when I lived in the Halls at one point where there were six girls and every single one of us was from a different country. And if I could get a chance to go back now I would really totally explore the whole, you know, what we had in common, what our differences were, where they came from, how they lived their lives.'

Perhaps the ease with which these young Muslims respond to cultural and religious differences in society is because their interpretation of Islam is one which accepts that human beings will follow different paths – that this is, indeed, what God has ordained. The Birmingham-based artist Mohammed Ali said, 'plenty of people are highlighting the political issues; I'm here to try and share some of the other principles that I think are beneficial for the wider society. To show people the certain *hadith*, the certain words and principles and virtues that are prevalent within the text, to say this is a guidance for everyone, for Muslims and non-Muslims, to say, live in harmony, treat your neighbour good regardless of what religion he is.'

He went on, 'In my affairs and in the way I deal with people, I'm happy to deal with all kinds of people. I enjoy it. It's not like a two-faced thing where I could go away [from dealing with non-Muslims] and just feel at home in the Muslim community or whatever. I enjoy and I prefer to work with non-Muslims. When I do workshops, I go up north, [in] Newcastle, I had a 100 percent non-Muslim kids and it was a pleasure to work with them, it really was, because I thought, "Well, these guys, I've been able to be respectful to them and they gave me respect back", and I thought that was a beautiful thing. The three days I spent when I went up to Newcastle, that was probably the best example. In Newcastle, in an area where they probably never come across Muslims, these guys were calling me by first name, "Mohammed! Mohammed!" and at the end of the day it just felt good to go away and see that these guys – there's three guys in that class, and I might have changed their perceptions slightly, and I think I did because they were young guys, and I think I really did break it down to them, – saw me as just Mohammed the artist, and I felt pleasure in doing so, in being able to show: what is Islam? What does it mean to me? Humanising Muslims and Islam as a faith, I think that's important.'

In sharp contrast to the conventional stereotype of Muslims as intolerant of *kuffirs* (unbelievers), as proselytisers intent on converting the rest of the world to their religion, this generation of young Muslims in Britain seems to be content to live and let live. In recent times, much has been made about the prevalence of anti-Semitism amongst Muslims. Whilst it is true that anti-Jewish feeling is very common in many Muslim societies, and that amongst British Muslims the rhetoric of resistance to Israel sometimes slides uncomfortably close to denigration of Jews (and does sometimes slip into outright anti-Semitism), I did wonder if young British Muslims were as anti-Semitic as they are portrayed.

Many, in fact, had had little face-to-face interaction with Jews living in Britain but they did not display any particular antipathy to Jews *per se*. A few, however, had encountered Jews to varying degrees. In Blackburn, Asif's partner, when he was doing voluntary work for a mental health group, was an orthodox Jew. Although their personal relationship never extended beyond their professional one, they did spend their lunchtimes together during which 'he used to ask questions about Islam and I used to ask him about Judaism […] You know, the Orthodox Jews, they're very strong in their belief but I wasn't thinking, like, oh I hate this person and he wasn't thinking the same. So, you just try to become friends, just try to get to know each other.' And there it was, said as matter-of-factly as one might talk about any other workplace relationship, without rancour or suspicion or any other inflection that might give one the impression that Asif saw his Jewish colleague in any other way.

A couple of the other Muslims I spoke to, however, had deeper and more profound encounters with Jews. Raihan had attended the City of London School in central London, and a lot of his friends and fellow pupils there were Jewish. I asked him if there had ever been any problem with them.

'No. It's always been a positive thing I guess,' he replied.

I said to him that a lot of people see Muslims as being quite anti-Semitic, and he seemed surprised by this. 'That's more of an issue to do with the politicisation of the anti-Semitism versus anti-Israeli thing but if you look at Muslims and Jews socially they have more in common than any other ethnic or social group. If we were having this conversation a few hundred years ago it wouldn't be the case, you'd think Muslims and Jews got on like a house on fire and then it was the Christians who were causing the trouble, and then if you go back before that it was Christians versus Muslims. The point is that we have similarities more so than differences. I've never felt so much about the Israel and Palestine kind of thing to have to speak to my [Jewish] friends about it and go on and hassle them about the whole thing because I just don't see it as positive. It's not something that can contribute anything to anyone.'

For Mohammed Ali, his encounter with one Jewish boy was one of the most pivotal of his whole life. He recalled with excitement how, at grammar school, he had been introduced to jazz by a boy called Joseph Tobias, who was Jewish. 'He was Iraqi – half-Iraqi – and he was Jewish. And that guy – I always tell people about this guy, Joseph Tobias, he was one of my other best friends, apart from Martin Barlow who died – Joseph Tobias was an amazing guy. He was a very eccentric guy. I remember in sixth form college people used to take the piss out of him and say like, "This guy's just weird", 'cause he'd like ripped out all the – he had a huge house, in this kind of Jewish area, Egbaston, where a lot of the Jews used to live, a huge house, with a big piano in his house and everything, and I'd be like, "Wow man," – I remember people used to take the piss because he ripped out the springs from his bed because he wanted it stripped down to the bare basics, he didn't want all this luxury life.

'He was an amazing guy, he influenced me a lot. Even though we weren't religious – none of us were at that time – but he was just amazing. He used to write a lot – in English, when he used to write an essay, the teacher used to just read it and say, "This is something else." His paintings were amazing – I still remember them. You could give him a block of wood in CDT lessons and all of a sudden there'd be a boat, a man on a boat – he'd just carve it.

'He used to always say, "I hate this country, I want to get out of here; I hate my family and blah blah blah", right? You could say a typical grammar school boy, really, and he used to say "I want to go and live in Brazil, and live on the beach and carve models and whatever." And the funny thing is, he did it, and he's just disappeared – he went to Brazil. No-one knows where he is. I'd love to hook up with him again. He just disappeared. He didn't want to communicate with anybody – just gone. After sixth form college.

'And I was very close to him. Like I said, I could go to see his family now I think we did chase him up once and his family were like, yeah he does call, and they gave us a number for him and I tried to call him but, I couldn't get through to him, there was some Portuguese woman and I couldn't really communicate with her.'

After telling me this Mohammed stopped talking for a while, and in the silence that ensued I began to think about how these stories of everyday interactions can so often be obscured by the larger narratives of conflict with which we seem to become obsessed. Perhaps Joseph Tobias had a seminal influence on Mohammed's art, inspiring in him the creativity out of which he has fashioned an exciting artistic career. From such little things, large consequences can follow. But these little chords of harmony are drowned out by the cacophony of raised voices, by shrill denunciations and articulations of large-scale animosities.

Given the enthusiasm with which these young Muslims spoke about difference, and about the value of living in a multicultural society, I was not surprised to find that conversion was off their agenda, even though they acknowledged that they had a duty as Muslims to spread knowledge of their religion to others. Muslims, said Ayman, must 'form an initial relation of humanity' with others – including, he said pointedly, Jews and Israelis. From this initial relationship stems all others. 'We have three levels of brotherhood and sisterhood [in Islam]', he told me, 'we have human brotherhood and sisterhood, we have Muslim brotherhood and sisterhood, and we have brotherhood and sisterhood of faith. Human brotherhood and sisterhood: I am the brother of the Jewish, the Christian [etc.]; he has rights on me and I have rights on him. Muslim brotherhood obviously is a closer relation because he's a Muslim just like me. Faith – because the Muslim might not be a practising Muslim – but the one that's practising and has the faith, he's even more closer to me.'

On this basis, Ayman believed that Muslims should not isolate themselves from others. 'What are we worried about or what don't we have that makes us isolate? Why can't I have a relation with my neighbours? Why can't I have a relation with my friends at work? And it doesn't necessarily always have to be a relation where I'm going to start preaching Islam.'

Raihan, on the other hand, did not feel there was any particular reason for believing that relations between Muslims are any closer than those between Muslims and non-Muslims. 'I have a lot of respect for anyone in any religion who has decided to live their life in an ethical and moral way, to give back to society, to do good things and work together, you know. I have a lot more time for these kinds of people whether they're Muslims or not. You know, if someone is not a Muslim but he's doing all that, why should I see him as inferior to someone who is a Muslim just by virtue of their name or their parents or something like that?'

* * *

What Raihan and Ayman have touched upon here, in their opposing ways, is an issue which is often central to debates about young Muslims' sense of belonging and identity. This is the *ummah*, the global community of Muslims. It is a key concept within Islam and is thus considered to be extremely important for all Muslims. It is not possible to convey the power of the concept except through the words of a believer. Ziauddin Sardar, in his wonderful book *Desperately Seeking Paradise: Journeys of a Sceptical Muslim*, writes, 'Muslim I am in the inmost existence of self, yet that self is never alone or singular but simultaneously part of the multiple and diverse body of the whole Muslim community. The *ummah* is not an added extra, not an aggregate after the fact of me. What point in seeking paradise if one is alone … ?'[16]

It appears to bother quite a lot of people that Muslims should feel such attachment to an identity that exceeds the borders of nation states and thus, in a way, eludes their jurisdiction.[17] A couple of weeks after the 7/7 bombings, *Sky News* commissioned a poll of British Muslims, which asked them if they considered themselves 'Muslim first and British second' or 'British first and Muslim second'. According to the poll, 46 percent agreed with the former and only 12 percent with the latter; 42 percent, however, didn't differentiate. Nevertheless, this was sensationally reported as representing some kind of crisis within Britain concerning its Muslim population, reinforcing the sense that their loyalty was 'suspect'.

As with most opinion polls, the question told us more about those asking the question than those responding to it. By framing the question in this way it purported to show the *underlying* strength of feeling towards Britain amongst Muslims in a way that may have been concealed by other polls, which asked them directly about their loyalty (and which showed that the overwhelming majority felt loyal to the country). 'How loyal?' is the question behind the question. The poll implicitly accepted that 'identity' has more than one dimension, that one could be both Muslim and British. But by asking respondents to rank their identities in order of priority it re-contained this acceptance of multiplicity within the singular frame of the 'flat' notion of culture and identity to which I have referred above. We may all have many sides to us but, it seems, we can only be properly and loyally British if we consider our national identity to be the most important part of us. That so many Muslims don't feel this way is read as being suspicious.

There are several objections to be made to this line of reasoning. First, it is clearly absurd to ask people to prioritise between different aspects of themselves. It would be a bit like asking them if they preferred their left or right hands. I am sure that left-handed people would prioritise their left hand and right-handed people their right; the point is that the question is beside the point. Also, our multiple identities encompass not just our 'cultural', 'religious' or 'ethnic' identities but many others besides. Would it not be futile to ask if someone was a woman first and British second or a man if he was husband first and father second? Such questions tell us nothing other than that those asking it seem to think that our national identity should take precedence over all others. This 'flat' sense of identity is, ironically, a mirror image of those Islamist totalitarians such as Osama bin Laden who insist that Islam must take precedence over everything else.

All the young men and women to whom I spoke were highly committed Muslims. Most of them would definitely have agreed or tended to agree that their religion was indeed the most important thing in their life. Some, such as Munizha from Slough, even spoke about being Muslim first and

British second, 'because obviously my Islamic identity is more a part
of me than the British society and culture'. This was echoed by others
and has been noted elsewhere.[18] On the other hand, Aisha told me how,
in the aftermath of the 7/7 bombings, the news showed an interview
with a Muslim Londoner whom they had picked 'out of the blue and
interviewed for his thoughts and opinions on 7/7, and he said, "Yeah, I'm
a Londoner and then a Muslim." And I picked up on that, in that he's
defining himself as first a Londoner and then a Muslim. You get the sense
that he felt the need to justify himself, like "We're British and then I'm
a Muslim."' This shows the extent to which flat notions of culture and
identity have been internalised as 'common sense' by Muslims and
non-Muslims alike.

Despite their common commitment to Islam, there were very different
responses when I asked them about their feelings towards the *ummah*.
Some, of course, felt a strong sense of attachment and identification
with it. Alluding to the way the *ummah* was spoken of by the Prophet as
a single body, Qadeer said, 'the Muslim world is such that if one is hurt –
if one part of the body is hurt, the whole body feels it. I'm Sunni, but if it's
Sunni, Shia, Wahhabi or whatever, you feel it when there's things going
on in Kashmir, in Chechnya, in Afghanistan, in Iraq, Palestine, things like
that … we feel it, most Muslims feel it.'

This empathy with other Muslims' suffering – 'feeling' their pain –
was certainly felt by all the young Muslims but this did not necessarily
determine their sense of attachment to the *ummah*, nor was it necessarily
seen as a *cause* of that identification. For Abdur-rahman, for instance,
the *ummah* was a 'strong thing' but 'it's like it's something that precedes
everything else, it's there in the background, it's part of your being,
so you can't differentiate it from anything else'. This 'core' of his identity
was certainly augmented by an empathy with the plight of others, 'when
you open a newspaper, for example, you might go to the world pages,
and you see what's happening in other countries, and sadly what news
reports come up with are trouble spots, and usually bad news, from
Muslim communities'.

But this empathy was not merely an abstract one. It derived also from
his sense that, had circumstances been different, he might have been in the
position of those about whom he was reading or watching on television.
'I mean, when I was growing up – 1987 – I was 11 or 12 or something,
and the *intifada* [the Palestinian uprising against Israeli occupation]
started off and you used to see pictures of kids your age throwing stones

against tanks and when they get caught by the Israeli police their bones getting broken because they got beaten up and you think, "hang on, that could be me."'

Others – generally women, but not exclusively so – tended to view the *ummah* through a more personal lens, in close-up rather than as a panorama. Razia believed that she had a certain bond with all Muslims regardless of where they came from because 'with all Muslims, no matter how religious they are, you can get on with them at some level okay? […] You can always find something to talk about with them, and you always have something in common with them, not merely just because you're named a Muslim. Every Muslim, I believe, does have a bit of faith in something, in some part of their religion and I think that's why, you know, I can get on with everybody.'

Similarly, Zainab said, 'I think I identify most with the Muslim community. I have lots of non-Muslim friends and work colleagues who are not Muslim but I think that … I identify most with Muslim Egyptians, you know, those that have been brought up here – which starts really pinpointing it down. I notice Muslims tend to do this and I guess to an extent it's good as long as they've still got non-Muslim friends and colleagues who they treat exactly the same. I think we just feel a sense of warmth and, like, bonding and, sort of, if I met another Muslim – probably if I met another non-Muslim as well – but I know if I met another Muslim, you know, another Muslim girl was to … if I was to bump into another Muslim girl, we'd just have that instant kind of bond […] I guess I kind of feel that bond with other Muslims [most].'

At the same time, Zainab also demonstrated how the idea of the *ummah* is always complicated by other loyalties, by ties to other communities and by other identities. The attachment of young British Muslims to their locality, and indeed their country, is one of those complicating factors. She would not say that British Muslims were more loyal to their religion than their country, for instance, because '[if] you define your country as your community, your local community or even the wider community, there's no need to even say something like that, do you see what I mean?' This in turn calls into question definitions of the *ummah* as well. It cannot be seen in splendid isolation, transcending or superseding all other loyalties and identities. Rather, the *ummah* is composed of those other identities and those other circuits of attachment, just as Britishness cohabits with the *ummah* within British Muslims. It works both ways.

An interesting example of this was described to me by Fahmida from Uxbridge. The Muslim community in that town, she said, is composed of a Pakistani community, a Bengali community and now a small Somali community, 'and because the Bengali and Pakistani communities are larger they [the Somalis] kind of follow them. It's still very traditional. It's not religious – it's just traditional, bringing all the Pakistani and Bengali elements into it.'

So it's more culture than religion? I asked.

'Yeah.'

What about the relations between the different groups? Do they largely stick together in their groups?

'I think the older population do, like my dad's age because he feels more comfortable with his Bengali crew, as you'd say, because he's had a business here and everything so he knows all his older friends. I suppose when they're praying together and there's a space they'll say, "Oh, come sit next to me", or whatever it is – and that is largely the same for Pakistanis as well. So I think the older group – you usually find them actually fighting each other, "Oh bloody Bengalis", or "Bloody Pakistanis", however it is, but the younger groups, like my brother's age, they just mingle more and they don't really have a problem, and they end up laughing at their dads.'

Not only does this corroborate the argument that the principal dynamic within British Muslim communities today is a conflict between first and successive generations of migrant Muslims, it also tells us a lot about the changing formulation of identity amongst British Muslim communities today. The *ummah* is clearly experienced differently by different generations. The older generation seems to be lacerated by old wounds, divisions that cut deep in the psyche (Fahmida admitted that her father has non-Muslim friends but no Pakistani ones, and it is worth speculating whether that is due to the painful memory of the Bangladesh war in 1971). In contrast, the increasing solidarity across ethnicities amongst younger Muslims shows us how for them the *ummah* may not be – as it seems to be for their parents – merely an ideal that is hopelessly compromised by the traumas of yesteryear. Nevertheless, this solidarity is engineered by their common location within Britain, and so we must not overlook the fact that this is due in part not just to a shared sense of Muslimness, but also to a shared investment in their common 'Britishness'.

Therefore, young British Muslims' appraisal of the *ummah* is often neither unconditional nor uncritical, neither romantic nor involuntary.

Fahmida recounted in exasperation how, 'with my mum and dad I usually find it's a loyalty thing where, "I'm going to back up the Muslims! We're Muslims so I'm going to back up the Muslims!" even though I don't think they necessarily have a viewpoint on [any given issue] or not. There is a solidarity [for me] but sometimes it's just a matter of logic.' She then cited a few recent controversies where she felt that she could not just 'back Muslims' because the logic of the situation demanded otherwise. For instance, she could not agree with women who refused to remove the *niqab* (the full veil) in court for identification purposes; nor did she agree with those women who argue that showing themselves uncovered on a photo ID, for instance, undermines their rights as Muslim women. These, she felt, were illogical, and she could not support them. Her 'solidarity' is conditional.

Others are very sceptical that the *ummah* actually exists in reality because of the divisions within Islam. Aisha noted that 'on the international scale, even within that, there's so many fractions within the Islamic *ummah*; obviously you know, there's Sunni this and Shia that so ... I know that it will never really be one, as long as these divides are there, the Muslim *ummah* will never really, really unite as one. Because obviously in Iraq, you have the Sunnis and the Shias and who's going to take power? It's like politics everywhere – you can't really escape from it.'

For her, the *ummah* only would have value if you saw it differently. 'I would like to better my community and I think there are plenty of other Muslims who think like that as well, and I think that falls under the umbrella of the *ummah* as well, you know?'

By that did she mean her local community?

'Yeah.'

Amina was also sceptical of the *ummah* as a reality but she saw it from the other end of the telescope. Divisions amongst Muslims in her local community made her feel that the concept of the *ummah* had no basis in reality.

'When they do say, *ummah*, and we're all Muslims and we're all one I don't agree with that because at the moment there's Wahhabis, Sunnis ... especially locally, there's two different ... like, Eid's two different days now as well, because of that, because of Wahhabis and Sunni – 'cos, I'm a Wahhabi, we celebrated our Eid on Monday and all the others celebrated on Tuesday. When we began our fast, our mosque did say that the fast is on Sunday, and the Sunni mosque agreed with that, but then our mosque changed their mind because they [the Sunnis] were going to do it on Sunday, so then our mosque said we're going to do it on Saturday because we don't wanna do it on Sunday like the Sunni mosque. That's just stupid, and I really disagree with that.

'So when they do say *ummah* and all the Muslims in the country are all one I don't agree with that 'cos they do disagree: whatever Sunnis believe, Wahhabis disagree, and whatever Wahhabis believe, Sunnis disagree with that. So I don't understand what *ummah* is. When you say, *ummah*, it's *all* Muslims, but if it's going to be all the Muslims, you should come together and solve it together as well. So everything's just falling apart now, I think.'

Some young British Muslims feel no affinity to the idea of the *ummah* at all. Their reasons for this stance were varied. Shaheen felt this was probably because she hadn't embraced Islam so completely as to be able to feel it but she was also sceptical that there was in fact an *ummah* to feel affinity towards. 'I guess membership of any kind of group or any society implies unity between the people and I don't see much unity in the Muslim community. You know, I don't feel that I could just go to a Muslim and rely on him in the street.' But her scepticism was not restricted to the *ummah*: it extended to other identities too. 'But similarly, I don't think I can do that with a Pakistani necessarily,' she added.

Raihan Alfaradhi, on the other hand, felt no equivocation about his Muslimness. He saw himself as '100 percent Muslim', but he still felt no particular bond with the notion of an *ummah*. 'I don't know why', he said, 'maybe it's because I'm a 100 percent British – a 100 percent Muslim, fair enough – but a 100 percent British in my upbringing and everything; maybe that's got a lot to do with it.' Perhaps, but it should be pointed out that all the others who did feel part of the *ummah* also felt this strong bond to Britishness. As we shall see in due course, this does have something to with it but not simply because of the strength of one's Britishness.

Yara el-Sherbini approached the issue differently. She has a 'problem' with the concept of the *ummah* because 'it's creating another defined little … I don't know how … it's putting someone in a little, you know, it's labelling people off: we're this, we're that, we're Muslims. Well, I think the point is we're people. My faith is my faith; we're people, let's interact in a world of other people. Don't try and put yourself in a little boot-camp over there and say, "Well, we're Muslims." I don't think that's positive.'

'My faith is a very private, individual thing so why are we having that thing about "this is who I am, I'm a Muslim"? I mean, even if I do end up saying I'm a British Muslim, I find that problematic. Why are we discussing religion, why? Why are people saying "I'm British Muslim"? Why? I'm British, or my father might be from Egypt and so on but why are we talking about being … we're not at the stage where people are saying "I'm British Roman Catholic or British Church of England", so why are we having or even using that as the deciding factor of who we are when that is part of our private, faith-based identity? Why is religion coming into it that way?'

In response, I suppose one might say that many people – not just Muslims – don't think of their faith in such privatised terms. It is as much a part of their public self as their private one. I shall turn to the reasons in due course but it is also worth noting that Yara draws attention – quite correctly, in my opinion – to the curious inconsistency in British public discourse which, until recently, spoke of *some* groups in religious terms – usually those from the Asian subcontinent – whilst others were spoken of purely in relation to their ethnicity or race. As I have argued elsewhere, this is changing now because people of faith – principally Muslims but also Christians, Sikhs, Jews and others – have begun asserting their religious identities within the public sphere.[19]

Many of these young Muslims who felt no particular loyalty or attachment to a global Islamic identity nevertheless could understand why people did feel it. Shahid, for instance, felt no sense of belonging to an *ummah*. 'The thing is, because of the way I am at home with my parents, it's a very Bengali tradition we have there, and then I'm always obviously around mainly English people at work and things like that, I can't say I've ever felt a global Islamic identity. I can understand where it comes from though […] It comes from the fact that when you see your own government fighting illegal wars there's a tendency to become totally narrow minded and always become pessimistic about everything, and there's no doubt that there are a lot of Muslims around the world suffering, and it's an easy trap to fall into, but I also do believe it's quite understandable because at the end of the day we always – we're always going to integrate with people we have most in common with. I think this is a natural thing and it's not something we should be surprised at. British people shouldn't be surprised that Muslims hurt more when there are other Muslims around the world being tortured etc.'

This idea that people feel a natural affinity to those similar to themselves seems at first to be based on sound common sense. But, like all things that seem like common sense, does it really explain anything? Where does that sense of similarity come from? Does it, as Abdur-rahman had suggested, inhere in a core Muslim identity that 'precedes' everything else? If so, what explains that core? Is it simply 'there' or can we adduce reasons for it being there? Alternatively, do Muslims feel their similarity as a result of circumstances, context, choice, knowledge and other factors? Even allowing for the fact that a Pakistani Muslim in Britain, for example, shares his 'Muslimness' with, say, a Muslim from Iraq, what else do they have in common? And why is this common religious bond more important than what they share with, say, the non-Muslims immediately around them: a language, a culture, a way of behaving and thinking, common physical reference points, a shared knowledge of their social and physical environment and so on? The religious 'bond' must be explained, not merely described.

There is no doubt that most practising Muslims conceive of the *ummah* using the metaphor of the body coined by the Prophet Muhammad. There is also no doubt that global mass communications have brought this body to life in a way that is quite unprecedented since the initial expansion of Islam from its Arabian heartland. The *ummah* has come into being as a proper marker of identity – as opposed to merely a descriptor of a notional form – in the modern, especially 'postmodern', period and, indeed, we may possibly speak of it as the first properly 'globalised' identity. But the Prophet was not referring to a 'global' identity when he first described the *ummah* as a single body. In fact, it was super-local, as it were, referring to the small band of companions who accepted his prophetic mission and accompanied him in his exile from Mecca to the desert oasis of Medina.

The rituals designed to fasten this vulnerable community of Muslims together in the face of more numerous, more powerful and implacably hostile enemies – and to mark them out as *distinct* – provided a practical symbolic core which subsequently held that community together through rapid geographical expansion. At first, it bonded the Muslim soldiers and then allowed non-Muslims to integrate easily once they had been conquered, despite the divergences of their pre-existing beliefs, which were more often than not tolerated and then accommodated – a necessary compromise which greatly facilitated the expansion of Islam.

Often the profession of faith – the *shahada*, 'There is no God but Allah and Muhammad is his messenger' – and ritual performance of the other four of the 'five pillars' of Islam – prayer, fasting, pilgrimage and the payment of a tax to benefit the needy – sufficed for converts to be considered Muslims. Belief very rarely entered the equation for ordinary folk (though it was extremely important amongst the learned), hence the rich profusion of heterodox views scattered throughout the Islamic world.

The symbolic power of such rituals is exemplified by the *hajj*, the pilgrimage to Mecca incumbent on every able-bodied Muslim able to afford the trip, at least once in their lifetime. The *Kaa'ba*, the black cube at the centre of the Holy mosque in Mecca, is the focal point for Muslims all over the world. When they pray, they face it at exactly the same time in the day (allowing for longitude, of course), and this symbolic centre is one of the highlights of the *hajj*. Muslims circle the Kaa'ba seven times during the *hajj*, their spiritual journey to the core of their faith made manifest in their perambulations.

Once again, Ziauddin Sardar's description of the pilgrimage on what is known as the Day of Arafat evokes well the power of the *hajj* to precipitate solidarity:

> The pilgrims leave early to cover the eight kilometres that separate Muna [a hill town just outside Mecca] from the Plain of Arafat, arriving before midday. When the sun passes the meridian, the ritual of *wquf*, or standing, begins. At the mosque of al-Namira, before Mount Arafat, the congregation of over two million prays as a single entity. Nothing in the world can match this spectacle; or surpass this experience. Already in the preceding days the pilgrims have experienced a brotherhood and humility the like of which they have never known. In ritual and reality they experience humanity as diverse, interconnected and united. Rich and poor, different races, different languages, male and female, the distinctions irrelevant in the commonality of endeavour, the shared effort and mutual support in which they come together for a higher purpose.[20]

Of course, modern travel has become increasingly available and affordable, thus enabling millions of Muslims who might not have had the opportunity before to experience the symbolic force of *hajj*. This has undoubtedly expanded the awareness of the *ummah* as a living community.

This is augmented closer to home by more mundane symbolic practices. Razia said to me that she had never felt part of the *ummah* before, even after she started wearing the *hijab*. 'But then', she said, 'all of a sudden I'd be like coming to uni or walking down the street and I'd see someone *hijabi* and they'd just see me, smile at me and they'd say *asalaam aleikum* and I'd be like, oh, *walakum asalaam*, and it'd kind of take me by surprise, but now I feel comfortable enough to do it to other people now. Whereas before I was a bit more reluctant, it's like, oh my God, would they actually say *walakum asalaam* back to me or will they think I'm crazy? But no, it doesn't matter anyway, you know, you can say it and people will always respond.'

It is almost as if she feels the bond with the *ummah* only after her Islamic identity – made *visible* by her *hijab* – has called forth a response from other Muslims. This has made her aware of her place in the community of believers in a way that she had not felt before. This is why symbolism is so important and so effective in Islam. Moreover, it is the tangibility of this feeling of belonging – manifested in the quotidian exchange of greetings, the visibility of dress or the wearing of beards and skullcaps – that also goes some way to describing the power and the attraction of the *ummah* as a concept and of Islam as a public identity (as opposed to a matter of private spirituality).

Nevertheless, one must note that other religions too have shared many of these symbolic features. Early Christians were also a small, persecuted group within the Roman Empire, and the idea of Christendom was somewhat analogous to the *ummah* until recently. Perhaps the Protestant Reformation, with its antipathy to ritual, its devaluing of pilgrimage and its commitment to the primacy of the individual's conscience may have weakened the notion of Christendom. The rise of secularism and nationalism then finished the job. On the other hand, the *ummah* was for much of its history only a notion, an ideal and not the real presence it is now. So what else might explain its force at this point in history?

One suggestion is mass migration, both voluntary and forced. In one sense, Muslim migrants simply become more aware of other Muslims, of the scope and extent of the Muslim community as a global phenomenon once they have moved out of their own country. But I would suggest there is a more profound and fundamental way in which migration has affected Muslim identity. This is illustrated by a character from Leila Aboulela's novel *Minaret*. When asked if he feels Sudanese, the character – called Tamer – says, 'I've lived everywhere except Sudan: in Oman,

Cairo, here [London]. My education is Western and that makes me feel that I am Western. My English is stronger than my Arabic. So I guess no, I don't feel very Sudanese though I would like to be. I guess being a Muslim is my identity.'[21]

Similarly, Shaheen told me about her old boyfriend, Haroun, a very devout Muslim who felt he was 'nothing' – not a Pakistani or British. Instead, he felt he was a Muslim. In both cases, simply being Muslim substitutes for a lack of an identity, a lack felt because they are literally *displaced*. It fulfils a role in their construction of 'selfhood' because those other identities are so fragmented – a little bit English here, a little bit Pakistani there, Omani this, Egyptian that; inhabiting each of them, they feel like they truly inhabit none. Migrants, writes Salman Rushdie, are 'haunted by some sense of loss'; they are 'obliged to deal in broken mirrors, some of whose fragments have been irretrievably lost'.[22] Therefore, the need to *imagine* an identity is more acute for those who have been displaced, precisely because they do not feel 'at home' anywhere.

Rushdie speaks of those who have left 'home' having to create 'imaginary homelands', but what of those who feel there is no home to recreate or who feel only 'nothing' as Haroun does? My sense is that the *ummah* is more important these days, more existentially important, for some members of diaspora groups than it is for more settled Muslims because it fills a void brought about by dispersal on the one hand and continued exclusion on the other.

In contrast, Raihan feels no particular affinity for the *ummah* because he feels '100 percent British'. He notes that there need not be a contradiction between that and being '100 percent Muslim', which is true enough, but he also gives the impression that he feels no particular loyalty to the *ummah* because he feels comfortably 'at home' in Britain. So it is not about either/or, and it is in fact not even about there being no contradiction – framing it in those terms is beside the point. It is about feeling 'at home' somewhere – and being allowed to feel at home.

I have discussed the ways in which young Muslims feel unable to feel at home in Britain – the myriad forms through which they continue to feel excluded. One other factor – an important one – needs to be added, especially in Britain: class. Perhaps Raihan feels so comfortably at home in Britain because he has been fortunate enough to have been educated in a public school, one of the best in London, from which pupils move into internationally renowned higher education institutions that are pillars of the British establishment: Oxford, Cambridge and the University of London. In his case, he attended the London School of Economics. From there, the City of London is a relatively short step both literally and metaphorically, and he has taken it successfully because he has dwelt in the very heart of Britain for such a long time; he has absorbed its nuances, its patterns of behaviour, its expectations and its social etiquette.

In Lancashire, Qadeer Ahmed feels 'at home' in Britain too, but he has not passed anywhere near the centres of power and authority. In Nelson, amongst the debris of a social landscape blighted by the end of the industries which sustained that community, he does his best to help others through his social work and interfaith activities. He hopes to go to university soon and complete the degree he once started but never finished. His class, his exclusion from the engines that still propel – and limit – Britain's social mobility, mediates his sense of belonging. He feels 'at home' in a very different way to Raihan, and his talent for noticing injustice and double standards against Muslims has been sharpened by his social environment. He notices these because he lives among the ruins of other inequalities. He thus feels the pull of the *ummah* in a way that Raihan does not.

Another public school–educated young Muslim, Abdur-rahman, summed it up quite nicely, 'I think, amongst Muslims, there's a class divide and a regional divide as well. People like myself are lucky; in the position I am, I don't feel as alienated as other people but I know for a fact that if you just go into communities in the north, with people who have not had that opportunity, they definitely feel alienated. You don't have to go up north, you can go to East London, Whitechapel, Aldgate, there's becoming a class distinction there as well because people who can afford to leave, amongst the Bengali Muslim community in East London, they're moving towards Redbridge and maybe a bit further out, to Essex and that sort of area, and leaving behind the people who can't move, so you're getting this class divide amongst Muslims now, which I think could be a big problem, and a gap in education.'

I agree – up to a point. The Muslims I spoke to from lower-class groups were not, in my opinion, particularly alienated. They were deprived of opportunity, yes, but they did not feel alienated. As I have suggested, if you had asked them if Britain was 'their country' – as some opinion polls have – they probably would not have agreed. However, ask them if Britain is their 'home' and they definitely say yes. In the difference between the two lies an enormous truth about lack of empowerment and social, cultural and racial exclusion, which is obscured by the obsession with loyalty and patriotism.

Both Raihan and Qadeer are remarkable young men, working incredibly hard – usually in their spare time – to 'put something back' (a phrase they both use a great deal) into the communities amongst whom they live. To think of one as less British than the other just because he happens to feel a loyalty as a Muslim to the global community of believers is both wrong and unfair. The strength of one's affinity for and attachment to that concept should be read not as a sign of loyalty or disloyalty but as the strength of the 'accommodation' that one feels in one's immediate environment. Conversely, being 'at home' in an abstracted global identity is a sign of not feeling quite 'at home' in Britain. For some young Muslims, it is a sign of not being at home anywhere. The ones I conversed with did not fall into this category but they undoubtedly exist, and it is those young men and women who are at risk from the vile seductions of political extremists. How they – and we – deal with that is another matter.

For the most part, however, the ways in which young British Muslims talk about identity confound the 'flat' conceptions of culture and identity shared by traditional nationalists and Islamic totalitarians alike. They seem to display an instinctive awareness that identity is not equivalent to *identical* but is part of a dynamic interplay of similarities and differences. In many ways, they may be exhibiting a sense of identity highly suitable for the globalised world we now live in, steering a course between an insipid consumer cosmopolitanism on the one hand and rigid local chauvinisms on the other, negotiating the 'global', the 'national' and the 'local' at the same time.

Chapter 4
Politics

Young British Muslims figure most prominently in the current public imagination as a political problem, and their politics is in a way what defines them according to many if not most non-Muslims. Their political views are in turn defined in relation to their position on violence. Are they likely to become terrorists? Do they support them or sympathise with their aims? A set of associations stitches together young Muslims in general with radicals and extremists, and the threat of violence, if not explicitly stated, is often implied.

But the way the issue of violence is approached is often highly provocative; in much current discourse, political violence or terrorism seem to be associated exclusively with Islam. Even when such associations are not consciously signalled, the accumulated weight of pronouncements on the ubiquitous threat from 'Islamic terrorism' exerts a powerful gravitational pull that prompts many to think and speak as if there is a specific and particular relationship between Islam and political violence. For example, the anti-terrorism legislation introduced in the wake of 9/11 and 7/7 is articulated as a response to a generic threat even though the specific address is clear: al-Qaeda inspired violent 'jihadism'.

Consequently, there is a demand that Muslims denounce all forms of violence to assuage the suspicion that they might in fact be harbouring some secret sympathy with such terrorists. Thus, when Muslims are asked to respond to terrorist-related incidents, a burden of representation falls upon them to demonstrate, on behalf of all 'peaceful and law-abiding' Muslims, that this is not the case. It is a burden that many resent. 'I'm really sick and tired of having to justify myself saying, "Oh, I'm really sorry about what happened,"' said Aisha. She was deeply sorry for what had happened, not just as a Muslim but also as a human being, but she was also frustrated by the cloud of suspicion that has gathered over Muslims. Others have been more forthright. 'I never have apologised', said Fahmida, 'I mean, why should I? I didn't do it, I didn't agree with it. I feel as bad as the next person. I totally condemn what happened.'

Conversely, any suggestion that there might indeed be situations and occasions when political violence may be legitimate is seen as confirmation by many of the propensity towards violence inherent in Islam and Muslims. This is most visible in relation to the closing down of any attempt to discuss suicide bombing in terms other than outright condemnation. Many non-Muslims have fallen foul of this ritual proscription, notably the Liberal Democrat MP Jenny Tonge and Cherie Blair, even when prefacing their comments with the equally ritualistic phrase, 'I am not condoning it but ...'; Muslims, however, feel the pressure most since suicide bombing has become exclusively associated with Islam.[1]

On the other hand, others seem to be exempt from denouncing all forms of violence. For instance, western political leaders and those who support them remain free to make discriminations between legitimate and illegitimate forms of violence, usually based on the distinction between state and non-state actions. But questions about when and how it might be permissible to use violence – whether as a state, as a group or as an individual – are common to us all, part of the ethical heritage of humankind. Responses to such questions have emerged at different times and in different forms – one thinks of the teaching of Jesus Christ, Thomas Aquinas and Just War Theory; the advice of the god Krishna in the *Bhagavad Gita*; of Gandhian non-violence; and of course, of the many meanings and disputations over *jihad* – but, in these times, Muslims seem to be excluded from this ethical heritage: not only does debate about the merits of violence seem impermissible if conducted by Muslims but also Islam has somehow been excluded from this ethical heritage because for many it is assumed to be intrinsically violent. Such people believe that it was violent from its inception, and it is argued that its spread at the point of a sword is of a piece with the violence inherent in its ethics, as evident in *Shariah* law's corporal punishments. Those Muslims who obsess and fantasise about *Shariah* law in these terms thus indulge this 'othering' of Islam. Quite why Islam and Muslims should be singled out in this respect is hard to fathom given that violence has been endemic in all human societies since the beginning of the species.

All the young Muslims I spoke to categorically rejected and condemned the narrowly violent interpretation of *jihad* espoused by those who promote it in the name of Islam. Qadeer summed it up. Speaking of the 7/7 bombers he said, 'the guys who did it, they're pointing to Iraq, Afghanistan and things like that. They're saying it's revenge for these things, but Islam's not about revenge. The West may talk about collateral damage, but there's no such thing as collateral damage in Islam, and there's definitely no such thing as an eye for an eye when it comes to innocent people. You don't go and blow up innocent people and say, "Well, because you did it, we're allowed to do it." That's rubbish, it's not in Islam and no scholar needs to tell you that.'

He added, however, 'I mean, you look at 9/11 and as a Muslim you're shocked at how anyone could do something like that and some people go straight to the conspiracy theory – there were no Jews in the World Trade Center, Muslims wouldn't have done that, they remote controlled the aeroplane and this and that – but unfortunately it's one of those things, the way it is today and the way you see Muslims, you can only see Muslims do something like that … you just think it can only be Muslims who are crazy enough, if you will, to do something like that. And by crazy I mean those extremists who, like I said, have been brainwashed to believe anything you do against the West is a good act.'

The point is that such attitudes to violence are not inherent in Islam, which is not to blame for these atrocities; rather, it is those Muslims who perpetrate such acts that are to blame. Equally, other Muslims – the vast majority, of course – should also not be blamed. One should not speak of 'Islam', one should speak only of Muslims – and not all Muslims should be stained by the actions of others since there is no relationship between them, either directly or through some putative thing called 'Islam'.

Shahid made this point very clearly, 'A few words that I really, really, do detest are "Islamist" and "jihadist". I hate them because I think Islam means peace and I think to go around calling terrorists "Islamists" is just ridiculous. The way the media's portraying things, it's essentially making it synonymous to being a terrorist and a Muslim at the same time. This other term, jihadist, which is used as another term for terrorist, I mean, I don't think that a lot of people appreciate the concept of *jihad*. Most people don't understand *jihad* completely, like, the greater *jihad* – *jihad* is split into the greater *jihad* and the smaller *jihad* and going around fighting is the smaller *jihad*. The greater *jihad* is the inner struggle in their soul. So to associate these terms with bin Laden I think is absolutely disgusting. They should just say "Muslim terrorists".'

This distinction Shahid made between different forms of *jihad* was echoed by others. Aisha spoke of *jihad* as a 'struggle, but a struggle doesn't necessarily mean go out there fighting a war, it can also mean a personal struggle as well – you, trying to find yourself. You have different types of *jihad*, like, for example, monetary *jihad* – not to be too selfish and materialistic.'

Omar felt 'really angry' that people used the concept of *jihad* to justify killing in the name of Islam. He wanted to know if such people looked 'first and foremost within themselves. I mean, are they practising Islam, first of all, are they performing their prayers, first of all? Are they doing the rights and responsibilities in their own personal life correctly?' This was because '*jihad* has lots of different meanings. Your first *jihad* begins from home, that's practising your faith and that's a *jihad* in its own self; by being patient, you know; patience is a great virtue but, you know, patience of actually going through struggles, performing your prayer at the mosque, you know, having good relations with people of other faiths, and doing honest and true dealings with other people. I think that *jihad* starts from home and not going out there and terrorising and killing people.'

There were others, however, who reserved the right to discriminate between legitimate and illegitimate forms of violence. For them, it was justifiable to undertake certain acts of political violence in certain contexts. Asif, for instance, was 'shocked' by 9/11. 'What's the point of doing something to people who haven't done anything?' he asked. 'Islam is not a violent religion but I think it's been defined as violent because of 11 September, and the July bombings in London, but that's because of a few people. I disagree with what happened there, completely disagree.'

Nevertheless, 'you've got the other side … Israel, what's happening in Palestine as well, where you've got suicide bombers. The suicide bombers' argument is that Israel have all the armoury, all the weaponry, everything comes from America, they get funded, they get supported to go out and attack and take away the land from the Palestinians and the Palestinians say, "we're just supposed to sit there and take it, with them killing our children? What are we supposed to do?" – I'm just trying to put myself in their shoes. I wouldn't be able to be a suicide bomber, I don't think I would be able to think about doing it but if people live in that situation, day in day out, repetitive, it's been happening for two years, you see your parents die, you see your mother die, see your sister die, see your child die, see your brother die and there's nothing you can do and now you're being enclosed in a land you're not allowed out of … I think they've no choice, personally, I mean with Israel the whole world's with them and there's no-one helping the Palestinians so what are they supposed to do?'

Asif therefore distinguished between acts of terrorism, looking at
the context of the Palestinian situation rather than condemning suicide
bombing outright. It is noticeable, however, that he does not go so
far as to endorse suicide bombing. Instead, he looks at the causes and
provocations, assesses the situation in which the action is being taken
and argues that all acts of political violence are not necessarily the same.

In London, Ayman argued that 'the religious person who understands
his religion properly, directly from the teachings of the Prophet, peace
be upon him, can make a division [i.e. discriminate] between different
areas and different things that are happening around the world, so I can
say, for example, I don't like the policies that are happening around the
world, I don't like the contradiction [between western governments'
domestic policies (which he thinks are good) and their foreign policy],
but I have different means of opposing this and different means
of standing against such policies. And I don't just mean terrorism
and not terrorism because obviously terrorism is completely out
of the subject [i.e. out of the question].

'There's a very clear verse that I really love – a verse in the Holy
Qu'ran – that says Allah does not prohibit you from having relations
with those that do not fight you in your religion, and do not stop you
from practising your religion, and to be kind and to be sort of passionate
with them and to have good relations with them; but God refrains you
from having relations with those that fight you in your religion and try
to prevent you from practising your religion. That's the simple principle
that everyone of my religion should follow.

'The biggest debate – it's not the only debate – that I would have with
people that agree with 9/11 and 7/7 and say, "But look at these people,
look what they're doing", is to say, "We don't change, our fundamentals
don't change regardless of what the situation is." If we don't kill civilians,
we don't kill civilians under any circumstances, under any situation. As
far as I'm concerned, if America – and they're not far from doing this – if
they invade five or six countries at the same time I – and I say this in front
of your recording – I will go and fight them on the battlefield, but this
same [American] soldier that is fighting [me] on the battlefield, if he
comes to London, to Edgware Road, I will not touch him because
the circumstances are different. Otherwise, you're going to have this
whole world as a battlefield.

'Palestine and Iraq is a different situation because that is what I call
jihad – defending your land and defending your religion – but like I say,

9/11, 7/7 and Madrid, this is terrorism, as far as I'm concerned it has nothing to do with my religion and my religion shouldn't have even been used to justify it.'

The key word here is 'battlefield', and Ayman sees it as a clearly defined and circumscribed theatre of operations; a battlefield in the old sense of a place where two conflicting forces meet under specific and highly limited rules of engagement with a rigid distinction between combatants and non-combatants. He believed that neither the terrorists nor the western governments were observing such rules of warfare, preferring instead to engage in indiscriminate acts of violence and wanton bloodshed. In other words, for Ayman, not only is violent *jihad* only justifiable as a defensive act, but it also further demands the observation of certain rules of engagement which must never involve the killing of innocent non-combatants even if the enemy is using methods that *do* kill non-combatants.

To reinforce his argument he said, 'we have a verse in the *Qu'ran* which says, "fight the non-Muslims as they fight you". Now, "as they fight you" could mean the *way* they fight you or the principle of fighting them back as they fight you, you know, defending yourself. Many Muslims, bin Laden is one of them, he's used this verse as "the *way* they kill you, kill them". So, like they're bombing, for example, civilians in Iraq and like they're bombing civilians in Afghanistan and elsewhere, we're now justified, as these people may assume, to go and bomb their civilians anywhere in the world – but that's not right obviously because this is a misinterpretation of what this verse means.'

For most young Muslims I met, all this is largely theoretical; fortunately, they had not encountered political violence directly. One young Muslim I met, however, had indeed known exactly what it is like to live with terrorism as an everyday threat, not in the sense we do now in Britain where the threat is still relatively marginal, but in the sense that it shaped every aspect of life on a day-to-day basis.

Taher had grown up in Algeria and left to take up a university scholarship in the United Kingdom in 1997. He differed from the other Muslims I spoke to insofar as the larger part of his life has thus far been lived elsewhere (he is now twenty-seven years old). Nevertheless, he has since settled here permanently, working in the City as a consultant. Indeed, he felt that since he had spent all his adult life in the United Kingdom, in many ways he related more easily to life here than in Algeria. To use the terminology of chapter 3, he feels 'at home' in Britain and he admires it greatly. Although he was aware of undercurrents of hostility towards Muslims, and was especially concerned about the portrayal of Islam and Muslims in some sections of the British media, he nevertheless felt compelled to state that he loved the everyday tolerance of British life, the ways in which it was possible for Muslims to practise their faith without much intrusion or comment. In many ways, he felt that Muslims in Britain were far better treated than even in Muslim countries – echoing a sentiment felt by others.

One particular aspect of British life he particularly admires is the right to freedom of speech, although like many Muslims he found the Danish cartoons, for example, personally offensive. In this context, he recounted to me an episode just a few days after his arrival in 1997.

'In Algeria, from 1992 to now we've had a serious terrorism problem because of particular fundamentalist groups,' he said. 'I lived through at least five years of it from '92 to '97, and even in the years after that when I was travelling home, I was travelling in fear. I know people who were very close to me who were killed. I wasn't just living through this terrorism from a distance. In my school they found a bomb and so on.

'When I came to London, I went to the central mosque, and outside was that group [from Algeria, which had been responsible for much of the violence] collecting money! And that actually was the first shock I had in Britain – it wasn't actually with Britain itself, not the British culture, or the British, it was actually with the people that a few days earlier I was worried that they were going to slaughter me or my family. I was still fearing for my family. Here I am, face to face with these guys – they're collecting money for their activities and there were a couple of policemen standing nearby as if protecting them. The joke was on multiple levels. One was the freedom of expression they had [here in the West that they hated so much] that they could do that; on the other hand I felt like saying [to the policemen], "Guys, these guys are terrorists! You've got to stop them!" There were all these contradictions. That was one of the biggest shocks actually.

'I went up to one of those guys and said, "Look, I can't believe you're not ashamed of yourselves. You're killing people and here you're collecting money to kill people." That's part of the freedom of expression that they have here. He just ignored me.'

One can only guess at the complex emotions felt by Taher during this encounter, rendered somewhat matter-of-factly some years after the experience. His amazement that such people could be allowed to do what they were doing had matured into a respect for the principles which lay behind that tolerance. Having said that, the question of whether they should have been allowed to solicit funds for their murderous activities was left open. It was not possible to gauge whether Taher's respect for British freedoms extended so far as to tolerating such people and their nefarious activities; following 9/11 and 7/7, such groups are not permitted anymore to operate as they once did. But something else is worth dwelling upon here. How successful was this group that day in obtaining money from Muslims in Britain for the purposes of killing Muslims elsewhere, albeit presented as a fight against a secular government and 'western' interests? If there were Muslims who gave money that day (and on other occasions) to such an organisation, it speaks to the moral and political confusion amongst many Muslims who simply cannot see beyond the simple Manichean dichotomies presented by such terrorist groups. Beyond that, there are many Muslims who never confront people like these because they are intimidated by them. Taher's courage in doing so was exemplary, and young Muslims are increasingly becoming emboldened to speak up against their radical fringe.

* * *

In the United Kingdom, most people are aware that groups proposing a radical political agenda in the name of Islam do exist but they are not aware, perhaps, of the disputes and differences between them. They are all stitched together in popular discourse under one rubric as 'extremists' or 'radicals' or, more problematically, as 'Islamists' or 'fundamentalists'. A few groups have acquired notoriety: al-Qaeda, of course, but also groups such as al-Muhajiroun and Hizb ut-Tahrir (HT), but it is likely that most people only know of them through their public faces, represented in the more lurid sections of the media – and sometimes even in more high-minded outlets – as a dark, ubiquitous threat of generic evil (Osama bin Laden), as raving fanatics (Omar Bakri Mohammed, an erstwhile leader of al-Muhajiroun) or as a pantomime villain (Abu Hamza al-Masri, complete with piratical eyepatch and hooks).

It must be stressed that very few young British Muslims have been drawn into contact with the nether world of Muslim terrorist groups. The greater number who have encountered extremist groups have only experienced the less clandestine and more visible groups such as al-Muhajiroun and HT, both of which were very active on university campuses in the mid-1990s and again in the early years of the following decade. HT is the more extensive organisation, and, indeed, al-Muhajiroun has since been disbanded by its leader, Omar Bakri Mohammed. Bakri Mohammed was in fact the UK leader of HT before he parted company with them to form al-Muhajiroun in 1996.

Peter Mandaville says of HT that it is 'a radical group in that its primary goal is the re-establishment of a global caliphate', which means they should be seen as a 'khilafist' rather than jihadist organisation. In the United Kingdom, HT has stressed its rejection of militant violence but nevertheless remains under suspicion as a possible ' "waypoint" on the way to violence'.[2] Al-Muhajiroun, on the other hand, seems to have aligned itself more closely to the 'Trotskyite' jihadism promoted by al-Qaeda.[3] Certainly, young British Muslims do distinguish between the two groups; in the words of the artist Mohammed Ali, 'HT are usually intelligent people; I disagree with them about a lot of things but generally speaking they're not like these ex-Mojo guys [al-Muhajiroun] – they're not like those guys; they're nutcases, they're just flippin' thugs, man, you know what I mean?'

Abdur-rahman first encountered groups such as HT and al-Muhajiroun when he began studying at the London School of Economics (LSE) in 1994.

'In the nineties it was just a mad time to be exposed in London to various ideas that were going around at the time. I joined in 1994 … and '94 was a particularly interesting year to start at the LSE because a particularly famous Muslim student was arrested back in Pakistan, Omar Sheikh, and it caused a big hoo-ha but that was just one angle – the Bosnian war had just finished so a lot of people were talking about that; we had a lot of different ideas, different groups were active all over the place. People who had older brothers, they knew what was going on anyway through their brothers and their connections, but I didn't really know what was going on so all this stuff was fresh to me.

'You had HT who were very loud and vociferous at that time. I think they had a big conference around that time, one of the big Islamic conferences, so they were out there being very brash and loud and very politically orientated; then you had the *salafi* Muslims who were quite hard line on a lot of things; then you had YM [Young Muslims], who were also active, bit more middle of the road … and that was it, really, on the campus because al-Muhajiroun didn't turn up until later.

'It was definitely buzzing. For me, a lot of the ideas were new because like I said I was never exposed to them before and I think there's something to be said to being exposed a lot since childhood, and then you sort of get an inoculation and you're used to it and then you can, like, debate with people on a level platform because if someone comes up to you and they appear to know a lot more than you then you're sort of a little bit cowed and you have no basis to go up to them and talk to them on a level playing field. So, on the one side it was definitely buzzing and you were learning lots all the time ... problem was, lots of it was just argumentation; religion is all about developing yourself and your spirit, your relationships with other people and if you've got argumentation that's not helping anybody – all you're doing is learning to debate. So, in a way, it was wasted years but I was glad I went through it.'

As for HT, Abdur-rahman felt that they resembled the revolutionary communist groups that also flourish on university campuses. 'HT are basically a political party although they don't want to come into power through the political process; they want it to come about through some sort of passive revolution. They've got their ideas from revolutionary communism, you understand. If you understand that sort of background, then you understand HT. They want a revolution, essentially, and they want to take over.'

According to Abdur-rahman, despite being vocal and highly visible, HT 'couldn't really infiltrate or dominate the Islamic Society in the LSE because they didn't have anyone clever enough to get in. They dominated a few universities like London Met or East London, no offence to them, but they had a bit more of a mass intake. So you only had like one or two people who were sophisticated enough to get in [to the LSE]. They were clever – obviously you have to be clever in terms of grades and stuff – and then once they got in they didn't have any support.' These few were, he said, 'thoughtful and intelligent and were not like the caricature of the group. They were quiet, very nice, very humble people and you just thought, "Why are you with them?"'

Far from the buzzing but august halls of the LSE, Munizha had also encountered HT and al-Muhajiroun in Slough, 'those were the two main groups, and both groups were fighting over this whole idea of an Islamic state and a lot of their talks were really, really radical. They didn't want to talk to people who were non-Muslim, they didn't want to negotiate within that society, they literally separated themselves from the *kuffir*, the unbelievers, the believers, and even from the Muslim community.

'So I think that's why I felt a resistance towards them because their views were really radical at that time; they didn't want to become a part of society, they just wanted to completely change it.'

Recently, however, she noticed that HT had changed. They are, she feels, 'not as radical as they used to be' because they have begun to invite people who are non-Muslims to speak at their events and seem to be trying to engage in dialogue. 'I wouldn't say I would be an active member of HT', she said, 'but I think there's a lot of good speakers amongst that group who actually give voice to a lot of Muslim feelings and sentiments about what's going on in society and what's going on in the news and things that Bush and Blair are doing.'

Her perception that HT has transformed itself somewhat in the following 9/11 is corroborated by observers such as Peter Mandaville, but many still suspect that this 'facelift' is nothing more than an instrumental ploy that gives the 'appearance of a "kinder, gentler" HT', whereas in fact the 'same old radical ideas lurk just below the surface'.[4] Whether sincere or not, the softening of Munizha's view of them suggests that it is paying some dividends even if it is not clear what those are.

Whilst groups such as HT or al-Muhajiroun have never really had the influence or reach that some have claimed, it would be churlish not to admit that they have enjoyed some success in appealing to some young Muslims. The nature of that appeal has been variously explained, but Raihan Alfaradhi believes that it is because they provide ready-made answers for a youth culture that demands 'quick-fire solutions, we want quick news, you know, give us that 60 second news on BBC3 and these kinds of things. We don't want to have to read stuff, we just want the information broken down bite-size, give it to us quick.' Such deep cultural determinants suggest to me that the government's 'hearts-and-minds' strategy, which aims to draw young Muslims away from extremist interpretations of Islam, may have to confront a much deeper issue than it perhaps realises – one that has very little to do with Islam. Raihan continued, 'different kinds of methods are going to have to be employed to counter these extremist views and, to be able to do that, we're going to have to sit down long and hard and come up with new, innovative ways to reach out to these guys, and that's going to take time as well; and I also think it's going to take a lot of effort'.

* * *

One of the key demands common to most Islamist groups is the implementation of *Shariah* law. For some this is only desirable in Muslim majority countries but for others there is a desire to introduce it in non-Muslim countries too, including the United Kingdom. Recent opinion polls have suggested that this desire is shared by a significant proportion of British Muslims, leading to yet more scaremongering about the threat of Islam to Britain's 'way of life'. As shown in chapters 1 and 3, such polls often provide somewhat misleading data. I wanted to find out what young British Muslims really felt about *Shariah* law, and I soon found out that whilst many did indeed exhibit a desire for it, what this actually meant was a lot more complex and subtle than the opinion poll figures suggest.

I met some who argued unequivocally against the implementation of *Shariah* law in Britain. 'If we lived under *Shariah* law what would the non-Muslims do then?' asked Amina from Nelson. 'Are they gonna live under *Shariah* law as well? 'Cos this is Britain [*sic*], and there's like all different religions out there. I don't think you will be able to change to *Shariah* law, and I don't think you should as well.'

Echoing her, Soumaya said that 'you have to look at what country you're living in and it should be their laws that should over-ride everything. Because in Pakistan, they'd have *Shariah* law and they wouldn't allow British law there because it is their country, so I don't think it would be practical here.'

Others did, however, exhibit a desire for *Shariah* law – with reservations and qualifications. 'You know when people mention *Shariah*, the first thing that people think about is the cutting off the hands', said Munizha, 'I just have to mention that because that is the first thing, Muslims and non-Muslims alike think of.

'I think if you're really strong in your Islam, if you really want to practise Islam fully, you wouldn't fear that because, at the end of the day, those are the laws that are set down by God and you want to follow them, so I think that in the sense of putting in place *Shariah* law, I think a lot of people who are practising would be for it and I wouldn't personally have a resistance to it because, at the end of the day, that's a part of the Islamic identity: becoming a realisation within that community.

'But I think if they did do that they would meet a lot of resistance from the non-Muslim community because, you know, obviously, people who aren't Muslim, who don't understand those values, they fear it, and they don't hold those values, and they fear that those values are instantly going to be imposed upon them, and they feel like they're losing their own right to live how they want to live. So I think it would raise a lot, a lot of issues, but I personally wouldn't have a resistance to it.'

But is there any need for *Shariah* law? I asked.

'You know, that is a good point because, I mean, if you're not living in a Muslim society but you're practising your Muslim identity, in some ways it's not needed because of the fact that, at the end of the day, even if *Shariah* law was there or not there, you know you can't steal, you know you can't indulge in adultery, and you know you can't do these things anyway so, regardless of whether *Shariah* law is there or not, you're still going to impose it upon yourself. I mean, you're still going to practise it, so you've still got it as part of your everyday life even though it is not part of the infrastructure of that society. I think that should be the main concern of a lot of Muslims that are living in non-Muslim countries.

'Because, living in this country, the laws in this country they don't actually make you do anything that is against Islam. So at the end of the day, if there is something in that society that is against your religious views or whatever and your religious values, you should just abstain from it, just abstain from it altogether and you've got the choice to do that.'

Like Munizha, Fahmida from Uxbridge felt that 'in principle it [*Shariah*] works well – in principle. If you read the outline of it, in principle it does work well – equality and all that. But it depends on the people who are going to be practising it – it depends on the leadership really – that's the worrying bit. Is it actually going to be carried out as to how it's supposed to be, you know, or are there going to be violations of it? So that's the worrying bit. I'm fine as it is unless you can find a perfect human who can carry it out, I mean.'

If you probe beyond the initial desire for *Shariah* law, then what you find is an incredible diversity of opinion about what *Shariah* law means, how it should be applied, the extent and scope of its application, which laws should be applied and which should not, and so on. Even from the small sample presented here it should be clear that there are considerable differences in the definition of *Shariah*, with some seeing it as a set of moral and ethical precepts, others thinking of it as a series of obligations and duties, some believing it to be divine law and others defining it as some combination of them. There are so many disagreements, qualifications or reservations that beyond identifying the desire itself amongst a certain group there is not much that one can say with any degree of certainty about how British Muslims feel about *Shariah* law.

One thing, however, seemed to be common to all of them. The discourse about *Shariah* was always laced with a certain degree of utopianism, summed up perhaps most succinctly by Zainab, 'You know, the whole point of *Shariah* is your complete obedience to God. Anyone who practises Islam wouldn't have a problem living in a country with *Shariah* law because I think if *Shariah* was enforced things would be pretty perfect, in terms of, you know, theft, and everyone would be completely safe.'

At the same time, this utopianism co-exists with a series of reservations and qualifications that typify a more realistic appraisal of the issue. Zainab also said, for instance, 'I think it would be too complex and difficult and it would cause a lot of problems if it was applied. I think it can only be applied if everyone believes in it.' The utopian nature of this desire can be seen as a symptom, rather than taken at face value. It is the reflex of Muslim diasporas living as minorities in non-Muslim countries as they engage in the slow and painful process of coming to terms with the consequences of a great historical transition from dominance to subordination. The new situation demands a rethinking of the 'triumphalist ideology' which permeates Islamic thought and which had its origins in that age when Islam was 'a political entity and empire'.[5] For contemporary Muslims living among what Ziauddin Sardar calls the 'wreckage of our heritage', the desire for *Shariah* expresses an elegiac yearning for a lost time – and is a signal that a historical reckoning with that loss has not yet been made.[6] On the other hand, young British Muslims are clearly aware of the new realities that need to be confronted, which suggests that the effort is underway.

* * *

Max Weber defined the modern state as 'a human community which (successfully) claims the monopoly over the legitimate use of physical force within a given territory'.[7] Political leaders in all countries therefore reserve the right to discriminate between legitimate and illegitimate forms of violence, but since the advent of the 'war on terror', it could be argued that this right has been globalised by western political leaders and mapped onto a discrimination between the violence sanctioned by them and that perpetrated against them, whether by states or non-state actors. The self-image of western political leaders rests on the notion that their violence (and that of their allies and proxies) is legitimate and virtuous, which helpfully deflects the troubling ethical questions that surround *all* forms of violence from the lowliest infractions of a child torturing an insect to the theatre of global geopolitics, even if accompanied by a UN Security Council Resolution.

Such discriminations lie at the heart of Muslim complaints about 'double standards'. These have been well documented in the media and in fact have been articulated by Muslims and non-Muslims alike. All those I spoke to echoed them in some form or another. Why was Iraq invaded – and why is Iran being threatened – for supposedly trying to develop nuclear weapons when the United States and its allies have them? Why was Israel allowed to bomb Lebanon mercilessly but Hizbullah condemned for doing the same to Israel? Why is Palestinian violence described as 'terrorism' but Israeli violence seen as legitimate self-defence?

The sense of injustice felt by British Muslims of all ages about the political situation in Israel and Palestine, or the war in Iraq, need not be rehearsed here. It is real and extensive and it runs deep. These grievances have been articulated a thousand times by others and, without exception, those I met opposed the war in Iraq and felt pain and anger on behalf of the Palestinians. A few felt that the war in Afghanistan was justified because of 9/11 but just as many, if not more, argued against this conflict as well. Most felt that the 'war on terror' was indeed a war on Islam, in effect if not intent.

One example, perhaps, captures the sense of bewilderment brought about by these double standards as they see it. Qadeer Ahmed pointed out that Israel was itself 'formed upon terrorism'. The British, he felt, should know this above all because during the British Mandate the Royal David Hotel in Jerusalem was bombed by the Stern Gang.

'Recently, Benjamin Netanyahu celebrated the event', he said, 'in England, I think – I think he was in England – and that seems to be fine even when it was British people, British soldiers who died in that blast, and there's no outrage, not even from the British. It was a terrorist act, and you get someone who's involved in politics in a big way in Israel, who's been in positions of power, and he's celebrating the event and there's no condemnation. If something happens on the other side of the world and a Muslim does it, every single Muslim needs to get up and condemn it. These things, they boggle my mind, honestly, they just totally, totally … if you start talking about them you feel outraged because it's obviously hypocrisy.'

It all contributes to what Abdur-rahman called a 'discourse of rage'.[8] He recognised that it creates a mental obstruction for certain young British Muslims and precludes them from participating in British civic and social life. He not only recognised that it fuels a Manichean sense of otherness but also cautions about taking it too seriously – at least with respect to the majority who do not follow up on the rhetoric. Anger, he felt, was a part of being young.

'Young people who aren't necessarily Muslims in this country might just drink and have a fight,' he said. 'Muslims don't drink – usually – but they see the news, they get angry, they might write a letter to their MP, or they might get politically active and join anti-war demos, that sort of thing, or if they're not that sophisticated they just get angry and talk amongst themselves.

'We are in danger of criminalising what's natural in being young these days. I know people who went through that period of rage, but they come out of it the other side, quite sane and rational people – they get married, settle down, have kids, get into a nine to five job and that's it. But now, if you get angry now, you probably get put in jail for it and that's the real worry because you just don't get an opportunity to pass through that phase anymore without somebody picking up on it or you getting on some MI5 file. Maybe it's my paranoia kicking in but I think there's some truth in that.'

It must be said that there were also small notes of dissonance against this larger chorus of complaint. Fahmida, for instance, said that 'I find that a lot of Muslims, they kind of jump … you know the whole Israel and Palestine thing. They focus on that more than they do on what's happening here. What I'm saying is that the country that you're living in, you need to kind of be more active in that than in Israel and Palestine, which is thousands of miles away. It's sad what's happening, definitely, but you can't really do much to change it.'

Raihan agreed that such issues are often a convenient distraction for Muslims which deflects them away from confronting the problems within their communities and 'you'll just turn to this kind of cycle of, "yeah, it's the foreign policy therefore anything I do wrong, therefore if I don't get a job because I don't have an education, because I don't do this or that, it's the government's fault because they did that to my brother"'.

At the same time, he found it 'preposterous' that the government could not admit that its foreign policy has led to the resentment and anger that contributed to 7/7. 'Even if it's the fat fanning the flames, they're still fanning the flames. They can't not accept that as a fact. Even if the fire is already there they shouldn't be in a position where they are adding to it or contributing to it. There's a lot of talk about how there was extremism before [the war in Iraq, so it cannot be a factor]. I think that's a joke. Who are they trying to kid?'

Nevertheless, the predominant political mood amongst young British Muslims is antipathy to 'western imperialism' in general and the United States in particular. As we have seen in chapter 3, this is not the abstract hatred of western society as a whole espoused by the radicals but rather opposition to what they see as the western *political* agenda. At the same time, they were careful to admit that there were non-Muslim political voices with whom they shared a common perspective.

Munizha, for instance, said that 'In Britain a lot of people are actually anti-war anyway so I think that helps because you don't just feel like the only person who thinks it's completely unjust and you know you're not feeling it because you're a Muslim but because it is actually unjust. Even more amazing was the march they had in America, because you have this feeling that they go with anything the President says and they don't question it all, so it was quite amazing they had this massive march there as well.'

What does she think of those people who call America the Great Satan? I asked.

'If I heard that I would probably laugh! Perhaps American policies and the American government, the kinds of things that they do, they are in a sense the Big Satan but you can't label the whole of America like that because obviously you have to think about the different communities and the different people.'

Asif in Blackburn managed to express his opposition to the American political establishment rather more directly. In 2006, during a visit to the United Kingdom, the American Secretary of State, Condoleezza Rice – one of the principal advocates for the war in Iraq – was due to visit a mosque in Blackburn.

'She was gonna come to my local mosque,' he said. 'The mosque committee, they were, like, for her coming, saying if we don't let her come then they'll think, "what's the mosque hiding?" But I thought that's completely stupid. I thought most of the mosque youngsters were against it, 99 percent, and me and three other people, we didn't want to bring her in so we thought we'll sit inside the mosque to go and pray *Fajr* [the morning prayer]. They wanted to clear everyone out but you can't really physically take us out of a mosque because it's a house of God. I think they had to cancel it, saying we're a security threat and all that.'

He resented the way his mosque would have been used as a publicity stunt to show local Muslim support for the United States and the war; he felt that because there would be no question-and-answer session, and that only selected people would be allowed inside; the local Muslims were being exploited for a political agenda they totally opposed. In the end, it seems he and his friends managed to notch a small victory against the might of the US political establishment.

* * *

Although young British Muslims overwhelmingly voice their opposition to a western political elite they feel is being unjust towards Muslims around the world, what may be more worrying for those political leaders is their level of disengagement from domestic politics. There are some young Muslims who clearly feel it is incumbent on them to participate in the political process, to make their voice heard and to try to influence the political direction of their country. They feel this duty not just as citizens but also as Muslims. On the other hand, they were largely outnumbered, in my experience, by those who feel no particular affinity for, nor show any willingness to invest in, political life.

Take, for instance, the most basic form of political participation in a democracy: voting. A few did vote and, despite their frustrations, were committed to the political system. Of these, a couple were politically active – or had been. Qadeer, for instance, had stood as a Liberal Democrat candidate in the local elections some five years before. In a Labour stronghold, he had narrowly failed to win, but he said he had wanted to do it not just to win but 'to get involved in my local community, to try and help the local community. Even though I didn't get in, until recently I've been quite active with helping others and canvassing and things like that. The political process is something Muslims need to be a part of so that they can be a part of this country. We need to be part of the system and not just be living here. I think if we're in the political process it shows how serious we are about this country.'

Earlier in his life, at school and at university during the 1990s, Abdur-rahman considered himself 'more of a socialist, and [back then] the

Labour Party was just coming into power so everyone was interested
in that. I joined the anti-poll tax demos and stuff and at school I was part
of Third World First and I was worried about Third World debt, and
other social justice issues, so I have always been interested in not just
Muslim politics but general politics.'

However, he had never really involved himself in party politics 'apart
from a stage when I was at university when I helped the Labour Party.
I was leafleting and campaigning against the BNP in the East End.
That was only a one-off specific issue because we all hated the BNP.
It was an interesting experience, because we were leafleting in ones and
twos and the BNP were marching around in ten, twelve giving their
leaflets and stuff, and I was a skinny teenager then!'

Despite this, he has never voted in his life because he lives in a
Conservative-dominated constituency and he feels there is no point. This
speaks to a familiarity with the political system that is not widely shared
by his peers, particularly those from poorer neighbourhoods. This lack
of political literacy was clearly demonstrated by Amina, from Nelson,
when I asked her if she would vote now that she had turned 18. She said
she would but 'I don't know anything about voting. My dad was like
"you're going to be voting now" and I was like, ok, so what is voting?
So I don't know anything about voting.'

Had anyone told her about what is involved?

'No. I do watch programmes on TV when there is the voting month …
there is a month, isn't there, a special month when the voting is done?'

'Well, we have something called an election,' I said.

'An election, yeah. And when it does come on TV, like Labour,
Liberal … and is it when they say that they're gonna do this they're
gonna do that, we'll make this better, we'll make that better, you got
to vote for one of them? Something like that isn't it?'

'Yes, it is', I said, 'but it sounds like you're not particularly interested.'
'No, I'm not. No.'

So despite the fact that she will vote, Amina displayed no enthusiasm
for it; most others I spoke to were not even going to vote. Some, like
Nazma and Saiqa, felt there was no point, although Saiqa implied that
she had voted before.

'I have no interest in politics,' she said. 'I have stopped voting.'

'I don't think I want to,' added Nazma, who is a few years junior
to Saiqa and thus may not have been eligible to vote before. 'You just
get put off don't you?'

'It doesn't make a difference, anyway,' said Saiqa.

'Because we're never heard anyway,' said Nazma. 'People's voices are never heard and they always say that they're going to hear us, that they're going to listen to us, but they don't. I think that's why people are getting put off and a lot of people on my street that I know, well, the majority of them didn't vote either.'

As a result, they were sceptical about government efforts to tackle extremism and promote 'community cohesion'.

'They always say it's to improve the local community, you know,' said Nazma.

'Community cohesion …,' said Saiqa.

'Yeah, all that … the favourite words but there's nothing done,' said Nazma.

They felt the government was getting it wrong by holding talks on 'Islam and Extremism'. This 'just put us off', said Nazma, because they felt that by putting these two words together all the time 'it's like saying that that's what we do'.

Such talks not only put people off by tying Islam to extremism but they also felt they produced little but hot air for media consumption.

'If you're having a talk you, don't really take it in 'cos I've been to conferences and they bore me, but if it's a fun thing, you want to go, you'll enjoy it and you can see the difference,' said Saiqa.

'We got money from Pendle Borough Council', she continued, ' 'cos there was money going for a community cohesion event so I organised one with help from Nazma and some other colleagues at Silverman Hall, and we had a group come over from Preston and do, like, the Bollywood songs, and we had an English group doing punk and rock and roll music and then we just had a chillin' out time and we had such a good mix, it was just ladies and kids 'cos obviously it's a women's organisation.'

'When things are done definitely you can see it's a nice environment, everyone gets on, but when all these talks are happening and when they put the two words together, I don't know, I think everyone just thinks of it as negative,' Nazma concluded.

Qadeer was also scathing in his criticism of government attempts to tackle extremism. 'I know Labour has set up these task forces since 7/7 but it's all a load of bullshit,' he said. 'Honestly, it is. I went to an event organised here where they wanted to know what we think but they don't care what we think. They want to make out as if they're doing something but, really, they don't care, they're gonna do it their way.'

He implied that certain members of the local community had ulterior motives for becoming involved in government-sponsored efforts to tackle extremism. 'The event I went to was not itself part of the task force but it was initiated through it and, no names mentioned, but the people who were there with the task force, I knew that it was a way for them to get ahead in the community [i.e. to increase their political standing].'

As for what should be done about extremism, Qadeer suggested that we should be a bit more forthright about confronting extremists. 'There's scholars – well, scholars in inverted commas, big time – like Abu Hamza and how long was he openly preaching and they were saying he's bad, he's bad? Bloody put him away. Recently on *Newsnight*, there was a debate between Anjum Chowdhury, ex-Muhajiroun, and Tariq Ramadan, who is an intellect, a very, very intelligent person who knows his *deen* [religion] well, from what I know, and this guy [Chowdhury] just ranted and raved and wouldn't let anyone else speak and they let him talk and talk. No-one stopped him. Throw him out. You know he's an extremist; his group has celebrated 9/11 – how ridiculous is that? If that's not inciting racial hatred … why give him a voice? Put him in jail, you've got the bloody terrorism laws.'

Disillusionment, detachment and disenfranchisement are the main words that come to mind as I reflect back on my conversations with these young Muslims about politics. Even those who did vote rarely felt that there was much point in doing so. Most were united in the belief that the mainstream political parties were 'all the same'. As Aisha put it, 'the faces may change but the policies will stay the same'. Some do feel attracted to the Respect Party, mainly because of its strong position on the war in Iraq, but many remain sceptical of them too. Fahmida, for instance, had previously been a Labour supporter but had deserted them and did not vote at the last election. Her nephew had pressed her to vote for Respect because they opposed the war 'and I was like "And? Is there anything else?" It's not just one issue that makes you vote, it's the whole range of issues.'

It would be a mistake to read this as apathy. As we have seen in previous chapters, young British Muslims are far from apathetic and do participate quite vigorously in civic life, much more so than their non-Muslim peers. Instead, a feeling of powerlessness has sapped their trust in the political process. They see politicians making mistakes but not admitting to them; they see grave injustices but feel no one is accountable. As Madeleine Bunting has put it, 'those in power accept no responsibility. Those who might have a sense of responsibility feel utterly powerless.'[9]

Mistrust and disillusionment breeds cynicism, and this perhaps explains why so many young British Muslims display a weakness for conspiracy theories. I heard many of them. Often it seemed like they knew they were being foolish but they could not help themselves, as if it were some kind of mental reflex. Of course, this is not confined to Muslims; many non-Muslims also indulge this particular habit, but it does seem that there is a difference in scale if not in kind.

The point is that the conspiracy theory, as a genre of thought, is a symptom of powerlessness. It imagines power as distant, concentrated in a few hands and unaccountable. Like God, it is ineffable; ever-present but invisible. Maybe this metaphysical aspect is also partly responsible for the attraction. In any case, conspiracy theories flourish in societies characterised by political exclusivity, hence their prevalence – and virulence – amongst the authoritarian and despotic regimes of the Islamic world. They are thus not necessarily motivated by ignorance, envy or prejudice (e.g. anti-Semitism), although these may be thrown in too – their purchase amongst Muslims and non-Muslims alike in the supposedly democratic and politically open societies of the West is a cause for concern and a testimony to the growing blockage within the arteries of the body politic.

* * *

One of the key themes of this book is the desire for empowerment amongst young British Muslims today. In this sense, the turn to Islam is obviously 'political', but it is not political in the sense usually spoken of in the media.

If we look carefully at what the young British Muslims I spoke to are saying about 'politics', it becomes apparent that *aside from the issue of violence* – which, strictly speaking, is not a political issue but an ethical one – there is in fact little to distinguish between the views of those who are considered 'moderate' and those who are labelled 'extremist'. It is clear, for instance, that there are continuities and commonalities in the political preoccupations and perspectives of the two groups. There are overlaps and affiliations in terms of the issues that concern them (the war on terror, Iraq, Afghanistan and Palestine, lack of faith in the 'West' and so on), the emotions they arouse (anger and frustration) and the ideological frameworks through which they interpret political events and structure their narratives of understanding (e.g. victimhood, utopianism, nostalgia for a 'golden age').

It would be problematic, therefore, to speak – as some are wont to do – of 'extremist' Muslims as being totally disconnected from the 'moderate majority'. That does not mean, however, that they are therefore the same. Some people may want to jump on this as evidence that there is in fact no such thing as a 'moderate' Muslim; that beneath the veneer of moderation there is always lurking an undercurrent of 'extremism'. This would be a serious misperception based on the assumption that 'moderates' and 'extremists' should be distinguished from each other by comparing their respective positions on just 'political' issues.

In fact, 'politics' is not actually the most significant dimension in determining how 'mainstream' Muslims differ from the extremists. There may be common ground in terms of their political views but, if we look beyond politics, what is more significant are the differences in their conceptions of identity and belonging (pluralistic as opposed to Manichean), their views on what being a Muslim is (exploratory and flexible as opposed to rigid and dogmatic) and their views on others (respectful of difference as opposed to intolerant). We have seen all these positive characteristics exhibited in previous chapters, and these, combined with an ethical position which disavows violence, are the values which set most young British Muslims apart from the extremists.

Chapter 5
Generational Conflict

As we have seen in earlier chapters, young British Muslims are
increasingly turning to Islam as part of a wider confrontation with
their elders, the first-generation migrants who settled in Britain during
the post-war period. For most of them, with family origins in South
Asia, this conflict hinges on the tensions between two forms of social
organisation that are largely incommensurable. On the one hand, there
is what is known as the *biradari* clan system and its variants; this is
structured around kinship networks of extended families which are
rooted in a particular region and locality. Close-knit and insular, the
biradari places the existence of the clan above all else. Individuals
are subordinated to its demands, and its economy – social, moral and
cultural – operates through the regulatory mechanisms of honour and
shame which police behaviour and inhibit actions that might threaten
the cohesion and self-identity of the clan. In short, it is a 'corporatist'
social system, one which will be broadly familiar in many respects even
to those young Muslims whose families migrated from other parts of the
Islamic world. On the other hand, there is the increasingly disembedded,
individual-oriented social structure of modern Europe with the nuclear
family at its core. Each has different values, norms of behaviour, patterns
of obligation and sets of expectations.

Young British Muslims have been socialised within both social
formations. Outside the home, in their everyday interactions at school,
in civil society and in their relationships with non-Muslims, they inhabit
the social landscape of modern, post-industrial Britain; at home, during
family gatherings or within the local neighbourhood and its institutions,
their social landscape is similar to those found in the rural hinterlands
of Pakistan, India and Bangladesh. The same is largely true of recent
Muslim migrants from Africa but less so for young Arab-Britons because
their social profile is somewhat different: more upwardly mobile or even
elite in origin, and therefore more urban.

These young men and women incessantly shuttle back and forth
between these discrepant and increasingly divergent worlds. This
constant movement, an unsettling oscillation across the threshold
of different social universes, is their existential condition, and

it is at the root of that psychic disturbance what we call 'identity crisis'. They are hybrid folk, neither one thing nor the other but something else besides, and this is the source of their social and cultural discomfort. Nevertheless, as they feel increasingly at home in Britain, they are resolving this conflict in favour of the culture and lifestyles they share with their non-Muslim peers.

As a result, the conflict which has been raging inside them has come out into the open as an increasingly bitter and acrimonious dispute with their parents and elders. Many expressed a general antipathy towards their parents' generation, although they were usually careful to avoid direct criticism of their own parents. Aisha summed it up when I asked her if she thought there was a generation gap, 'There is, there is. I think most of the people like that, who are running the mosques and who have set up these little societies or parties are mainly Pakistani men who are quite old and have those cultural holds that stick to them and are loyal to them, and then obviously you have the new generation emerging, like my generation, you know – there is a need to actually get rid of … because that's what the conflict is about, isn't it, out with the old and in with the new? I think that as long as that generation difference exists there won't be any progress, I can't see any.'

Soumaya did try to strike a more conciliatory position, 'There is [sic] certain things which a lot of the elders do – those who really, like, got knowledge on Islam – you understand where they're coming from and you know they're right and maybe that would be my belief when I get to their age, but some of our elders they use their own beliefs, what they've been taught is right and wrong, they try and back up that with religion – and I don't think I'll be doing that when I grow up to that age. Some manipulate it for their own opinion. Because they think girls shouldn't work, they should be housewives; that's not Islam, is it? That's just their belief and opinion and they try to twist it.'

She added, 'I think in the end, no matter what your elders say, you should respect them no matter whether it's right or wrong, but, in the end, it's up to you that you believe in what you do. But there's no point in having a conflict with them, so respect them in their place and do what you feel is right.'

I can't help but notice a covert dismissal of the elders here in the same breath as she advocates respect for them. It is as if they should be respected not because they are 'right' (or wrong) but merely because they are elders. They should be respected 'in their place'. And yet the prerogative is with the younger generation, who should believe in themselves and do what they feel is right regardless of what the elders think. They are reduced to an irrelevance.

It must be said that Shahid did offer a more genuinely respectful view of the elders, although it is perhaps significant that he did not grow up surrounded by them in a predominantly Bengali (in his case) neighbourhood. 'I haven't really grown up with Muslims around me so I can't really vouch for that much. I haven't even had my grandparents in this country but going by my parents I think they are a great example of how to live in this society. To a certain extent, I also think there's actually a danger that if this slide towards modernisation means giving up on the elders completely, I think that's also very dangerous because sometimes, like from a Bengali perspective, we just completely ignore some of the great values that their traditions have left. And I also think it's contradictory in Islam if you completely leave out the elders' opinion.'

There were specific flashpoints around which these general antipathies and dissatisfactions gathered. Through them one can see this inter-generational conflict being played out. For instance, nearly all those I spoke to grumbled about the state of Britain's mosques and were highly critical of the *imams* working within them.

'If I had a choice I would go to a particular mosque rather than the one I go to locally,' said Abdur-rahman. 'Yeah, I'd definitely be more discerning mainly because of the qualified scholarship issue and the communication. It's sad but it's true when people say that a lot of the *imams* can't communicate properly or effectively. Either they can't speak English properly and they focus on giving a lecture in Bengali, Gujarati or Urdu, or they don't understand what it's like to be a youth, or to grow up in this country or society.

'It's a fair point they make – when I say "they" I mean the media or Ruth Kelly [the Minister for Communities] – and they do bang on about it but what you've got to remember, we're immature and a relatively recent group of people coming into this country; I see myself as part of the middle generation, if you like, going through a transitional phase. My parents didn't have any problem about knowing who they were and going to a mosque and listening to *khutbah* [Friday sermon] in Bengali. I sort of can adjust, if you like – I know what they're saying when they speak in Bengali or Urdu, even Arabic I can basically understand. But I know there are a group of kids who I call the third generation, who don't know what's going on, and see it as a waste of time, and I see myself as part of a transitional generation definitely, who will have to do something about it.'

It is clear that the problem is not confined to small- and medium-sized mosques. When she was younger, Zainab attended the grand mosque in Regent's Park, the largest and most well financed of all mosques in Britain. She cited a number of complaints against it, from the inadequacy of the toilets ('always flooded') to the chaotic management. 'There's a lot of disorganisation, like you never know when the *imams* are going to be available, there's no sort of timetable, they have events and things like that but they are not properly advertised, you might go and it might start late or it might completely ... they might not adjust the timings according to the prayers, for example – the prayer could be at 3 p.m. and the talk could start at ten to three – so it's not really that appealing to young professionals, that kind of environment.

'I don't know what the problem is, it's an efficiency thing and I know there's lots of politics regarding especially Regent's Park mosque, but I think there's lots of people working there, full-time administrators and things, so it just needs to be planned properly and completely restructured, no sort of Asian or Arab timing, everything just very clean, very efficient. I don't think it's that hard work, and some *imams*, if they have to bring them from abroad – I think in Regent's Park mosque they like them to be al-Azhar trained – then they just have to be a bit more in touch with what's going on.'

The age gap is thus also a cultural gap; the two intersect so that the age of the imam does not matter so much. Even young *imams* would be ineffective if brought in from abroad by mosque committees dominated by elders who prefer their *imams* to perform according to the traditions and expectations 'back home'. As Fahmida put it, 'the local *masjid* [mosque] is basically our dads and our uncles and I don't think they'd agree to accept a younger imam brought up here because it would be like "Well, what would you know?" kind of thing.'

As a result, said Zainab, 'they come from abroad, they don't speak English, and they don't have the mentality of young people. I have often gone to *imams* and not been very happy with their opinions. They're not accessible enough; it's hard, it's difficult for whatever reasons to talk to them.

'I think mosques think that if you've got a question on marriage or divorce or whatever, then it doesn't really matter where the imam's from, he's going to answer your question with the religious knowledge, but

I really think it's more than that – a lot more than that. Life is lived here, and sometimes you need to be aware of the situation here not just hear about it, because the other thing is that they live in the mosque, they live on site, and I get the impression that they don't kind of go out very much ... everything is very convenient for them and they don't really need to travel very much, and mix with people.'

There is, therefore, an urgent need for British-trained *imams* – an opinion shared by all the young Muslims I spoke to. But this will cost money. Part of the problem is that remuneration for *imams* is very poor, and the imam is often at the mercy of the mosque committee that employs him. These committees are themselves rather informal and under-resourced, often dependent on individual members' *ad hoc* financial contributions. Informally employed, poorly paid and dependent on the good will of the community for basic necessities – including accommodation – it is not altogether surprising that amongst young British Muslims the queue to become an imam is rather short.

'Why would you want to be an imam in this country?' asked Shahid. 'If you're British, why would you want to be an imam? I just don't think it's very attractive. That's why most of the *imams* are from foreign countries ... because *imams*, they get paid probably from voluntary donations by the congregations. As a British Muslim you'd be a lot better off finding a job somewhere else.'

The isolation of most mosques from British life – physically, culturally and socially – means that young British Muslims are increasingly turning to other organisations and institutions for guidance. For the main part, these are not, however, those organisations belatedly established by the older generation to come to terms with the myriad schisms and fractures within Britain's diverse Muslim communities. The Muslim Council of Britain (MCB), for instance, was formed in the mid-1990s as an umbrella group of Muslim organisations to liaise with and lobby government more effectively by representing British Muslims as a unified community that could speak with one voice across a range of issues. But, as Philip Lewis suggests,

> any attempt to organise Muslims in Britain, especially those with roots in South Asia, is always going to be hostage to an entrenched sectarian division within the Sunni tradition imported from those countries. Because one of these schools of thought – Deobandis – has aligned itself with the MCB, only a few

people in the other – Barelwis – feel comfortable in the same organisation. Indeed, both the British Muslim Forum and the Sufi Muslim Council are largely home to this latter tradition.[1]

Recently, the government has distanced itself from the MCB in the light of concerns raised about its links to 'extremist' groups, and it has encouraged other avenues of representation.[2] Notably, both the British Muslim Forum and the Sufi Muslim Council have been courted by the government as alternatives to the MCB. It is not my intention to rehearse the claims and counterclaims about the MCB that led to this repositioning. All I can do here is to consider the ways in which the young Muslims I spoke to felt about the MCB, which presents itself as being representative of the 'Muslim community'.

There was a range of opinion about the MCB and its claims to representativeness. Many simply did not know anything about it and a few had never even heard of it. Others felt it to be too distant and aloof with little relevance to their lives. 'Before this year', said Munizha, 'I wasn't really aware of the Muslim Council of Britain. I knew about the Racial Equality Council, and I sort of knew about the Islamic Council of Britain, but I wasn't really aware of the MCB and of, like, these big Muslim organisations. Even though I have heard of them I don't know what it is they actually do and I think they're more representative of places like, in London, like central London sort of thing as opposed to the wider areas of England.'

Similarly, the Birmingham-based artist Mohammed Ali felt that his ignorance of the MCB was a symptom of their failure to engage with those whom they claim to represent. He felt it was a little odd, given his high profile as a British-Muslim artist, that no one from the MCB had ever approached him to work with them. He had been interviewed by a number of international media outlets such as the CNN and he had been promoted around the world by the British Council, but the MCB seemed to be unaware of his existence. 'I've never ever met or spoken to anybody from MCB – shouldn't we really be communicating at some point? Muslim Council of Britain – whenever I go abroad, I'm promoted as a Muslim from Britain, so Muslim Council of Britain, I've never met them and they've never contacted me. Shouldn't we be trying to work together here?'

Some of those who *had* encountered the MCB had been less than impressed. Aisha told me that she had been to the *IslamExpo* exhibition that year, 'and there was an MCB stall there and the guy was just standing there. He wasn't very, you know … he just pointed out some leaflets, "take this and take that", and that was it. He didn't bother to say what the MCB is about because I didn't know that much about it – and I still don't know that much – but he didn't really make much of an effort to say "This is what we're about or do you want to participate in any other way?"'

This distance and disinterest has left the field open for others. At the exhibition, Aisha had been approached by a freelance magazine called *New Civilization*. 'The guy basically came up to us and we started talking and he was telling us that if we wanted to participate or do something or if you knew anyone this is how to do it. If we wanted to write a little article, submit it, by all means, contact us this, that and the other – he actually made an effort, whereas the MCB, no.'

To be fair to the MCB, there were other voices that offered a more supportive assessment of the organisation. 'Well, the thing is', said Shahid, 'the MCB doesn't stand for anything. All it's saying is that whenever all the Muslim groups that are under our umbrella, whenever they have a problem we will negotiate with the people they have a problem with to help them out. It doesn't have an identity because Muslims, you have Sunnis and Shias and different schools of thought, and you have Sufis as well. MCB hasn't said "we're representing a certain sector of Muslims" or something like that, all they're saying is "we're an umbrella organisation and we're going to help with co-ordination". I personally can't see what the problem is in being a part of that; it's not like "whose side are you on?"'

But he added, 'I remember reading in *The Guardian* about the Sufi Muslim Council, I don't think they're too happy with the MCB affiliation. I think this is the one chance for Muslims in the country to have a common voice but again differences get in the way; I think it's crazy.'

These sentiments were echoed by Abdur-rahman. The question of its relevance to young British Muslims needed to be approached with a sense of perspective, he felt. 'I think, at what they do, people just leave them to do what they do – liaise with government, try to lobby on a few issues, things that may help. What have they done? They've prepared leaflets on praying at work, you know, to help employers understand what Muslims need, they tried to create some sort of *imams* bodies to co-ordinate how you train *imams* and that sort of thing. They're the best of what we got. There are plenty of other "upstart" organisations,

if you like … Sufi Muslim Council, you probably heard of them, they've
been courted now by government as a rival to MCB, but they've come
out of nowhere and they've got no history within the community, unlike
people like Dr Abdul Bari [the current chair of the MCB], who has
roots and has been working and been active for thirty, forty years.

'You have to remember, the MCB is a new organisation, from
1997, so it's not going to be perfect. The Jewish Board of Deputies has
been around for, how many years? Hundreds of years – it's a lot more
sophisticated, got a lot more resources behind it, it's a lot more plugged
in. I don't know if it's fair to compare them with the MCB which has
been around for only nine years now. MCB is basically the best of what
we've got, I think; it's not perfect, no organisation's perfect. I've heard
of Dr Abdul Bari before and, on a community level, he's highly respected,
but everybody knows that his downfall is that he's got an accent.
He might be the most super-intelligent man, and he is, but just because
he comes across as an Asian, in effect, an immigrant, people think that
because he can't speak English properly – without an accent – that he's
not an intelligent man, he's not articulate. So, that will have to change,
in terms of professionalism, and the quality of the spokesmanship will
have to change a bit, and there are people around him who are very
articulate, like Inayat Bunglawala, I'm sure you've come across him.
He's very articulate.'

Wittingly or unwittingly, Abdur-rahman raises here once again the
generation and culture gap that so bedevils attempts to organise the
Muslim communities in Britain. The MCB's attempts to position itself
as a representative of these communities to government continues to fall
foul of this chasm, and it is fair to say that the issue of leadership and
authority, who speaks for Britain's Muslims (particularly its youth),
is at something of an impasse. This is a liminal moment, a moment
of transition, as the elders – so long accustomed to the mantle
of 'community leaders' – are gradually being pushed to the margins
by a new generation of leaders and organisations who are beginning
to articulate new visions of Islam that are more truly representative
of the younger constituencies to whom they are addressed.

* * *

In December 2007, I finally met Asim Siddiqui, chair of the City Circle,
a remarkable organisation set up and run by young Muslim professionals
working in London. Asim had been instrumental in finding me some

professional young Muslims to speak to and now I wanted to ask him about the City Circle. Appropriately enough, our rendezvous was at a café near Moorgate station, deep within the City of London and a stone's throw from where Asim works. Bespectacled and dignified, he recalled to me the beginnings of an organisation that many wish to put forward as a model for Muslims in Britain. It has been lauded in the press and even courted by the government, but it remains fiercely protective of its independence.

'The City Circle is a pretty loose network of individuals. It came together in 1999, almost 10 years ago. Many of the people who founded it were activists themselves, from different backgrounds, whether it was Muslim organisations or others, and felt that existing organisations weren't providing a space for people to ask fresh questions. Many of the organisations already had a doctrinal template, they already had all the answers or they thought they had. Obviously because we were all graduates in fairly good jobs, we all had the brains and the intelligence to say, "Hang on a minute, all this stuff may have been relevant 50 or 60 years ago in India and Pakistan but what on earth has it got to do with our situation here?" So that basically led to this feeling that there was a need to create an independent space – neutral, informal.'

There are two 'threads' to the work that the City Circle does. One is what Asim calls '*constructive* citizenship', and this refers to the community projects that it undertakes. These include a Saturday supplementary school, located in Westbourne Park, which helps inner-city children with 'mainstream curricular subjects' and a 'Helping London's Homeless' project.

'The way that started', said Asim, 'was that homeless people literally stumbled into our meetings, drunk or whatever. Then we began to raise money to feed people on the streets, and then we felt we shouldn't be doing that we should be working with hostels – for a number of years, from 2002 to last year we would raise money during Ramadan to feed homeless people in hostels.

'What was so interesting about that, and what was so moving about that, was that we approached hostels and said "we want to feed people in your hostel" and when they realised we were a Muslim organisation they asked us, "do you want to feed Muslim people in the hostel?" and we were like "My God, of course not. Whoever comes to the hostel, it doesn't matter". The fact that they had to ask that question was a poor reflection on us – Muslims are just so obsessed with helping their own bloc, where's the universal compassion gone?'

The other strand, which Asim calls '*critical* citizenship' involves the weekly Friday night discussions and debates. The City Circle provides an 'independent and open public space which allows communities to get together and talk through difficult issues in a self-critical manner. We do all our critical thinking in public and have as much non-Muslim engagement as possible.'

It is this idea of an 'enabling' space which Asim tried to get across to me as the key characteristic of the City Circle. He said, 'As an organisation we will not hold positions on anything, really; as individuals we can, I as an individual will write articles, give interviews etc. City Circle does not claim to be a representative organisation, we claim no representative mandate and neither are we a lobbying group. We're not aligned to any movement, any party, any organisation, any overseas doctrine. It's an absolute clean slate and people have always struggled to place us – other than to say we're progressive, but that's about it.'

Nevertheless, this is precisely what attracts such a broad spectrum of people to their meetings. 'We've had meetings with a full house where you've had people from 7/7 sympathisers to 7/7 victims – it can be that broad. We have all the extremists who also turn up – and that can be good as long as they're prepared to engage with the ideas, because you need to move people's minds.'

This is a point which should be absorbed by many who seem to think that merely associating with those whom they deem to hold 'unacceptable' views is a heinous surrender to 'extremism' or 'terrorism'. What comes to mind, for instance, is the vilification of the Mayor of London, Ken Livingstone, for inviting the Egyptian scholar Yusuf al-Qaradawi to speak at City Hall. Whatever one thinks of al-Qaradawi's views on certain topics, the main point is that the 'critical space' that organisations such as the City Circle would like to open up would be pointless if it only included those who hold 'acceptable' views. Preaching to the converted is of little value if the aim is to engage 'hearts and minds'.

Taken together, 'constructive citizenship' and 'critical citizenship' can provide 'thought leadership'. A striking example is the pressure City Circle has brought to bear on the MCB's controversial boycott of Holocaust Memorial Day, to the point where the MCB has now reversed its position. This, said Asim, shows that they are having an impact on the thinking of other Muslim organisations.

'In 2006, we held our own Holocaust Memorial event jointly with the Holocaust Educational Trust; we brought in a Holocaust survivor to make the point and let a Muslim audience hear a Holocaust survivor speak. Partly it was to provide reassurance to the Jewish community that we want to work with you, that we're not a monolith and that the MCB's position is not representative, but also it was about putting pressure on Muslim groups. It obviously had an impact – it was on Radio 4's *Today* programme, and that's obviously quite embarrassing for them [MCB] isn't it?'

In terms of the behaviour and attitudes of those who attend the City Circle weekly meetings, Asim recalled, 'When we started, it was absolutely normal for women to be sat at the back. I know it sounds silly but this is how it was back then. And then it was side-by-side, and now it's mixed. And what you will see is that other traditional Muslim groups have followed this.

'A lot of our early projects were actually led by Muslim women, young professional women. I mean, that's what you'll find – a lot of women are involved in the projects at City Circle. Why is that? It's because a lot of them are on the management team. Why are they on the management team? Because they're involved in the project, because we don't believe we should tell them what to wear, or tell them where to sit, nothing, we don't impose any theology on anyone. A space where they were equals, and what you find is that they headed up all the projects. And of course, once you're in charge you can help set the agenda as well, which I think helps keep us as open-minded as possible.'

In terms of thought, the City Circle has tackled head-on issues that were not being discussed. '7/7 happened on the Thursday', he said, 'and our events take place on a Friday. There was a lot of pressure on Muslim groups that people should stay at home, there's going to be a lot of backlash and that women definitely should stay at home and all the rest of it, yeah? Really a kind of siege mentality. Once the mayor and the head of the police had made a statement saying, "no, no no we cannot be defeated by these people, we have to come out and act almost as if nothing had happened, life has to continue", we decided we would go ahead with our Friday night talk, and our Friday night talks take place on Edgware Road, metres away from the blast. So basically we reacted in the same way as any Londoner would have reacted. So that was one small example of thought leadership. We went ahead and it was a full house.

'The following week we said we have now had a bit of time to absorb what had happened and we now wanted to think about it and the title of the talk was "The criminal distortion of Islamic texts". We were going to talk about how is it that Islam can be manipulated to justify acts of terrorism. People couldn't breathe, there were so many people in that hall. Madeleine [Bunting] covered it as well in *The Guardian*. She said it was upsetting to see so much self-flagellation but we wanted to speak about the problems with certain interpretations of Islam. I mean, it's too easy to talk about foreign policy. Face it, I'm not saying it's not a factor, but obviously a framework, a justification, exists to allow people to do that. I mean if you have 1 percent doubt you're not going to blow yourself up. They had to be 100 percent certain within Islamic scriptures to do what they did. So you've got to discuss that. And that was dynamite – excuse the pun – no-one was discussing that. That's a topic I would have liked to have discussed a bit earlier, but after 7/7 it was like, "no, no, no, the gloves are off now". After 7/7, we had to go beyond the "Islam is Peace" argument – forget that, been there, done that. We needed to talk about why Islam *can* justify terrorism – let's talk about that. Not about "Islam condemns it", but "why can Islam also be used to condone and encourage it?" That's thought leadership because no-one else was prepared to talk about it.'

The City Circle has come a long way since its inception in 1999, but perhaps a general lesson to be drawn from their example is not to expect Muslim organisations like it to emerge overnight. There is an understandable impatience with the pace of change within Britain's Muslim communities. For every step taken forward, it seems there is also a step back. That is what happens, however, during historically significant transitions, and there is no doubt that we are witnessing one right now. Reform is a slow and uneven process and even those who embody its spirit bear the scars of the effort.

Asim mused on the gradual emergence of the City Circle as it is now and said, 'It still means different things to different people, which is good, I'm happy with that. I think it has broadly crystallised in a certain direction but in those early days … I recently met a girl who said to me, "Is this the same City Circle which was set up in '99 in East London?" – we were in East London in those days – "because that was really religious, really conservative and you guys don't seem conservative now". It *is* the same City Circle – and I almost wouldn't recognise it, well, I would because I was there, but it would be a different meeting: it was segregated, fairly religious topic, the whole feel – we have *really* changed. A lot of the organisers, we were almost there [i.e. where they are now] anyway, but you have to take people with you and that takes time. We couldn't hold a meeting the way we do it now back then. Even the speakers that we had – we used to have pretty orthodox *salafi* speakers – those speakers have grown with us as well. The way they speak now any normal person would accept – so they themselves have changed. Everyone has been on a journey.'

* * *

Most of these new organisations operate outside the mosques, which remain bastions of conservatism. Run by mosque committees dominated by men from the older generation whose world views have been immersed in the *biradari*-style social networks of their countries of origin, the mosques continue to represent a kind of Islam that is largely being ignored by Muslim youth. However, even here the need for change is beginning to be recognised, and there are promising signs that a new generation of *imams* are transforming the idea of what a mosque can and should be.

In Burnley, Qadeer's mosque has appointed an imam who is 'really, really good – not a typical Asian *mufti* or whatever you want to call him. He's well in touch with young people.' Although he is not born and bred in the United Kingdom, and his English is not quite as good as Qadeer would like – 'I'd want him to be fluent but he can easily get his message across' – he is nevertheless a vast improvement on the previous *imams*, and Qadeer has begun to attend the mosque, which he previously avoided.

To the south, in Slough, Aisha also spoke of the new imam in her local mosque with approval. In his mid-thirties, the imam delivers his sermons in English and has won over the youth through his use of humour and parody. 'His sermons are really quite funny because he's mimicking like the older lot or the younger lot, like these radical Muslims, you know, like these boys who want to convert everyone and this that and the other, and he tries to reach out to those people and say, "Look, you need to calm down, you know, this is not the way to go about things".'

This has won him many admirers amongst the Muslim youth in Slough as he is offering them a new way of practising Islam, one which avoids the discredited traditionalism of the elders but also the hot-headed radicalism of groups such as Hizb ut-Tahrir. Much has been made of the activities of such groups and their putative successes in attracting disillusioned and disaffected Muslim youth, but even if they had made the running before, there are now alternatives from within the 'mainstream' which are confronting them and challenging their ideas and methods.

Part of this challenge has involved a transformation in the kinds of instruction on offer in mosques. Shahid said, 'I've been going to mosques from quite a young age and I've noticed that, in the last few years, there has definitely been a creative movement towards understanding the Qu'ran, and paying more attention to scholarly writing and things like that instead of this rote learning of Arabic that used to take place. Now there's more emphasis on the English rather than the Arabic and there's definitely a movement to put a lot of things into context, especially after, you know, recent events. I think it's definitely a step in the right direction.'

This will certainly foster the kinds of critical thinking needed to revitalise the practice of *ijtihad*, which is the basis for dynamic new interpretations of Islam suitable for Muslim minorities in multicultural societies. Abdur-rahman observed that the scholarship available for such communities has only just begun to emerge – a consequence, of course, of the traditionalism of the older generation of Muslim migrants to Britain and Europe. Effective scholarship of this kind can only be formulated by Muslims living within such societies; it cannot be imported from Arabia or South Asia, where the issues and dilemmas faced by Muslims are very different. If a new generation of *imams* can help incubate new ideas which address this lack then they should be supported.

In turn, this will transform mosques. This process has already begun to happen. In the genteel Essex suburbs that skirt the edges of greater London, Leila told me about her local imam and how he has transformed the mosque. 'Our imam is not an Asian imam – he's Egyptian – his children are born and brought up here, his wife is a doctor, he's very relaxed with both males and females – he can have a proper chat with you about shopping or going out or whatever – and he does counselling for married couples, he's very approachable for every issue, he's not like narrow minded, so if you wear *hijab* it's fine, if you don't wear *hijab* that's fine too, he's not going to judge you,' she said.

'He is a good representative of the way I think an imam should be – speaks fluent English, he's actually a professor and he runs a nursing home, so he's very versatile. This is a very non-Muslim area but more Muslims are moving here because it's much nicer [than London's East End] so there was obviously a need for an Islamic area to worship in and there was none. The mosque has been going since the last six or seven years or so and it's had its ups an downs; don't get me wrong, it's still got some people on the board who are stuck in the archaic ages but the actual *imam*, you know, his involvement – he's very forward thinking. They do talks, they do a monthly youth thing, marriage instruction, they do lots of different things there.'

These sentiments were echoed by Munizha in Slough. 'The *masjid* isn't just a place of prayer, it's a place to gain knowledge. To actually sit there and to study; to actually provide places for the Muslim community. There's a lot of *masjids* that are quite isolated in the sense that they don't actually reach out to the community, and I think things are starting to change like the *masjid* in Slough, they are actually, you know, organising things for the community. They have a Saturday school – and not just to teach Islamic lessons but also maths, science and English – and this is to raise the standards of the Muslims in the community because they've seen in the league tables and stuff the most disadvantaged communities are Muslims who have got the lower levels of achievement. So they're actually trying to address that issue in the community and they're trying to help that community. There's other things that are going on – Sisters' circles, brothers' circles, football and stuff like that. – I think that's how a *masjid* should be; It should be reaching out to the community.'

All this bodes well for the future of Muslims in Britain. As they begin to increasingly feel at home here, as their participation in British social and civic life increases, so too will their institutions and organisations reflect this greater level of engagement. Already, the process of change is underway. The cultural obduracy of the elders is giving way to new ideas and new ways of practising Islam. Young Muslims are beginning to develop their own networks which transcend the insular and divisive fiefdoms of the *biradaris*, and they are beginning to forge alliances with one another across sectarian, geographical and social divisions, passing ideas and inspiration along a chain of innovation that may one day be seen as the prelude to a groundbreaking and much-needed British or European Islam, at ease with itself and others in our increasingly diverse and ever-changing society.

Chapter 6
Women

The generational conflict we have witnessed throughout these pages is a gendered one, which is to say that it plays itself out differently according to gender. The overall picture is, however, not as clear as it might seem to those who are accustomed to viewing Islam as being inherently oppressive of women. The reality of gender relations for young British Muslim men and women is highly complex. Some young male British Muslims are complicit in upholding those very same clan or family-based structures in relation to gender that they otherwise contest in other spheres of life. Even amongst young female Muslims, responses to *biradari*-style patriarchal structures are at times highly contradictory. There is little doubt, however, that such structures bear down most heavily on women.

This is most apparent in relation to education and marriage. With regard to the former, Munizha from Slough spoke for many when she said to me that 'the culture of our family, all our family here, my uncles and aunties, [is that] the girls, when they're 16 or 17, have been married off and they haven't paid any sort of attention to getting their daughters educated'. However, she and her sisters have been rather fortunate. 'My dad, he had seven daughters, and most people would think that he had that same mentality but he didn't, which we're really grateful for. He's always, always driven us on to be educated, which is quite an anomaly for our family.'

Most young women I spoke to had been educated up to college level (that is, post-16 further education: sixth form or college). Some of them had not gone further, although this was not always because of family pressure. Nazma, for instance, had not gone to university. Instead, she had left college and started work. Although quiet, she was nevertheless a very thoughtful and, in fact, highly intelligent young woman. It was clear that it was her choice to begin working as soon as she did – in itself a statement of independence. Moreover, she made it clear to me that her family was not in the habit of preventing its young women from acquiring an education. 'My brothers and sisters have all been to university. With each and every one of us our parents have supported us all the way. They never said, "No that's not for you. Girls shouldn't be out." You do get some backward …'.

At this point, her more garrulous colleague Saiqa (I spoke to them together during their lunch break) interjected, 'My sister, she was the first one of us to go to uni. It wasn't seemly for a girl to go to uni but because she's gone each of us has gone and each of us is getting better degrees. You can see the pride and stuff in my mum and dad's face when they're talking about it.'

Her words implied that it was considered inappropriate within the Muslim community in Pendle for women to attend university until relatively recently. Although that is now changing, and parents are taking 'pride' in their daughters' educational achievements, Qadeer Ahmed was quick to point out that many parents who did allow their daughters to go to university nevertheless still imposed limits and restrictions on them. 'Around here you get a lot of Asian families saying "If you do study you've got to commute to Preston." You get a lot of that, Preston or Manchester, so they can commute.' He acknowledged, however, that his parents were liberal enough to let his sisters study wherever they pleased.

Although class is often taken to be a significant factor in determining educational opportunities and aspirations, some middle-class women experienced similar restrictions. We have seen in chapter 1 how Zainab resisted her parents' entreaties (and bribes) to live at home during her university years and chose instead to live in halls of residence, even though both her university and her home were in London. Shaheen, on the other hand, recalled that 'my parents were quite … they didn't like me going out, like to nightclubs and that sort of thing, so my university days were literally driving to university, attending my lectures, at most having a coffee with friends or doing a bit of shopping in town, and then coming back. I hear all these crazy things about people at university, and my university days weren't really like that.'

Marriage, however, is the site of most intense inter-generational conflict and tension for both men and women. Surveys indicate that the right to choose one's own spouse is a general grievance that many young Muslims hold against their elders. According to Philip Lewis, 'more than eight out of ten males and females would prefer to select their own marriage partner'.[1] Leila, a solicitor working in Essex, summed it up when she said, 'Obviously I'd like to meet someone I really like because I can't be doing with all this introduction thing. Because I've made my own decisions all my life, really, and that is a major decision that I can't just let somebody else make for me.'

Although there is a significant discrepancy between such widespread desire and actual marriage practices, many young Muslims are getting their way. Asif told me that he and his close friends – there were about eight of them in total – had all married recently and 'none of them were arranged marriage [*sic*]. My wife, I used to go out with her for about three years, and then I told my uncle, my uncle told my dad and my dad said, "Yeah, that's fine, what's the family like?" And vice versa for her and we just got married.'

In Slough, Aisha told me that she would be looking for her partner because her parents were quite relaxed about it. In many ways, they were somewhat exceptional, not because they did not mind their children finding their spouses (the same was true for Asif and others as well) but because of the scope of their liberality. 'The thing is my parents, they're not the type to … unless we tell them I don't think they'll actively look for us. They're like, "If you find someone then that's perfectly fine, let us know. Just don't do anything stupid." From day one they have trusted us. With my parents, colour wasn't an issue for us and it never has been so my parents really don't mind if we get married to someone outside of our culture or to someone from a different race. The thing is God doesn't distinguish between black, white, blue, Asian or whatever, so why should we?'

Despite these examples, most young Muslim women I spoke to were having their marriages arranged for them by their parents and elders. Some were happy with this, others less so, but they were all at pains to point out that they were not going to be forced into marrying someone against their wishes. Soumaya's brothers had had arranged marriages, and she would be happy to have one in due course because she trusted her parents. Speaking of her brothers, she said, 'They were arranged, like my parents actually found the girls but they weren't really forced upon 'cos it's not really like that in our family. I have seen some Asian families that call it "arranged" but the child has no choice in the end, it doesn't really work like that in our family, though. My brothers were asked whether they were happy with it or not and they went ahead.'

Unwittingly, Soumaya's words here reveal the spectre that haunts the scene whenever arranged marriages are discussed in Britain. This spectre of the forced marriage is like a background *tableau* which throws into relief the balance between compulsion and choice in any arranged marriage. That balance shifts according to individual circumstances but in general there is greater latitude of choice for males than females.

This was clearly illustrated by Fahmida from Uxbridge. 'My older sister, she actually married my cousin. My brothers, as well, both of them, my mum and dad chose – "do you like her?" [they asked]. In my sister's case it was a lot different, it was a family obligation I think. She was only 19 at the time. I suppose she felt, because she's the oldest, that she had more responsibility. She's the oldest out of the wider family as well after my cousin that she actually married. I think she felt not just responsibility, not just with my mum and dad and brothers and sisters, she felt a wider responsibility to the rest of the family. I think in that way I would say there was more pressure on her. She wasn't forced into it but she kind of sacrificed her ... not well-being but her, like, choice, for everybody else.

'[With] my brothers, it was like, "Oh we found somebody for you", you know, "do you like her? If not ...". My older brother, we spent like a year looking for him and then they finally found someone. My sister was the only, I suppose, "responsible" one; we had to think of all sides but with my brothers it was like, "your choice".'

For herself, Fahmida has changed her mind as she has grown older. Whereas she had wanted to find her partner before, she is now less worried about that because she has realised that the western tradition of romantic love 'is not really all it's made out to be'. This despite her awareness of the pressures: 'when the rest of the family choose him first, and they all like him and you're the last one, you feel obliged to say yeah. Nowadays ... I suppose as you get older you think about it a bit and actually I'm more than happy for them to look, I'm more than happy, because it takes the stress off you and you know your parents brought you up, you've been brought up with your parents' ideals as well and they want the best for you – they're not exactly going to fob you off to any Tom, Dick or Harry – you definitely have the last say, so it's like, yeah, I mean ...'.

She tailed off. As I listen to her interview now, I am left wondering; it is almost as if she did not continue because she did not quite know where she was heading with this line of thought. Perhaps she was not quite as comfortable with this idea as she was trying to suggest; the tone of her voice indicates that she was not exactly sure about what she was saying, about whether to believe herself or not.

Perhaps she should take note of Shaheen's story. It is a story which vividly illustrates the pressures many young Muslim women face during the process of betrothal. At university, Shaheen met a young man called Haroun and, although she was initially cool towards him, eventually fell in love with him. They had much in common – he was from Pakistan and a Muslim. He was even from the same region, the Punjab. However, he was not from a wealthy family and, before she fell in love with him, Shaheen had made the mistake of telling her mother (her father had died) that she had found him 'quite obnoxious'.

'My mum's got lots of – yeah, now I guess I rationalise it and I try and think, well after what she's been through and the politics she's had to deal with and the pressure she's had from people – she's always wanted to impress. Always. Me and my brothers have this issue with our mum, it's all about impressing, like her family, you know?

'So when I proposed that guy, who didn't come from a wealthy family, of course she remembered all that stuff and she was like, "That guy who wouldn't leave you alone, who pestered you? He's the one that you now want to marry?"

'It was a very distressing time for me, it was awful, because at the time – there are times I look back and I thought … well I thought I was in love with him, but now I know I really was, so he's left his mark. My mum was so desperate that I wouldn't progress with him that she … there were two proposals from Pakistan and she said "you have to pick one of those two". And my mum's quite clever and I think she knows that I have a soft spot for her, you know; she doesn't really keep too well, she hasn't kept very well for a while now, and every time I would see her getting distressed and crying I'd say, "I'll marry whoever you want, whoever you want." And then of course the tears would stop and she'd say, "Right then, we'll get you to marry this guy." And it got quite far with one guy, Khalid. I went to Pakistan and met his family, and my brothers met him. All the time I was still communicating with Haroun and telling him I was really unhappy and I didn't know what to do, my family were forcing me to meet with these people. And he stuck by me through all of that.

'And when I came back, it was just that same dilemma. As soon as I came to my senses I'd say, "Mum I can't marry this guy, I don't know him, I don't want it, I don't want to marry him", and she'd start the tears and say, "I'm going to die soon", and that sort of thing, and I'd be like, "Okay I'll marry him, I'll marry him". It literally went like that back and forth. I met this guy, he was okay, nice guy, and I basically said I'd go ahead with it. It got to the point where it was the engagement and he came to our house, and I just froze, I just couldn't do it. I got all dressed up and I just couldn't go downstairs where they were all waiting. So we cancelled the engagement on the day.'

What happened next? I asked.

'It was a melodrama, it was awful, it was awful. My mum's always been quite … with the pride that she gets about me and my brothers, she's always never thought anyone's quite good enough, and that extended to my sisters-in-law. Afterwards, they would say comments like, "You thought we were bad, and now look at the track that your daughter fell on." So my mum felt a great sense of shame when I cancelled on the day; the whole family were there, my sisters-in-law were there, my aunt was there, so my mum felt this absolute shame that on the day I wouldn't go down. Of course the poor guy was sat downstairs, I was in tears, I just couldn't go ahead with it. My mum was physically going to kill me, she literally came … she was hitting me. My sisters-in-law had to pull her off. It was awful. My little nieces were there and they were watching and they were crying. Very, very distressing … in some respects I think it really damaged family relations.'

It took Shaheen a long time to recover her poise and to repair the breach in relations with her family. Mercifully, her story ends happily. Her family had realised how much the whole episode had distressed her, and they began to make conciliatory efforts and 'laid off the pressure'. Moreover, she realised that there was a silver lining to the whole incident and that marrying Haroun might indeed have been a mistake.

Looking back on it she said, 'I just think I have to be practical, you know, about Haroun and I; for example his family and I were very different. His mum and I probably wouldn't be able to communicate that much because they were quite traditional and his mum didn't speak much English.

'Practical things, like there was a lot of rigidity with Haroun, you know, it would be very black and white, for example with *halal* issues, "You're not eating this, you're not eating that." And whilst I was with him I'd respect that because I'm happy to make those compromises for someone that I love, but he would sometimes go very far, you know, like, "I don't want you to go to the theatre because there are men there." And I'd say, "I think you're very, very rigid. If you come to that conclusion after a discussion, after a debate, fine, I respect that. But if you just come to that conclusion without even talking about it, it's not fair." I don't think that's fair.

'And although one of the things I loved about Haroun was the fact that he had opinions – it was something I always admired in him: his principles really guided his life, you know – he didn't move on them, and I was thinking you know, five years down the line when he's working crazy hours and I've got screaming children, will that model work? And it's very hard to rationalise an emotional issue like marriage and your partner, but I think you have to do that.'

Since then she has met someone else and was engaged to him. Her feelings about her fiancé indicate why she feels that she is ready to marry him, 'He's someone I can go home and talk to at the end of the day and tell him what's happening at work and have a discussion with him. If he disapproves of something we'll have a debate and he'll change his mind if he agrees, or he won't, it's a bit more … I guess a bit more of an equal relationship. As far as my parents are concerned he's the perfect guy, you know, great job, nice family, all of that kind of stuff.' She made one final comment before she let the whole matter rest: 'I met him on my own account. I liked him. It just so happens that my parents also like him.'

* * *

Unlike Shaheen, many other young Muslim women continue to feel compelled to accede to their parents' desires rather than their own. These are small tragedies that fall within the grey area which lies between an 'arranged' marriage and a 'forced' one.

'I can't imagine being with a Bengali guy,' said Razia. 'Because I've always fancied typically white guys really. My oldest sister, she had to have an arranged marriage. My brother, he said I'd have to have an arranged marriage. I spoke to my mum and I was like, "Mum, am I not allowed a love marriage?" She was like, "No", and I was like, "Why? What if he's a Muslim?" And she was like "No, I don't care." I was like, "Why? If he's a Muslim therefore it's not actually a sin." She was like, "No it has to be someone I found." I was like, "For God's sake, what if you met him quite a few times and decided you really liked him, and then afterwards I told you about us?" And she was like, "No." So basically I have to have an arranged marriage with some Bengali guy. Obviously, I am allowed to say no to whoever they choose, but at the end of the day at some point I will have to say yes to someone they choose.

'Also, I think it would be best for everybody if I did have an arranged marriage,' she added after a thoughtful pause. 'Because if I do have a love marriage, chances are … obviously my parents have already said they would not approve, and I would not feel right marrying someone, even if I did love them, hurting my parents like that. If it is a love marriage, it doesn't matter who I marry; people will never accept it, even if he is a Bengali, even if he is a Muslim.'

I found it sad that such a spirited young woman like Razia should be resigned to her fate. This was the same Razia who enjoyed fighting because of the thrill it gave her, who played football with gusto and who had wanted to be a car mechanic when she was younger because she liked fast cars. Her robustness was quite deflated as she spoke of the pressures bearing down upon her.

What really irritated Razia, however, was the fact that her brother *did* manage to secure a love marriage – 'after many years of fighting' – and to a non-Muslim as well. Complaints about such double standards were aired by many Muslim women I spoke to (though not by many young men). They felt a profound sense of grievance about this.

Razia, for instance, made no attempt to hide her frustration and anger. 'One thing we always fight about is the way that my mum favours my brothers over me and my sisters. I think this is the case with like most Asian families I'm sure, but in my house it's really terrible and I can't stand it, and I usually get into a fight with my mum about that. For example, she'd say something to me like … when I first started covering my head she was really proud of me, she was like, "Oh my daughter's covering her head, oh my daughter's so good." But then my oldest brother, he had such a major problem with it, and then when he said to my mum that he doesn't like me covering my head, my mum was like, "Yeah, why are you covering your head? You shouldn't do that, you're only little – blah-blah-blah-blah-blah." It's like, "You just said like twenty minutes ago how proud you are of me." Oh I really can't stand that!'

At other times she recalled, with a certain degree of understandable bitterness, the pettiness of some of these everyday discriminations. Once she openly interrogated her mother about the inequality she and her sisters faced compared to their brothers. 'So I said to them, you know, you have to start treating us equally. And she said that she is, and it's like, "no, you're not". If that was the case then when guests come round and they give you like biscuits and stuff like that, if that's the case then how come my brothers are allowed to open, you know, the good things but I'm not allowed? And also if we are treated equally how come their photos are put in really nice gold frames but ours are in like those little rubbish ones? It's like, "Mum, explain that", and she doesn't say anything.'

Such imbalances have led many young Muslim women to pursue a secret life, one that is daily negotiated within the parameters of the restrictions imposed upon them. Razia said of her elder sister, 'She does all these things, like misbehaving with boys and drinking and smoking, yeah? And these little things that she does which are bad, if our parents later found out not only would they kill her, they'd kill all of us lot as well because obviously they would know that we knew about it.'

Despite her reservations, Razia's complicity in her sister's secret life is part of a more general phenomenon common to many young Muslim women. They often close ranks and cover for each other in the face of their parents' (and sometimes even their brothers') suspicions. Razia also led a secret life, and no doubt she relied on her sisters' discretion as well. As she made clear, the whole process involves a certain amount of duplicity.

'In this country I can go out here just to the shops or whatever or with my friends or whatever. In Bangladesh that's not really allowed, and my cousins are like, "Oh you can do that but in this country you can't really do that." And I was like, they don't really understand that in this country I'm not actually supposed to be doing that either, because my parents they don't allow that. I don't think I'm doing anything bad by going out with my friends, but my parents they think I am because I say to them, "Oh yeah I'm going to uni", and then I just stay out with my friends or whatever. The thing is, I don't like lying to my parents, they're the only people I actually lie to because I hate lying. I have a really guilty conscience. The thing is, I feel like my parents they restrict me too much and they just don't trust me, and I really hate that. And me lying to them doesn't make it any better because obviously if they do find out that I'm not actually wherever I said I was then they won't trust me even more.'

I wanted to know what she actually did when she went out with her friends behind her parents' back. 'Just little things like shopping or bowling or cinema, or just going out to restaurants,' she replied, and then added, 'I usually do that because my parents are very restrictive, so if I'm constantly going out they make a really big deal out of it. It doesn't matter if my brothers go out all the time though, that's not an issue, but for me it is, apparently. So I try not to go out too much and if I do, I make sure it is actually worth it, you know?'

It is the structure of the extended family – the *biradari* and its
variants – and the demands it makes of individuals which is key
to understanding both the pressure that young men and, particularly,
women feel over marriage and the double standards in their treatment.
As Razia made clear when discussing her marriage, all that mattered
was that the patriarchal authority of the elders was upheld. 'Culture'
and religion had very little to do with it – it did not matter whether she
chose a Bengali or a Muslim; what really mattered was that she did not
arrogate to herself the right to choose. Similarly, the greater freedom
and scope for individuality enjoyed by the men – often endorsed by the
parents – is also an expression of this patriarchy. It is not a culture which
promotes equality between the sexes.

This is yet another dimension of the 'turn to Islam' amongst many
young Britons of Muslim parentage. It is particularly pertinent for
young women. 'It says in the Qu'ran, you know, that sons and daughters
should be treated equally and those that don't treat them as equals will
get punished,' said Razia pointedly. This was something I often heard,
and it shows why young British Muslim women would contest the view,
commonly held in the West, that Islam is inherently oppressive of
women. In fact, they find it liberating; for them it is a means of leverage
by which to resist the patriarchal imbalances of their parents' culture.

A couple of points need to be noted here. First, young British Muslims
draw a distinction between culture and religion with regard to gender
issues as with much else. When I asked Aisha, a student, whether she
thought Islam oppressed women, she replied, 'People think that Muslim
women, especially, haven't seen outside the four walls of their own
houses and that's not true. I mean, I don't deny the fact that you do get
some people who are very traditional, and they enforce these things like
the woman should stay at home, she should be a housewife – that is
where the misconception is, because people confuse religion with culture
and you need to make that distinction: culture and religion are two
separate things, you can't get them mixed up.'

Qadeer Ahmed made a similar point but illustrated it in a way that
illuminated the rationale behind why so many seek the necessary
resources for tackling gender oppression within Islam. 'Islam in itself
doesn't oppress women', he said, 'but the cultures where Muslims are,
whether it's Arab culture, whether it's Pakistani culture, Indian culture,
do. I think, honestly, if you look at how women were treated, like, worse
than animals before Islam in the Middle East and the Prophet, peace

be upon him, gave rights to women. I mean, this is how bad it was: the Quraysh [the tribe to which the Prophet Muhammad belonged], when they were against the Prophet, peace be upon him, someone came back and there was all this news coming in that the Prophet's done this, the Prophet's done this, peace be upon him, and this guy said "he's given rights to women, he [the Prophet] said they're equal to men", and one of the Quraysh guys said, "What's he going to be doing next? He'll be giving rights to horses." So they were considered even less than the animals. I mean, I'm sorry to say it, if anything, it's moving back towards that in certain parts of the world.'

So young British Muslims see themselves as being engaged in a battle for cultural authority against their parents, and for them Islam is a means of doing that most effectively. As we have seen before, the 'turn' to Islam is thus an expression of their affiliation to British and western ways of being expressed in an idiom capable of being understood by their parental antagonists. But with respect to their reappraisal of gender relations, they face certain limitations based on the 'discursive tradition' of Islam because that is the ground on which they are articulating their opposition. Therefore, they do not enjoy an entirely free hand.

What they have done is to interpret that tradition as broadly as possible to achieve their desired aim of gender equality within the framework of Islam. The result is a conceptualisation of gender equality that is different to that commonly assumed in the West. There is an emphasis on equality but there is also an emphasis on the difference between men and women.

It was put most succinctly by Munizha, 'Your rights and responsibilities are different in the sense of your responsibilities in the community, in your family and things like that. But the end goal is the same. The end goal is that, after all, you want to worship Allah, you wanna be a good Muslim. But the responsibilities are different. Like for a Muslim man, his responsibility towards providing and caring for his family is a lot bigger than the responsibilities of the woman. But then the responsibilities of the woman in the upbringing of her children and the education of the children is a lot stronger. The point of it is that they have different responsibilities but it's so that they complement each other and I think that's the main thing.'

To some in the West this may seem like the same old gendered division of labour characteristic of patriarchal oppression, but currently most young British Muslim women do not see it that way.

* * *

In October 2006, Jack Straw published a short article in the *Lancashire Telegraph*. In it he reflected on the full veil (*niqab*) as a 'visible statement of separation and of difference' that was 'bound to make better, positive relations' between Muslim and non-Muslim communities more difficult because it obstructed face-to-face communication. 'So many of the judgments we all make about other people come from seeing their faces,' he argued.

The remarks sparked a controversy and acted as a lightning rod for polarised debates about the integration of Muslims in British society and the position of women in Islam. Although Straw was addressing the former issue, others were quick to link the two, merging anxieties about the supposed divisiveness of multiculturalism and the threat posed by Islam to the 'British way of life' with persistent and widespread perceptions about misogyny and gender inequality in Islam – as though misogyny and gender inequality were completely alien to Britain before the arrival of Muslims.

The vast majority of young British Muslim women who adopt Islamic dress do not wear the *niqab*, which covers everything but the eyes. Rather, they wear either a *hijab*, which leaves the face uncovered but is wound fairly tightly around the head, or a *dupatta*, a loose headscarf. As with all fashion, there are many styles and different ways of wearing both of them, the subtleties of which often escape the untrained eye.

My first visit to Lancashire coincided with the Jack Straw controversy. I spoke to some young Muslims from his Blackburn constituency as well as from neighbouring towns at that time and, unsurprisingly, there was much discussion of his comments. I did not notice many *niqab* wearers. In fact, in Nelson I saw only one, although in Blackburn there were more. At a guess, I would say most young women were wearing some form of *hijab* or *dupatta* but there were in fact quite a few whose heads were totally uncovered.

In the course of my conversations across the country, the issue of the *hijab* and the *niqab* was raised several times. Most women I spoke to wore the *hijab*, and their reasons for doing so varied. Nevertheless, there was a common emphasis on *choice*. They were all at pains to point out that, contrary to popular opinion, they did not wear the *hijab* because they were being forced by their menfolk. Beyond that, they spoke about the *hijab* and its significance for them in many ways.

'It is not just about covering up but it's a whole attitude and mode of behaviour and stuff ... it's about modesty,' said Munizha. For Aisha, 'it sort of calmed me down and made me a bit more humble and it made me aware of how I was acting towards other people.' For Zainab, on the other hand, it helped to reinforce her sense of being a Muslim and the discipline that goes with it, 'you have always to be constantly aware that everybody knows you're Muslim so you can't do anything, sort of, wrong that's going to change people's perceptions of Muslims but also you kind of ... you just know where the barriers are in terms of relationships with the opposite sex, going into pubs and that sort of thing. You couldn't just stand there and drink, you know, do something like that for example. So it just really helps you to set the barriers.' She also emphasised a more practical side to its appeal, 'It's more comfortable not being harassed, and guys respecting you more.'

For many, wearing the *hijab* is seen as a sign of commitment and fortitude. It is a decision not to be taken lightly. 'It was a really difficult step to take at first,' said Fahmida. 'I'd been meaning to wear it for quite a while but I suppose I felt that I didn't have a good enough reason to wear it, 'cos obviously when you start wearing it, it's a commitment that you have to carry on – you don't just wear it at uni or when you go outside, you wear it even when you go to relatives' houses as well. I wanted to, I had that intention but I felt like I didn't have a good enough reason or standing to wear it, and then like last summer I went and did *umrah* [the lesser pilgrimage to Mecca], and I thought ok, this is a spiritual enlightenment, and I thought now is my time.'

Some who had not yet covered their heads nevertheless did aspire to do so, and their comments made it clear how they too saw the *hijab* in such terms. Leila, a solicitor, spoke about wearing the *hijab* in terms of courage and confidence, 'It's an Islamic principle so I'm not going to say it's wrong to wear *hijab* because it's clearly not, and it's mentioned in the Qu'ran. I think you should wear it, and hopefully Allah gives every woman the chance to wear it but I have to say I haven't been brave enough to wear it yet. I hope one day I will be able to.'

She told me that the reason she had not yet done so was based partly on the experience of a friend who had 'worn the *hijab* for years' and was unable to secure a position even though she was highly qualified. She had received many interviews but never been appointed. One day she removed her *hijab* for an interview and she secured the job. Leila felt that she did not yet have the confidence to take on the system on those terms.

'I don't judge her at all – she had to pay the mortgage', she said laughing, 'but if I did it I would want to do it properly. I wouldn't want to put it on and have to take it off. It's about being confident enough about your decisions and actions. So, I suppose I'm not confident enough to wear it.'

What I noticed about the way these young women spoke about the *hijab* is that there has been a shift in the meaning and function of covering up for them. Hitherto, covering up was part of the symbolic economy of clan patriarchy. The hiding away of a family's women from *public* view – *purdah* – protected the 'honour' of its men. Now, the rationale for covering has been uncoupled from that and has become what you could call a 'metaphysics of covering'. The emphasis is on the personal meaning of the dress, to which the person is attached regardless of the social context. Hence, these young women insisted on wearing it not only in public but also inside the home and in all social contexts. The meaning of the *hijab* is both individualised and ontologised: it is an emotional attachment which confers a particular sense of being on that person. As Zainab put it, 'if I didn't wear the *hijab* I wouldn't feel myself.' From this point of view, its purpose is not a social but a personal one. It delivers a sense of well-being, and it reflects (and deepens) one's faith.

None of the women I spoke to wore the *niqab*. They agreed that there was a distinction between the *hijab* and *niqab*, that whereas the *hijab* represented an Islamic principle, wearing the *niqab* was not obligatory. They emphasised the same *laissez-faire* attitude to the *niqab* as they did with the *hijab* – in terms of personal choice and the freedom to wear whatever you want. However, there was considerable debate and dispute about the value of the *niqab* and whether it is necessary. Some thought it was a step too far, and none could actually envisage taking this step. Amina's comments were fairly typical: 'It's up to them. For myself, I don't think I can wear a veil on. I just don't feel comfortable with it but if they wanna wear the veil they should be able to wear the veil because it's up to them.'

Nevertheless, some did view the *niqab* quite positively and sympathetically as an expression and measure of the strength of one's faith. Munizha said, 'the main view in Islam is that the woman should cover everything but the hands and the face, and if she wants to cover her hands and her face then that's at her own discretion, basically, and, obviously, that shows her greater strength in her faith and wanting to abide by the laws of God and, like all faiths, the more you do within that faith the greater it is for your own self, for your spirituality, and the more you feel you're getting your reward from God, basically'.

The idea of the *niqab* being a step too far was elaborated extensively by Sameena from Leicester. She said, 'I actually feel sorry for the women that do wear it because in my opinion – and they wouldn't agree with me because obviously they wear it, but in my opinion – they have added something that isn't within the tenets of Islam and made it Islamic.

'I think on the whole the issue is about modesty and about expressing your modesty through the way that you choose to dress. And whether that be in a suit or whether that be in a skirt, trousers, *shalwar kameez*, a *sari*, whatever, or the *jilbab* even, the sort of long cloak thing; and whether that be by covering your hair or covering your face or doing neither, you know, it's about expressing your sense of modesty. And I think modesty means different things to different people. And this concept of modesty applies to men and to women. Where it says in the Qu'ran to dress modestly, it actually clarifies men and women. So if some women choose that covering their face is their idea of dressing modestly, then so be it. But I feel that it's a bit of an extreme step to go towards. I don't feel that we live in a society where you need to cover yourself up to that degree in order to express the fact that, you know, you have a sense of modesty. Because I think modesty resides within you, much like spirituality.'

Fahmida felt that it was not the *niqab* itself that was a step too far but rather that it was inappropriate in certain contexts. She recounted a story about a woman in the United States who would refuse to take her veil off even in court. 'She wouldn't take it off and afterwards, she was saying it was violating her civil liberties, but I think it's logical, though; if you're going to stand up in a court you should be able to take the *niqab* off.' She went on, 'I think there was another story about a woman and how she wanted to wear the *niqab* on her driving licence in America, and I thought that the whole point of the driving licence is for identity and if you wear the *niqab* you can't identify yourself.'

Zainab also said, 'Not just for non-Muslims, even for myself sometimes, with women who wear *niqab* it's a bit awkward – it's a bit absurd sometimes when someone comes up to you and says "Salaam Aleikum" and they're wearing the *niqab* and you don't really know who they are. It's a tiny bit impractical.'

Some young Muslim women even wanted the *niqab* banned. Munizha told me that at the height of the controversy, Radio 5 Live ran a vote

on whether it should be banned, and there was a concerted effort by
her friends to organise a vote against. However, one friend replied back
that she felt it should be banned, 'because it's causing all these problems'.
They had a long text message debate and eventually agreed to disagree.

Having said all this, Jack Straw can take little comfort from the
responses of young Muslims. Despite the disagreements and debates
about the *niqab*, there was a general antipathy to his comments. Even
those who generally agreed with him took issue with the manner and
timing of his comments. 'I have reservations about whether it [the *niqab*]
is conducive to a cohesive society and a cohesive community, and I don't
believe that it is,' said Sameena. 'I do believe that it acts as a barrier.
I would ask Muslim women who do wear the veil, "think about what
you're trying to achieve and what you're actually achieving. You're
trying to blend in and not be conspicuous but actually you're standing
out like a sore thumb." Having said all of that, I don't agree with the way
that the subject was brought into the public domain. I'm originally from
Blackburn, I grew up in Blackburn and he [Jack Straw] lived just a couple
of streets away from us. So he lived in the heart of the Asian community
and was familiar with the women wearing *niqabs* around him and
communicating with them and, you know, I'm sure he's had to learn
how to deal with that.

'I feel that his comments were hijacked by primarily the media, and
the media loved it. Every bit of it. I think if he really wanted to bring this
issue out into the open he could have in a much more subtle fashion.'

It soon became clear that much of the scepticism was due to the
sensationalism of the press coverage, and indeed many of those I spoke
to were responding to bowdlerised versions of his comments that
had been relayed through many intervening mediations. The current
process of reporting such events clearly does not help in fostering
mutual understanding and resolving misunderstandings; in fact,
it helps polarise debates and hardens positions on both sides.

Zainab, for instance, changed her mind because she was fortunate
enough to hear Jack Straw explain himself at a meeting of the City Circle.
She said, 'At first I was very angry and I thought, you know, "how could
he say that?" – you can't tell someone how to dress – but then I went
to the City Circle event and he was talking and he said that if the woman
felt comfortable and wanted to, then, she could take it off – apparently
that's all he ever said. He was saying it's completely been blown out of all
proportion. If that's what he said then it was ok; still, perhaps it wasn't

the best thing to have said but I don't think he was saying anything as extreme as "I don't want women in society to veil their faces." ' She added, however, 'if that's all he really meant then surely it's kind of up to the person themselves? You don't need to necessarily tell someone it's ok to do that if you want to.'

Many did, however, take issue with the specifics of what he said whilst trying to give due consideration to the nuances of his position. They pointed out that those women about whom Jack Straw made his comments were fully participating in the democratic process by visiting their local MP's surgery. Far from being a sign of 'separation', did this not show that these women were highly integrated? As Aisha put it, 'The thing is, wasn't it the woman who came to him to talk to him about whatever grievances that she had? If she was so subdued, if she wasn't allowed out of the house or whatever, then why did she come to him? This whole issue of the *niqab*: people say it makes it difficult for integration and stuff, and I was like, "why?" The only reason it's making things difficult is because you're the ones that have the problem with it.'

As I reflect back on these conversations about the *hijab* and *niqab*, two things have struck me as being particularly noteworthy. One is the way that some of the young women spoke about the *niqab* as denoting a higher or stronger level of faith. We have already seen it, for instance, in Munizha's and Leila's comments. Aisha too spoke of it as follows: 'The *niqab* is not compulsory; it's optional for the woman whether she wants it or not. If she wants it, then by all means, go ahead, but that is her level of faith; that shows she's strong enough, she's confident enough to be actually able to do that and at the moment I would say that I don't think I am.' Those who were not covered at all spoke in similar terms about the *hijab*. Thus Saiqa said, 'I don't wear the *hijab* because I don't feel I am ready to wear it; so once I feel I am ready to wear it I will wear it.'

There is an implied hierarchy of faith here as expressed in the manner of one's dress. At the top are those who wear the *niqab*, then those who wear the *hijab* and finally those who do not cover their heads at all. When quizzed about it, they are adamant that this is not the case. Aisha replied, 'there are certain things within any religion which are optional. Whether you want to do it, you'll get extra blessings. Or if you don't, you're not going to be condemned for it, you know. At the end of the day, I don't think it's for the individual to judge whether someone's a good

Muslim or not because, at the end of the day, it's not for me to decide. So I wouldn't say that a person who's wearing the *niqab* – yeah, she may be more knowledgeable than I am – but I wouldn't say she's more sincere than I am because at the end that's not for you to judge.'

Nevertheless, the impression still remains that the *niqab* is an ideal towards which one *should* aspire. Why the 'extra blessings' if not? I raise this point not because of any particular antipathy I might have towards the *niqab* but because it seems to be in tension with the *laissez-faire*, wear-what-you-want attitude, which in turn is part of the wider attitude which we have encountered in earlier chapters: that young British Muslims take for granted that there are many different and equally valid ways of being a Muslim. In other words, if there is an implicit hierarchy of faith denoted by dress, then is an uncovered woman's way of being Muslim *equally* valid? This tension is, I think, seldom noticed, but now that young Muslims are indeed forging new ways of being Muslim, it perhaps deserves to be thought about.

The other point is that the culture/religion distinction that is deployed by young Muslims across a range of issues is seldom applied to the *hijab* or the *niqab*. They are thus taken to be *intrinsically* Islamic on the strength of a Qu'ranic verse which says that women 'should not display their beauty and ornaments except what (must ordinarily) appear thereof; that they should draw their veils over their bosoms and not display their beauty' except to their family (which extends quite broadly as the verse proceeds).[2] The verse offers evidence, by virtue of its ambiguity, for those who claim that the *niqab* is obligatory and for those who claim it is not. It depends, of course, on how 'beauty' is interpreted; the edition I have referred to, completed in 1934, interprets 'beauty' as 'figure', which would support Sameena's claim that the verse tells 'the women of your family to cover their hair and torso but it doesn't mention the face'.

The *hijab* and the *niqab* predate Islam and can be found in a wide range of cultures across the Mediterranean, Asia and northern Africa, both Islamic and non-Islamic. Moreover, the wearing of the *niqab* has been traced back to antiquity and was enforced upon the women of classical Athens.[3] These are clearly 'cultural' practices that were prevalent in the Arabian peninsula when Islam arrived and were subsequently accommodated within it. It is up to Muslims to decide whether the reference in the Qu'ran means that the culture/religion distinction does not apply here or whether there is a case for suggesting that the universal 'principle' behind the historically specific reference to such prevailing cultural practices is that men and women should dress 'modestly' however they choose to dress.

The point is, however, that only Sameena seemed to be aware of this. 'In terms of it [the *niqab*] being more of a symbol of your faith, and a lot of people comment on this, it doesn't come from the sources of Islam, the texts, it comes from a cultural setting during the time of Prophet Mohammed when he brought the message of Islam and at that time there was this notion that the woman who covers her face is more respectful. Much like covering the hair is a symbol of being respectful in other faiths. I think it was Madeleine Bunting in *The Guardian* who highlighted the fact that as a child she was taken to visit a place of Christian worship and the woman had her face covered. But it's funny how other faiths and other cultures haven't been drawn into the debate.'

This is perhaps because most Muslims as well as non-Muslims see the covering of the hair or the face as being specific to Islam, and the debate is being conducted in a vacuum of historical knowledge. Given the current emphasis amongst young Muslims on the historical contextualisation of Islamic teachings (and the culture/religion distinction they deploy is part of this emphasis), it remains something of an anomaly that it is not being applied to matters of dress considering the symbolic importance it carries amongst all parties to the debate about Islam in the modern world.

* * *

Young British Muslim women are becoming increasingly independent, assertive and self-reliant. They are wresting educational opportunities from those who had traditionally sought to deny them, and they are outstripping their male peers in educational performance when given the chance. A new generation of highly educated women are emerging who will, inevitably, shape what future generations of British Muslims will take to be the proper role and function of women in society. Nevertheless, this is a transitional generation; they still feel the need to negotiate the cultural pressures imposed upon them by their parents. They show clear signs of impatience and frustration with these pressures but they are not yet ready to throw them off. I think, however, that is only a matter of time.

Chapter 7
Prospects

These are difficult times for Britain's Muslim communities. They are under pressure as never before, living in the glare of a media spotlight that is often harsh and unforgiving. Young British Muslims in particular sometimes arouse fear and suspicion. To some extent, this is understandable; after all, five young British Muslim men did blow themselves up in London in July 2005, killing and injuring scores of innocent people. Others have tried to follow suit, whilst others have expressed hostility and hatred for the country in which they live. On the other hand, almost every week a controversy involving Islam and Muslims flares up, often fuelled by ignorance and prejudice. As I write this, a furore sparked by the Archbishop of Canterbury's words on *Shariah* law rumbles on. Lurid headlines raise the spectre of an incomprehensible barbarism insinuating itself into the fabric of British social life at the invitation of the 'liberal' establishment. A good and thoughtful man raising a complex and difficult subject is mercilessly pilloried by those who have neither the time nor the inclination to consider his arguments before rushing to judgment.

Such a febrile and polarised atmosphere is bound to have an effect on Britain's Muslims. Although young British Muslims demonstrate a great deal of confidence in both their Muslim and their British identities, they are also anxious and nervous about what the future holds for them. This ambivalence was summed up very well by Qadeer Ahmed, who saw 'a lot of good and a lot of bad' in the years to come.

At the end of every conversation, I asked each one of them about their thoughts and feelings about the future. Would life become easier for British Muslims? Did they feel that the pressure under which they live now would slowly subside?

'Things aren't *bad*', said Abdur-rahman, 'but I think they're gonna get worse before they get better. There's a long road ahead, but I'm an optimist.' This general sense of anxiety about the short term coupled with hope for the long term was echoed in some form by all them.

'I don't know what else can really go wrong,' said Zainab. 'More people are talking about British Muslims and what can be done to accommodate us, to make British Muslims feel more part of society, so I hope things are going to get better – I don't see what else can really go wrong. Individually, I don't see any barriers in terms of being Muslim and practising; I think things are getting easier, there's improvements in the way employers are thinking.'

Much of this division in the young Muslim attitude can be mapped onto a distinction between large-scale, general anxiety about macro-level problems in the world at large and a positive attitude towards more local concerns.

Munizha said, 'in terms of international affairs and the war on terror, it will get worse […], but I think that if you let that sort of negative atmosphere overwhelm you, then yes, your future does look pretty bleak. But I think, you have to think of yourself as an individual, you have to take each day as it comes and you have to think, at the end of the day, "what am I working towards? And why am I here?" And I think that everybody, individually, can have a positive impact.

'Things like actually helping your community, things like trying to get people to actually understand Islam, actually making a difference … just little things, you can do things to make a difference and I think if you take each day as it comes and try to make a difference and combat people's [negative] views with a positive attitude the future can look bright.'

Others also articulated this positive emphasis. Speaking of his children Mohammed Ali said, 'I would like for them as Muslims to be strong in their identity, strong in their faith, Islam prominent in their life, but that doesn't mean you go into your own shell – you engage with people, have friends who are of different faiths, and interact with people of different faiths, good people of society in general.' From this perspective, strength (of character and faith) combined with open-mindedness will enable young British Muslims to take charge of their lives, to prosper in a diverse society.

Nevertheless, there were a few instances when their general anxiety was startlingly focussed into a more concrete fear. Quite a few expressed a concern that the situation would deteriorate to the extent that they would either feel compelled to leave Britain or, in fact, be expelled.

In London, Shahid said to me, 'I can only see things going downhill, to be honest. My dad's always telling me, "Make sure you've got a back up plan. Say one day they won't let you be in this country anymore, you have to think about where you're gonna go."'

'I think Muslims are going to reach a juncture where we have to make a choice about whether we become *completely* westernised and behave like the English or whether we have to emigrate. I mean, that might not necessarily happen in my lifetime. It's still quite a long way away, I think. I think that might happen first in western Europe rather than Britain but we'll have to wait and see.' He pondered this for a minute before adding, 'I have no idea where I could live because in Bangladesh I'm not sure I could adjust to that sort of lifestyle. But I think this country's our biggest and best hope in all of Europe.'

This was echoed by Saiqa in Lancashire. 'I do think, like, when our parents used to say "Send your money back home and make your houses there because one day [they'll kick us out]". I have thought about it and maybe there is that question – there's a question mark over that now. We wouldn't *want* to go but obviously if they say we have to go, we'd have to wouldn't we? There's a difference.'

This was her only anxiety about living in Britain. 'With everything else, I'm perfectly fine', she said. 'I'll go into pubs and sit with friends while they're drinking, I'll have an orange juice. I'm getting used to their culture and they'll learn about mine.'

Others are thinking along similar lines and have considered pre-empting the possibility of expulsion. Shaheen just could not believe the situation that she and others now faced. 'What's happened recently has been on such a big scale, a scale I could never have imagined ten years ago. You know, we're on top of the BNP agenda now, whereas ten years ago it would have been black people. It's grown so much I don't see it dying down.

'And my brothers, especially the one in the middle, he's quite sensitive. Anything that happens in the news, he immediately emails my older brother and me and says the UK's not safe for us any more, next year we're going to get kicked out, just like what happened with the Partition, and you know, Muslims were told to leave India, it's going to be the same in the UK. He genuinely feels that the day is going to come when Britain … I don't think that will ever happen, I don't think that will ever happen in a country that calls itself, you know, like, a liberal country, a diverse country.

'But I speak to my fiancé about what we're going to do in the future – he does a lot of work in Dubai. And I would be really happy to move to Dubai because I think it would be safer. I don't like it as a country, I think it's very artificial, there's no culture there, but for bringing up children I just think it would be safer.

'It's sad because this is where the whole identity thing comes back into play, because Britain is in many respects … you know, like London, I love

London and I love Manchester, it's where I grew up and I'd always want
to keep ties to this country. But I certainly do feel a sense of uncertainty
going forward, and for children to grow up in. I wouldn't like my
children to be ashamed of the fact that they were Muslim.'

It is worrying that the shadow of ethnic cleansing hangs over the
young British Muslim imagination to such an extent. Perhaps it is just
a reflex of the hysterical times in which we are living, in which lurid
fantasies of nefarious threats conjure up equally lurid imaginings from
the residual memory of past historical traumas: the Holocaust, the
partitions of India and Palestine, Rwanda and the former Yugoslavia –
the record of the twentieth century does not bequeath particular
grounds for optimism as we look ahead to the twenty-first.

The very least that can be said is that the situation presents a challenge
to young British Muslims. The artist Yara el-Sherbini said to me 'We need
voices that are prepared to debate, challenge and put themselves on the
line, to rearticulate what it means to be a British Muslim, what those
definitions are, what it can be, what it can mean. One of the fundamental
things that needs to happen is that Muslims need to look at their
understanding and interpretation of Islam – what it means.'

The evidence presented in this book suggests that this challenge is being
taken up with enthusiasm and determination by young Muslims from all
kinds of background. I do not think that they will shirk this responsibility.
Young British Muslims are on the move – spiritually, intellectually, philo-
sophically, culturally, ethically and politically – and there is a dynamism
amongst them which is not being noticed by the wider society. As Bob
Dylan remarked in one of his songs during a similar period of profound
social change, 'Something is happening here but you don't know what it
is, do you, Mr Jones?' Where this particular restless generation will end
up is not known, but they have begun a journey that may one day be seen
as a highly significant moment in the development of new ways of being
Muslim, not just in Britain but elsewhere.[1]

However, the situation presents a challenge for non-Muslim Britons
too. There is much talk of social cohesion these days and much of it is
spoken with relations between Muslim and non-Muslim communities
in mind. If this is to amount to anything then as a society we must begin
to address the poisoned public discourse through which we currently
speak about such things. Is Britain really ready not just to tolerate
difference and diversity but also to accept it as an integral part of its
social fabric? At the moment it would seem not.

To make progress on this front, there must first be a recognition that Britain's Muslim communities – and especially the youth within these communities – are not as different as some people imagine them to be; nor are they as alienated as some people claim. But there must also be an acknowledgement that there are genuine frustrations and grievances and that some of these may be justified. In particular, there are particular frustrations concerning the way Islam and Muslims are talked about: as an 'alien' way of life that threatens the British 'way of life'; as a barbaric, backward and intolerant faith; as though it could offer nothing of value; and as though British Muslims faced a stark choice between becoming British or remaining outsiders. The overwhelming majority of British Muslims do not see their situation in these polarised terms.

There also needs to be an acknowledgement that most Muslims do not necessarily want to conform to what others perceive to be an acceptable way of being British. They want to forge this for themselves. They do not want to become secularised in the way that many non-Muslim Britons are. They do not wish to see their religion as purely a private matter. For them, being a Muslim is a public identity and it entails social, ethical and political responsibilities. The challenge facing British society – both Muslims and non-Muslims – is how to fashion a sense of Britishness that would allow them to do this, to be British *Muslims*.

How all this plays out will depend on how non-Muslims deal with and respond to these aspirations. As for myself, I have learnt a great deal from the many young men and women I have spoken to over the last couple of years. From them I have taken great confidence that the struggle within Islam will not be surrendered to those who shout the loudest or those who seek constantly to reduce the lived complexity of life to a set of rigid doctrinal prescriptions.

I have become aware of the sheer number of pathways into and through Islam – the Islamic term for this, incidentally, is *Shariah* – and I must admit that I too have undertaken something of a journey. There are some things that I once believed that I no longer believe. Principally, I have learned to speak of Muslims rather than Islam. In one sense, there is no such thing as Islam. Sure, there is a discursive tradition comprising a core set of ideas and principles which is known as Islam, and all Muslims relate in some way or another to it, but a 'thing' called Islam that has inherent qualities that result in general consequences and determine what all Muslims think and feel? No, there is no such thing as that kind of Islam. 'Islam' only exists as the sum of all Muslims – over a billion of them; as a lived reality, it is vast and heterogeneous, and is manifested in different ways according to what different Muslims make of it.

So when it is said, as many do, that 'Islam is misogynistic' or 'Islam is violent', what exactly is being said? That all Muslims are misogynistic and violent? And if some are not, are they then still Muslims? Moreover, if Islam is *intrinsically* misogynistic or violent, then surely reform as such is impossible? When 'Islam' is spoken about in such terms, the implicit desire is not for 'Islam' to be reformed but for it to be removed. There is no possibility of a middle ground; it is either what it is or it must become nothing. Such a way of thinking, as encoded in such ways of talking, brooks no difference. There is no possibility of nuance or flexibility. It is black and white. The call for reform is itself negated by the manner in which it is made. 'Reform' comes to stand in as a code for 'become like us', which in turn expresses a desire for annihilation, for the outright 'victory' of 'our' ideas over 'theirs'. If that is how the 'battle for hearts and minds' comes across then it is no wonder that Muslims become defensive.

If the task of establishing a new Britain at ease with its racial, cultural and religious diversity is to be achieved – if Muslims are truly to be accepted as *bona fide* Britons and if Islam is truly to be seen as an integrated part of Britishness – then as much care must be taken over how things are said as to what is said. A national conversation must take place, and it must be a proper dialogue. Non-Muslims need to hear what Muslims have to say and vice versa (the evidence of this book is that most young British Muslims are doing just that) – and not just hear, but listen, and not just listen, but absorb and understand. It is a conversation that needs to begin urgently and in earnest, to be undertaken with good will and in good faith.

A Brief Profile of Britain's Muslims

The 2001 census records 1.6 million Muslims in Britain. There are probably more now. Most live in and around the major conurbations of London, Birmingham, Glasgow, Leeds, Bradford, Manchester and Leicester. Many live in the industrial towns of Lancashire and Yorkshire such as Blackburn, Oldham, Burnley, Dewsbury and Keighley. The most significant Muslim communities in the south, outside London, can be found in Slough, but there are communities of varying sizes in many of the commuter towns such as Woking, Uxbridge and High Wycombe.

Most British Muslims are of South Asian origin, from Pakistan, Bangladesh and India, but there are also Muslims from the Middle East, Turkey, north Africa (Algeria, Morocco and Tunisia), Kosovo, Bosnia, Afghanistan, Somalia, Nigeria and, in fact, virtually every Muslim country. They speak over 50 different languages and pursue a wide variety of cultural and Islamic traditions. Most are Sunnis but the proportion of Shias is not accurately known. Those from Pakistan constitute the largest bloc (some 660,000 of the 1.6 million recorded in the census), and they are split doctrinally between two branches of Sunni Islam – the 'Barelwis', as they are colloquially known (Ahl As-Sunnah wal-Jama'at is the formal name of this school of Islam), are very closely associated with Sufism, and the 'Deobandis', taking its name from an Islamic seminary in the north Indian town Deoband. Deobandis are relatively more 'orthodox' than the Barelwis.

This diversity means that it is not accurate to speak of a British Muslim 'community' in the singular. Rather, this heterogeneity compels us to bear in mind that there are several British Muslim communities.

Note About Names and Persons

The young men and women I spoke to were given a choice over anonymity. Some were happy to be identified by their real names, others were not. Some of the names of the people in this book have therefore been changed.

Notes

Chapter 1: Why Islam?

1. Munira Mirza, Abi Senthilkumaran and Zein Ja'far, *Living Apart Together: British Muslims and the Paradox of Multiculturalism* (London: Policy Exchange, 2007), p.37.

2. Ibid. p.46. Of course, as we shall see in a later chapter, it all depends upon what is understood to be *Shariah* law – a much misunderstood concept – by both those posing the questions and those being questioned.

3. Ibid. p.15. The report is something of a curate's egg. Much of it is useful, and there is plenty of good insight, but its arguments are not convincing, not least because its primary concern seems to be with 'Islamists' (i.e. those who espouse 'political Islam') and 'extremism'. Despite acknowledging the need to distinguish between 'Islam' and 'Islamism', it is interesting, and significant, how quickly the report's 'Introduction' settles upon explaining the rise of such 'extremists' and how much space is devoted to them. Thus, although the research concerns all Muslims, often the attention of the authors is drawn towards the problem of 'extremism'. The probably unconscious – and sometimes little noticed – slippages between 'Islam' and 'Islamism' can be seen in various passages. For example, they cite an interpretation of why young Muslims in the west might turn to religion offered by the Australian Muslim psychiatrist Tanveer Ahmed (ibid. p.32). This explanation is clearly meant to apply to *all* young Muslims, not just radicals. They quote him as saying, 'In lay terms, they cannot carry their inconsistent selves through to adulthood … This often involves a dramatic shift to either side of the cultural divide, perhaps committing to an arranged marriage or seeking refuge in deep religiosity. Or it can occur in the opposite behaviour, such as eloping with a partner against their parents' wishes.' It is sandwiched between two glosses which suggest that this is generalisable to all young Muslims, 'Tanveer Ahmed … has written about the way in which young Muslims growing up in the West may feel caught between two different cultural systems with competing values' and 'It seems embracing religion can help some Muslims overcome this sense of alienation from the mainstream, and give them a sense of belonging.' It is only on a second (even third) reading that one notices that all this is supposed to explain 'Islamism' not just the appeal of Islam in general. The suggestion that multiculturalism is responsible for accentuating differences and separation is also problematic, based as it is on certain assumptions about multiculturalism and its impact which are not fully substantiated through evidence or by a clear, logical delineation of cause and effect.

4. Ibid. p.12.

5. Followers of this orthodox tradition are thus known as *Sunnis*.

6. Shiv Malik, 'My Brother the Bomber', *Prospect*, June 2007, pp.30–41.

7. What the young Muslims I spoke to thought about this will be dealt with at length in chapter 6.

8. The Tablighi Jamaat is one of the largest Muslim organisations in the world. Founded in north-western India in 1926 by Maulana Muhammad Ilyas, its vision of Islam was moulded by the needs of the peasants to whom it principally addressed itself. Eschewing intellectualism and politics, it distils Islam into a simple six-point formula that emphasises ritual performance.

9. *Living Apart Together*, p.52.

10. Ibid. p.32.

11. This is what the Policy Exchange authors advocate on ibid. p.88.

12. Ibid. p.52.

13. This is explored in greater detail in chapter 2.

14. The generational conflict within Muslim communities will be explored again in chapter 5.

Chapter 2: Being Muslim

1. This is not a new motif. In his wonderful book *Desperately Seeking Paradise*, Ziauddin Sardar notes that 'In classical Islam the quest for knowledge had always been intimately linked with extensive travel, a fact endorsed by none other than al-Ghazali' (p.85). Al-Ghazali (CE 1058–1111) was one of the most formidable intellectuals of medieval Islam. For him, travel involved a journey in both literal and metaphorical, material and spiritual, senses.

2. Julian Flanagan, 'Prophetic Voice of a Modern Messenger', *Times*, 5 May 2007, p.74.

3. Even more fundamentally, it rests on who wields the greatest political clout. Historically, the settlement which has determined the ideological balance of power in Islamic states centres on the 'ruler' as the final arbiter. Perhaps this is why many *salafis* of a more literal persuasion – and even some reformists – find themselves unable to resist the appeal of the Islamic state as a guarantor of their vision of Islam. What they cannot achieve by force of argument, they hope to achieve by force alone.

4. She is actually wrong about the title here. It is Martin Lings, *Muhammad: His Life based on the Earliest Sources* (London: Allen & Unwin, 1983).

5. For Freud, of course, the unconscious can be spoken about – hence, the very possibility of therapy – but only in a displaced or 'translated' form. For some contemporary philosophers of religion, the 'name' of God is also a 'translation' into language of that which cannot be expressed by it – John Caputo distinguishes the 'name' of God from God as 'event' (precisely that which cannot be spoken). See John D. Caputo, *On Religion* (London: Routledge, 2001).

Chapter 3: Identity

1. This suspicion is manifested more in the reporting than the data, in the selection and framing of questions and in the subsequent emphasis given in news reports and publications. The general question about loyalty seems to have disappeared in later polls (presumably because they told a rather unsurprising and mundane story that the overwhelming majority of British Muslims did indeed feel loyal to Britain) to be replaced by questions calculated to elicit sensational headlines. So, for instance, attention has shifted to such issues as support or sympathy for the suicide bombers, on how many Muslims would like *Shariah* law to be implemented, or an Islamic state in Britain, or are 'anti-freedom of speech' or believe in conspiracy theories concerning 9/11 and 7/7. Alarming – and alarmist – headlines inevitably follow, and reports constantly overlook the proper perspective on the data or the fact that many questions are often ambiguous or lead the respondent to answer in a particular way. For a commentary on some of the most sensational of the polls, see the Policy Exchange report *Living Apart Together*, pp.61–63. See also Anthony Wells's blog on the infamous GFK NOP poll for *Dispatches* at http://ukpollingreport.co.uk/blog/archives/291 (cited 2 May 2008).

2. A survey by GFK NOP commissioned for the Channel 4 documentary *Dispatches* in April 2006 found that whilst 55 percent of British Muslims aged 45 or over felt that Britain was 'my country' only, 44 percent of 18–24 year olds felt the same. The total figure, without age profiling, was 61 percent. However, this poll represents something of a statistical anomaly compared to other polls of British Muslim opinion. A couple of months earlier, in February 2006, an ICM poll for *The Sunday Telegraph* found that 91 percent of British Muslims felt loyal towards Britain. A poll conducted by ICM for BBC Asian Network a year later in July 2007, which included all South Asian communities but which also broke down the findings by religious group, showed that in response to the question 'to what extent do you feel British?' 64 percent of Muslims replied 'completely/a lot' and 38 percent said 'a little/not at all'. At first glance, this might seem comparable to the NOP findings, but the 64 percent figure for Muslims is, in fact, higher than for Asians taken

as a whole, of whom 59 percent felt 'completely/a lot' British. The same poll had 88 percent of Muslims saying that they were satisfied with life in the United Kingdom (compared to 84 percent among Asians as a whole). Another NOP poll for Channel 4 News in April 2007 shows that 93 percent of British Muslims feel comfortable that their future lies in Britain – which puts rather a different complexion on the results of their 2006 poll. As I suggest below, the framing of these questions is pivotal in determining the response, and the NOP/*Dispatches* question from the April 2006 survey is perhaps one of the most revealingly symptomatic of this.

3. In 2001, I edited a collection of articles on Britishness which took the metaphor of interlocking braids as the guiding principle through which to explore the multidimensional multiculturalism of Britishness, focussing on regional and historic cultures and identities as well as on the newer strands contributed by recent migrant groups. See Anshuman Mondal, *EnterText: an interactive interdisciplinary e-journal for cultural and historical studies and creative work*, 2.1, 2001, http://arts.brunel.ac.uk/gate/entertext/issue_2_1.htm (cited 2 May 2008).

4. For more on the patterns of Bangladeshi settlement in the East End, and on the everyday racism they encountered, see the detailed research produced by The Young Foundation, published as Geoff Dench, Kate Gavron and Michael Young, *The New East End: Kinship, Race and Conflict* (London: Profile, 2006).

5. By 'coconut', he means an Asian who has become westernised to the extent that they are brown on the outside but white on the inside. It is a pejorative term used amongst young Asians.

6. See Tariq Modood, *Multicultural Politics: Racism, Ethnicity and Muslims in Britain* (Edinburgh: Edinburgh University Press, 2005), p.27.

7. Kenan Malik, 'Islamophobia Myth', *Prospect*, February 2005, pp.28–31.

8. Melanie Phillips is a columnist on *The Daily Mail* who has published some notoriously anti-Islamic articles and a book, *Londonistan: How Britain Has Created a Terror State Within* (London: Gibson Square, 2006). Richard Perle was former Chair of the Defense Policy Board Advisory Committee in the George W. Bush administration, a notable and influential policy advisor and neoconservative 'hawk' who argued strongly for the war in Iraq in 2003.

9. The subsequent trial of the men was picked up by the BBC and other national media outlets but not much attention was given to it. Given the context, it might have warranted at least a report from the Courthouse on the 6 o'clock news but this, sadly, was not forthcoming. After a retrial, one of the men was acquitted and the other, the BNP candidate Robert Cottage, was found guilty of possessing explosive materials but not guilty of conspiring to cause explosions after the jury failed to reach a verdict on this charge.

10. 'Only 1 in 400 Anti-terror Stop and Searches Leads to Arrest', *The Guardian*, 31 October 2007.

11. Yara el-Sherbini, *Sheikh 'n' Vac* (London: Book Works, 2005).

12. I think we should hesitate to use the term 'alienation' here. The young Muslims I met did not feel as if Britain was alien to them; nor did many of them feel alienated in the classical socio-economic sense. They feel integrated, but they feel that there are continuing obstacles to their becoming *accepted* as Muslim *and* British.

13. GFK NOP, April 2006. See note 2 above.

14. Populus, Muslim 7/7 poll, for *The Times* and ITN News, 4 and 5 July 2006. The poll can be accessed at http://www.populuslimited.com/the-times-itv-news-muslim-77-poll-050706.html (cited 2 May 2008).

15. Muslims are often singled out from other migrant communities in this respect – another sign of the subtle contours of Islamophobia. See Anshuman A. Mondal, 'Multiculturalism and Islam: Some Thoughts on a Difficult Relationship', *Moving Worlds*, 8.1, pp.77–93.

16. Ziauddin Sardar, *Desperately Seeking Paradise: Journeys of a Sceptical Muslim* (London: Granta, 2004), p.183.

17. In fact, there is a link between *identity*, as we understand it, and the formation of the modern state. See Michel Foucault's seminal essay 'Governmentality' in Graham Burchell, Colin Gordon and Peter Miller (eds.), *The Foucault Effect: Studies in Governmentality* (Chicago: Chicago University Press, 1991), pp.87–104. I discuss the implications of Foucault's essay for conceptualising *identity* in my book *Amitav Ghosh* (Manchester: Manchester University Press, 2007), pp.66–68.

18. Ethnos Research, *Citizenship and Belonging: What Is Britishness?* (London: Commission for Racial Equality, 2005), pp.38–39.

19. See my essay 'Multiculturalism and Islam' (see note 15).

20. *Desperately Seeking Paradise*, p.130.

21. Leila Aboulela, *Minaret* (New York: Black Cat, 2005), p.110.

22. Salman Rushdie, 'Imaginary Homelands', in *Imaginary Homelands: Essays and Criticism 1981–1991* (London: Granta, 1991), pp.12–13. It may seem inappropriate to many that I should at this stage refer to Salman Rushdie but it should not be forgotten that, despite *The Satanic Verses* controversy, Rushdie has been one of the most insightful commentators on the effect of migration on the imagination and on one's sense of self.

Chapter 4: Politics

1. This association, though given credence by the work of al-Qaeda and other Muslim terrorists, is actually belied by a wide-ranging study of suicide bombers by Robert Pape, which concluded that there is no *intrinsic* relation between Islam (or any other religion for that matter) and suicide bombing. See Robert Pape, *Dying to Win: Why Suicide Terrorists Do It* (London: Gibson Square, 2006).

2. Peter Mandaville, *Global Political Islam* (London: Routledge, 2007), pp.266, 269.

3. Ibid. p.270.

4. This is the view of Dilwar Hussain, cited by ibid.

5. E. Moosa, cited in Philip Lewis, *Young, British and Muslim* (London: Continuum, 2007), p.6.

6. Ziauddin Sardar, *Desperately Seeking Paradise: Journeys of a Sceptical Muslim* (London: Granta, 2004), p.156. I would highly recommend the chapter in this book entitled 'The Laws of Heaven' for a clear exposition of the historical development of the *Shariah* (wrongly assumed to be 'divine law' when it is not) and for an interpretation of *Shariah* appropriate to our times. See also Sami Zubaida, *Law and Power in the Islamic World* (London: I.B.Tauris, 2003).

7. Max Weber, *Politics as a Vocation* (Philadelphia: Fortress Press, 1968).

8. This phrase was originally coined by the American Sufi scholar Sheikh Hamza Yusuf, whom Abdur-rahman admires a great deal. Hamza Yusuf is distinguished by his command of both Islamic and modern western disciplines as well as being a fierce critic of the kind of mindset which lies beneath the 'discourse of rage'.

9. Madeleine Bunting, 'The Iraq War Has Become a Disaster That We Have Chosen to Forget', *The Guardian*, 5 November 2007.

Chapter 5: Generational Conflict

1. Philip Lewis, *Young, British and Muslim* (London: Continuum, 2007), p.67.

2. These claims were made by Martin Bright in his highly influential report for Policy Exchange, *When Progressives Treat with Reactionaries: The British State's Flirtation with Radical Islamism* (2006). It received acclaim within policy circles and clearly made its mark on the government decision to move away from the MCB. However, it should be pointed out that the report is deeply flawed and shows a somewhat superficial understanding of the phenomenon of 'political Islamism', stitching together various movements, organisations

and ideological currents as though they were all part of an unproblematically identifiable 'radical Islamism' – with both the term 'radical' and the term 'Islamism' left open to question. Philip Lewis, among others, has critiqued its usefulness and the validity of some of its most alarming claims; see *Young, British and Muslim*, pp.66–68.

Chapter 6: Women

1. Philip Lewis, *Young, British and Muslim* (London: Continuum, 2007), p.54.

2. Abdullah Yusuf Ali (trans.), *The Holy Quran* (Maryland: Amana Corporation, 1989), 24:30–31, pp.873–874.

3. This is a monumental historical irony given that 'the West' traces its liberal democratic lineage back to classical Athens, and the way the veil is deployed as a sign of Islamic backwardness and barbarism in some quarters of the West today.

Chapter 7: Prospects

1. Many Muslim thinkers are convinced that the most creative and rewarding efforts to revitalise Islamic thought and behaviour will occur not in the Arabian heartlands or in the Middle East but on the peripheries of the Muslim world: in South East Asia (Malaysia or Indonesia), in southern Africa or in Europe and America. Foremost among them is Professor Tariq Ramadan.

About the Author

Anshuman A. Mondal has published widely on national identity, religion and politics in the modern world, particularly South Asia and the Middle East. He is the author of *Nationalism and Post-Colonial Identity: Culture and Ideology in India and Egypt* (RoutledgeCurzon, 2003) and *Amitav Ghosh* (Manchester University Press, 2007). He is the Deputy Director of the Brunel Centre for Contemporary Writing (BBCW) and has appeared as a commentator on cultural, political and religious affairs on BBC radio and television. He lives in London.

Index